Chaplaincy

Chaplaincy

Contemporary and Global Perspectives

Edited by

Grace Thomas and Kim Wasey

scm press

© Editors and Contributors 2024

Published in 2024 by SCM Press
Editorial office
3rd Floor, Invicta House,
110 Golden Lane,
London EC1Y 0TG, UK
www.scmpress.co.uk

SCM Press is an imprint of Hymns Ancient & Modern Ltd
(a registered charity)

Hymns Ancient & Modern® is a registered trademark of
Hymns Ancient & Modern Ltd
13A Hellesdon Park Road, Norwich,
Norfolk NR6 5DR, UK

All rights reserved. No part of this publication may be reproduced,
stored in a retrieval system, or transmitted,
in any form or by any means, electronic, mechanical,
photocopying or otherwise, without the prior permission of
the publisher, SCM Press.

The editors and contributors have asserted their right under the Copyright,
Designs and Patents Act 1988 to be identified as the Authors of this Work

Scripture quotations marked (NIV) are taken from the Holy Bible,
New International Version®, NIV®. Copyright © 1973, 1978,
1984, 2011 by Biblica, Inc.™ Used by permission of Zondervan.
All rights reserved worldwide. www.zondervan.com The "NIV" and
"New International Version" are trademarks registered in the
United States Patent and Trademark Office by Biblica, Inc.™
Scripture taken from the New King James Version®. Copyright © 1982
by Thomas Nelson. Used by permission. All rights reserved.

British Library Cataloguing in Publication data
A catalogue record for this book is available
from the British Library

ISBN: 978-0-334-06621-7

Typeset by Regent Typesetting

Contents

List of contributors ix

Introduction 1

Part One: Chaplaincy in Organizational Contexts

1 A Critical Reflection of NHS Chaplaincy: Governance, Organizational Context and a Story of an Unexpected Ministerial Opportunity 7
   Nik Hookey

2 Trans-Atlantic Concepts for University Chaplaincy 19
   Ian Delinger

3 Police Chaplaincy: Diversity, Inclusion and Welcome 29
   May Preston

4 The Place of Healthcare Chaplains in Hong Kong: Organization, Governance and the Emergence of an Unlikely Role in Suicide Prevention 36
   Tak Hang Angus Lin

Part Two: Inhabiting Public Ministry

5 Exploring Hospice Chaplaincy Through a Christian Understanding of Mortality 49
   Andrew Webster

6 The Prison Chaplain as a Pastoral Prophetic Presence: Perspectives from a Prison Chaplain in Nigeria 58
   Basil Odenore

7 Pioneering Community Chaplaincy 66
   Heather Farrow

8 Dementia, Social Care and Chaplaincy: Lessons Learned on
   One Lay Chaplain's Journey   78
   Abigail Ogier

Part Three: Multifaith and Secular Dimensions

9 'How Shall I Sing the Lord's Song in a Strange Land?'
   Christian Biblical Perspectives on Theological Integrity in
   Inter- and Multifaith Chaplaincy   91
   Andrew Jyothi Isaac Susan

10 Baptist Prison Chaplaincy: A Divided Duty?   105
   Simon Hollis

11 'Do we really need 500 crosses?' Chaplaincy Administration   118
   Carol Thorne

12 Identity, Ministry and Healthcare Chaplaincy: Reflections
   From a Black, Female, Assemblies of God Minister   121
   Agatha Ngambi

13 Mystic Sweat: Unveiling Spiritual Dimensions of Music-
   infused Workout Classes and Their Implications for
   Chaplaincy   128
   Arek Malecki

Part Four: Chaplaincy and Christian Mission

14 Cross-cultures: Hospital Chaplaincy as a YWAM Missionary   143
   Carol Hatton

15 The UK Oil and Gas Chaplaincy   152
   Lee Higson

16 Chaplain as Fire-tender: Envisioning a Model of Chaplaincy
   for Clinical Pastoral Education in the USA and Beyond   160
   Anjeanette Roberts

17 A Personal Reflection on Chaplaincy for Older People in
   Botswana and Scotland   173
   Oarabile Molaodi

18 Retail Chaplaincy and a 'Ministry of Encounter'   179
    Deborah Dalby

Part Five: Research and Reflective Practice: Chaplain Theologians

19 The Story Behind the Transformative Anti-racism
    and Faith Schools Project 'Shades': A Case Study and
    Personal Reflection   189
    Ni-Cola Scott

20 Toxic MasKulinity and Gender-Sensitive End-of-life Care:
    A Research Proposal   199
    Andrew Webster

21 Organic Chaplaincy: Supporting the Spiritual Care of
    Persons with Learning Disabilities   207
    Andrew Jyothi Isaac Susan

22 Re-writing the Play: Reflections on a Theodramatic
    Approach to Decolonizing my Teaching of Chaplaincy
    and Pastoral Care   223
    Grace Thomas

Index of Names and Subjects   233

List of Contributors

Editors

Grace Thomas is Canon Missioner at Manchester Cathedral, having previously been Programme Lead for Chaplaincy Studies at the Luther King Centre. She is Diocesan Environment Officer and a regular presenter on Radio 2's *Pause for Thought* and Radio 4's *Daily Service*. Prior to her ordination, Grace had a career in nursing, including in clinical research, before taking roles in youth work and family support.

Kim Wasey is College Principal at the Luther King Centre and tutor on the Chaplaincy Studies programme. She holds Theology degrees from the Universities of Manchester and Birmingham (BA, MPhil and ThD). She has extensive and varied experience as chaplain at the universities in Manchester, Salford and Bolton and helps facilitate the Symposium on the Faith Lives of Women and Girls.

Contributors

Deborah Dalby enjoyed a 30-year career, mainly in leadership roles in the community and voluntary sector, before entering ministry. This career path, coupled with her faith, led into the sphere of social and environmental responsibility at a diocesan and national level. Deborah is now a CofE parish priest in mid-Cheshire.

Ian Delinger is Rector at St Stephen's Episcopal Church in San Luis Obispo in California. He was ordained in Manchester, where he served his curacy. He then served eight years as chaplain of the University of Chester. His MA thesis explored the intersection of radio and ministry.

Heather Farrow lives and works in the north-east of England. Her work currently involves connecting with a wide range of community practitioners, seeking ways of working together. This includes exploring theology and the integral uniqueness of place and context on human flourishing. She is due to complete her MA with the Luther King Centre this summer (2024).

Carol Hatton currently serves with Youth With A Mission (YWAM) in the UK. After a career in teaching, she joined YWAM in the Asia-Pacific region, studying Christian Counselling and Pastoral Ministry in Australia. Carol is passionate about bringing her cross-cultural international missionary experience to her healthcare chaplaincy.

Lee Higson is a pioneer curate leading an estate church in Bolton. Previously, Lee worked deep-sea and offshore for 22 years in the energy industry at all levels up to Offshore Installation Manager. He served from 2022 to 2023 with the Oil and Gas Chaplaincy. He holds MAs in Mission and Christian Leadership.

Simon Hollis practised as a solicitor for 30 years before being ordained as a Baptist minister. He currently serves as a sessional chaplain in a prison for people convicted of sexual offences.

Nik Hookey is an NHS Healthcare chaplaincy manager and an accredited Baptist minister. Following pastorates in Oxfordshire and Staffordshire, he has worked in Manchester hospitals since 2019 and has a particular interest in the intersection of sexuality and faith.

Andrew Jyothi Isaac Susan is an ordinand in the Diocese of Manchester. He has experience in healthcare chaplaincy in the NHS as well as in India. He has also worked with Persons with Learning Disabilities as a care assistant, which motivated the research shared in this collection.

Tak Hang Angus Lin is a chaplain in a retirement-living community in Leeds. He was a certified hospital chaplain in Hong Kong and has ten years of chaplaincy experience in Hong Kong's public and private health sectors. He holds an MDiv and has completed four units of CPE.

Arek Malecki is an ordained Unitarian and Free Christian minister by day, and a certified group exercise instructor by night. He is especially interested in embodied and contemporary expressions of spirituality, and similarities between ministry and coaching, worship services and fitness classes, and gym and church communities.

Oarabile Molaodi is a volunteer chaplain at Methodist Homes (MHA) and leads care-home ministry at Kings Church Motherwell. She is originally from Botswana and relocated to Scotland in 2005. She holds a PgDip in Chaplaincy Studies, PhD in Statistics, and previously worked in health research at Glasgow University.

Agatha Ngambi is a healthcare chaplain and an ordained Assemblies of God minister, associate pastor of Authentic City Church. She has more

LIST OF CONTRIBUTORS

than five years of chaplaincy experience. Agatha holds an MA in Practical Theology, BA Hons in Theology and Biblical Studies and a PgCert in Chaplaincy.

Basil Odenore is a mental health and psychosocial specialist, offering over ten years of experience in clinical and pastoral care in hospitals, faith and non-faith-based organizations and prisons. He holds MAs from Liberty and Tilburg Universities and a BA from Trinity College of the Bible and Theological Seminary, Indiana.

Abigail Ogier is a chaplain and Area Support Chaplain for MHA, working in the north of England. She is a Licensed Lay Minister in the CofE, and has a particular interest in the spirituality of people living with dementia.

May Preston is a Chief Inspector based at West Yorkshire Police and was the Vice Chair of the Christian Police Network for Greater Manchester Police (GMP) until 2023. In addition to her background in operational policing and investigations, May was, for a time, the GMP Equality Lead, with responsibility for chaplains.

Anjeanette 'AJ' Roberts, PhD, transitioned into chaplaincy from a career encompassing scientific research, education, writing and public speaking. AJ has co-authored over 40 peer-reviewed research articles and co-authored two books and many popular-level articles in Christian Apologetics. AJ is passionate about theology, chaplaincy and micro brewing.

Ni-Cola Scott is the Shades Lead for the Children Changing Places project in Bolton, Greater Manchester. The Mobo-nominated singer songwriter and recording artist brings fresh approaches to chaplaincy and discipleship using her creative style with passion for racial justice, and supporting children and young people to take the lead in this.

Carol Thorne taught in a primary school for over ten years before beginning work as Secretary to the Chaplaincy and Spiritual Care Service at Manchester Foundation Trust hospitals in 2019. Carol is due to complete her studies on the Postgraduate Diploma for Healthcare Chaplains programme at the Luther King Centre in 2024.

Andrew Webster is a presbyter in the Methodist Church. Currently working as a chaplain at St David's Hospice Care in South Wales, he served for 18 years in a variety of local church ministries with ten years as part-time prison chaplain. He holds degrees in Psychology (Sheffield) and Theology (Manchester and Cardiff).

Introduction

This book reflects the privilege the editors have of working with a wide range of richly talented, reflective and spiritual students and practitioners of chaplaincy through the teaching and learning taking place in the Luther King Centre's Chaplaincy Studies courses.

In 2020 we were partners in creating a brand-new Chaplaincy Studies programme, sitting within the Common Awards programmes at Durham University. The course was launched in September 2021, with United Kingdom Board for Healthcare Chaplaincy (UKBHC) accreditation gained for students beginning to study with us from September 2022.

These exciting developments in the growing field of Chaplaincy Studies in the UK were taking place at the same time as movements such as #BlackLivesMatter, which made even more prescient the Luther King Centre's existing commitment to worldwide perspectives in theology and the need to constantly strive towards decolonizing the curriculum.

The fact that the new course was offered through real-time online teaching and learning meant that we were soon welcoming students into our virtual classrooms from Nigeria, South India and the USA, as well as experienced leaders in various chaplaincy fields who contribute to teaching. As with our on-site teaching of other programmes, the presence of people from across the world, with a huge range of experiences, frameworks, perspectives and expectations, made the learning process always fresh, invigorating and positively challenging for everyone involved, including lecturers.

This collection offers readers the chance to hear and engage with that rich variety of voices, working and researching in chaplaincy globally, including writers from Botswana, India, Hong Kong and the USA, as well as practitioners from various denominations (including Baptist, Assemblies of God, Anglican, Church of South India, Methodist and Unitarian) and diverse backgrounds within UK contexts. The chaplaincy contexts explored vary from the NHS, prison, police, hospice and nursing homes to retail and oil-rig chaplaincies, and reflect the ways the sector is expanding and diversifying.

Part One offers insights from chaplains regarding the interplay between the organizational context within which they practise and the structures and expectation of their faith and/or denomination. Issues of professionalism, accountability and integrity are explored from the very different perspectives that the chaplains inhabit, beginning with Nik Hookey's candid and inspiring journey into healthcare chaplaincy (Chapter 1), and reflecting on the role of the United Kingdom Board for Healthcare Chaplaincy. Ian Delinger (Chapter 2) reflects holistically on how his life experiences and commitments can helpfully shape chaplaincy for educational contexts both in the UK and the USA. Then May Preston (Chapter 3) evaluates the role, position and development of police chaplaincy in a northern police force, considering the factors that influence this, asking whether a multifaith model is most helpful and, if so, how such a model might most effectively operate. Finally, Angus Lin (Chapter 4) offers a perspective from the context of Hong Kong and the impact this has on expectations of chaplaincy ministry.

Part Two examines the public and representative role of chaplaincy ministries. Contributions from Wales, Nigeria, the north-east and north-west of England look at the role of the chaplain through very different lenses. Andrew Webster (Chapter 5) explores how theologically informed understandings of mortality can shape the public ministry of hospice chaplaincy, arguing that such an understanding is needed as a counter to some prevailing societal attitudes, and that it can offer a powerful contribution to the formation of chaplaincy itself. Basil Odenore (Chapter 6) shares his story of a pastoral and prophetic approach. Heather Farrow (Chapter 7) negotiates the complex demands of pioneering chaplaincy, with particular attention to power, trauma and context, and Abigail Ogier (Chapter 8) focuses on dementia and her position as a lay chaplain.

Part Three explores working within diverse chaplaincy teams, reflecting theologically on the complex, unpredictable and ambiguous realities of chaplaincy in multifaith and secular contexts. Andrew Jyothi Isaac Susan (Chapter 9) draws on his background and experience to engage with biblical texts and examine ideas of truth in relationship with others. Simon Hollis (Chapter 10) wrestles with his ecclesiological framework and contextual realities to similarly ask about integrity in chaplaincy. Carol Thorne's reflection (Chapter 11) reminds us that, in many contexts, chaplains do not operate in isolation. Good teams need not only good leaders, but good support structures and administrators can also be crucial. Agatha Ngambi (Chapter 12) interrogates the place of identity in chaplaincy as a black, female Assemblies of God minister, and Arek Malecki (Chapter 13) dives deep into secular spirituality in 'Mystic Sweat'.

Part Four reviews a number of models of chaplaincy in relation to church and society, together with the nature of mission and calling in contemporary chaplaincy. Carol Hatton (Chapter 14) provides a unique perspective from her background as a career missionary, and Lee Higson (Chapter 15) another very different context, experienced by few chaplains, that of offshore chaplaincy. Anjeanette Roberts (Chapter 16) develops a new model of chaplain as fire-tender, highlighting the significance of creating space for social bonding and intimate attention in spiritual care. Oarabile Molaodi (Chapter 17) reflects on the different positions of older people in Botswana and in Scotland and the implications for chaplaincy, while Deborah Dalby (Chapter 18) shares the story of a more responsive chaplaincy approach in her local community.

Part Five provides a glimpse into chaplains as academic researchers and reflexive practitioners, shaping the field of chaplaincy studies and impacting the practice of chaplaincy. Ni-Cola Scott (Chapter 19) outlines the very practical impacts of proactively addressing racism in school contexts, empowering others through these communities to create change. Andrew Webster (Chapter 20) provides a research proposal, showing how a question can be identified and a practical project shaped, considering purpose, literature, methodology and ethics. Andrew Jyothi Isaac Susan (Chapter 21) provides a view from the 'other side' of a research project, giving an overview of the project as a whole and the impact and outcomes such practical engagement in the field can generate. Finally, Grace's use of theodrama in Chapter 22 provides a creative conclusion to this book, framing the commitments of all those who have contributed to it, and of the Luther King Centre, through a fresh way of thinking about theology as practitioners, students and educators, and its importance for chaplaincy studies.

We celebrate the fact that the chapters and reflections use a variety of written styles and approaches. This demonstrates our commitment to a decolonial approach, where the importance of story and enabling difference in voice is foregrounded. We hope that the diversity of voice will encourage others to find their place, their voice, and to share in the genuinely inclusive conversation which can create and enrich genuinely inclusive chaplaincy in our contexts and communities.

We hope you will find this book useful, whether you are thinking about chaplaincy for the first time, teaching or studying chaplaincy, offering training for others or reading to enrich your own practice.

Grace and Kim

PART ONE

Chaplaincy in Organizational Contexts

I

A Critical Reflection of NHS Chaplaincy: Governance, Organizational Context and a Story of an Unexpected Ministerial Opportunity

NIK HOOKEY

There are complex, interwoven and overlapping guidelines, policies and procedures that impact upon the practice of a Christian minister and NHS chaplain in England and Wales. At times the different frameworks reinforce one another and at other times they stand in opposition. The organizational landscape of healthcare chaplaincy has changed significantly in the past few decades, as it travels on a journey of professionalization and seeks to establish its place and role within the NHS. This chapter begins by giving a brief, yet detailed, overview of some of the most significant organizational issues that outline the life and work of the healthcare chaplain today within the complex context that is the NHS. As I explore this multifaceted governance framework, I will draw into the narrative parts of my own journey from Baptist minister, to healthcare chaplain, to chaplaincy manager. I shall show how the different governance frameworks in the NHS enabled a new opportunity for ministry when the denominational route appeared closed off to me.

Chaplaincy and governance within the NHS

There were chaplains connected with hospitals in England and Wales many years before the creation of the NHS. Initially the chaplain's role was very much focused on moral improvement as well as administering the sacraments, especially within the workhouse model. When the NHS was formed in 1948, chaplains gradually began to be directly employed by the NHS. In the early days they would have been almost exclusively from either the Church of England (CofE) or Church in Wales (CinW), but over time this began to widen out to other denominations and religious groups. The change in the employment status of healthcare chaplains to that of NHS employees meant that chaplains were increasingly managed in a similar way to other NHS employees and greater professional expectations were placed upon them. Swift identifies the greatest surge in this professionalization as taking place in the second decade of the NHS, 1958–68 (Swift, 2014).

The professionalization of chaplaincy

Van Dijk (2021) charts the history of the professionalization of chaplaincy within the NHS in England in relatively recent times. While the NHS was formed in 1948 it was not until the 1990s, with the introduction of NHS Trusts, that the professionalization of chaplains began to take off. Before this point, chaplaincy had largely functioned on a religious model; chaplains were there to meet patients' religious needs and perhaps to bring them some comfort. However, with individual NHS Trusts managing their budgets, the appointment and employment of chaplains needed to be justified. A representative body, the College of Healthcare Chaplains, was formed and became part of a trade union. Chaplaincy was established within the NHS as a graduate profession and chaplains were employed on the same Agenda for Change terms as all other NHS staff. Instead of simply looking to the CofE to supply chaplains, new posts were advertised on an open (though still largely restricted to Christian) basis, leading to more ecumenical representation within chaplaincy teams.

The NHS Chaplaincy guidelines define chaplains as those who 'promote pastoral, spiritual and religious well-being through skilled compassionate person-centred care for patients, their families and their carers, NHS staff, volunteers and students' (NHS England, 2023). The guidelines identify several roles for the chaplain: spiritual, religious and pastoral care, involvement in initial response to major incidents, roles within multi-disciplinary teams and employee health and well-being support. The chaplain is paid by the NHS Trust and is expected to supply a specialist spiritual care service. The guidelines also discuss recruitment of chaplains under contract as spiritual care specialists and seek to place chaplains firmly as a professional discipline within the NHS.

The benefits of professionalization are:

- There are clear frameworks within which to work.
- There is a commitment to continuing professional development.
- There is an expectation that chaplains will adhere to the policies and procedures of the Trust.
- There should be clear criteria for access to the service.

- The chaplains should be recognized as having a professional status by other professionals within the Trust.
- The service should be measured and evaluated regularly.

The drawbacks might be perceived to be:

- Missing the 'calling' to chaplaincy, where it is seen as a vocational imperative rather than a job to be done.
- Too restricted by processes and administration, which can be time-consuming and take the chaplain away from the more recognized work of 'bedside' care.
- Inflexible when some situations need a degree of flexibility that would not be possible within a policy framework.
- The benefits and activities of chaplaincy are not always easy to describe or quantify and so they resist statistical measures.

The power and position of chaplaincy

It can appear from organizational structures that chaplaincy has very little power within NHS Trusts and can be seen as a small cog within the large and complex structure. However, it does seem to have a disproportionate role, partly as a result of the unique and specialized nature of the service. Trusts undoubtedly employ many hundreds of band 6 nurses but, for example in my context, there are only a handful of band 6 chaplains shared across four main sites and seven in-patient hospitals. Thus, if a committee or a multi-disciplinary team (MDT) wants a chaplain to attend their meeting, there are far fewer to choose from. None the less, the relatively small number of chaplains compared to other professions within the Trust can make it feel as though the chaplain is powerless to influence change or policy.

The location of the chaplaincy department within the NHS Trust is also interesting in terms of how its role and position are perceived. Many NHS Trusts will have their chaplaincy in the same part of the organization as palliative care or bereavement departments. While this can appear to make sense, as chaplaincy, palliative care and bereavement often work closely together, it is ultimately not helpful. Placing chaplaincy together with either of these services helps to give the impression that it is primarily related to death and dying. Chaplains may be highly skilled at dealing with patients and their families towards the end of life and they may be highly skilled in offering bereavement care, yet this is just a part of what they do and not the whole. Even though there is a perception that if a chaplain has been called it means that the patient is approaching the end of their life, there is much more to the chaplain's role. Furthermore, placing chaplaincy with either or both palliative care and bereavement focuses only on the patient side of chaplaincy work.

In the NHS Trust where I work, chaplaincy sits in quality and patient experience (QPE). This is interesting as it reflects two different aspects of chaplaincy: the role of chaplains in supporting patients and staff, and the contribution chaplains can bring in the improvement of the quality of care provided. As well as 'patient experience', which incorporates chaplaincy, and 'quality improvement', the QPE department includes those working under the remit of 'professional practice'. This means that we have close relations with the quality-improvement team and professional accreditations. This helps the Trust to understand chaplaincy as a professional grouping, with the importance of professional accreditation, as well as a service that strives to improve the quality of its provision.

In every area of the NHS there are guidelines and policies and, as the professionalization of chaplaincy has become the norm, there exists a growing number and variety of governance documents that healthcare chaplains are expected to adhere to. Various guidelines for chaplaincy have been published, the most recent being in 2023. Because this chapter is exploring the nature of this multifaceted governance structure, it is pertinent at this point to give a summary of the main governing papers.

NHS Chaplaincy Guidelines 2023

The NHS Chaplaincy Guidelines (NHS England, 2023) are mainly written for NHS employers, to help them understand the role of chaplaincy within the NHS and to be able to provide appropriate levels of chaplaincy support within each hospital Trust. They explain the nature of the support that chaplaincy offers, affirming that chaplaincy within the NHS is to be provided not just for patients but also for carers and staff. The guidelines are specifically focused on the provision of the service, rather than describing how chaplains will work from day to day. As such, they describe best practice in a variety of settings, and focus on governance and quality assurance. There is guidance on staffing, recruitment, training and volunteers, as well as the resources required. These might be seen as high-level resources, most suitable for managers who oversee or who commission chaplaincy.

United Kingdom Board of Healthcare Chaplains (UKBHC) Code of Conduct

UKBHC was established in 2009 to be a register of healthcare chaplains that is recognized by the Professional Standards Authority. It emerged as chaplaincy became more professionalized and recognized the need for a body analogous to the other professional bodies within the NHS. Its responsibility is to maintain professional standards, whereas the College of Healthcare Chaplains exists as a union for chaplains. Their Code of Conduct (UKBHC, 2014) provides the ethical framework and professional boundaries within which I am expected to operate as a healthcare chaplain, including the duty of candour and the requirement to raise any concerns with the appropriate authorities when I observe them. These are directly relevant to the day-to-day conduct of a chaplain.

Membership of UKBHC is not required for NHS chaplains, but most job descriptions for chaplains at band 5 and above will expect them to work to UKBHC standards. Full membership of UKBHC requires a postgraduate-level qualification in healthcare chaplaincy, and to have 'evidence of a recognised or accredited status within a mainstream faith community or belief group' (UKBHC, n.d.). This can present barriers to entry for those who do not have the necessary academic requirements and for those from faith traditions that do not have formal registers of accreditation. It is well recognized that people from less affluent backgrounds are less likely to have higher-level academic qualifications and so this can also mean that UKBHC-registered chaplains may not necessarily be as diverse as the communities that we serve in.

Standard Operating Procedures (SOPs)

SOPs are documents that are local to a department. In our chaplaincy we have about 15 such documents, covering such aspects of our work as ward visiting, record keeping and on-call. The principle of an SOP is that someone who is new to the department can pick it up and follow the directions closely to complete the task that is described. For example, we are currently writing a volunteers' SOP. This is following a few occasions where volunteers have potentially acted outside their remit, but there had not been complete clarity of the boundaries for their tasks. It had been assumed that the volunteers would either know the right thing to do, or that they would be trained correctly and retain that knowledge. These showed the importance of writing a SOP for the volunteers' work but there could be a danger that volunteers who felt confident in their tasks will now feel that they are not trusted to get on with it. Healthcare chaplain volunteers are required to adhere to the UKBHC Code of Conduct as well as all relevant local policies and procedures for volunteers.

My status and responsibilities as an NHS employee

When I was a minister of a local church I was regarded as an office holder, so I did not have a contract but rather a 'Terms of Appointment'. I was paid a stipend designed to cover my living expenses and was classed as being self-employed rather than employed by the Church. As an employee of the NHS, I have a contract that sets out what is expected of me in a work setting. It outlines my place of employment and terms and conditions. It commits me to following NHS and Trust policies and guidelines and determines how many hours I should be working each week, including Sundays and out-of-hours on-call. The policies I am expected to adhere to cover all aspects of conduct within the Trust. The ones most immediately relevant to chaplains are the Human Resources policies. These relate to our conduct at work: sickness, annual leave, equality at work and so on. However, as we are patient-facing, some of the clinical policies, such as the infection prevention and control policy, also apply.

The policies make clear that chaplains are expected to adhere to the requirements of the Equality Act (2010). This legislation details nine protected characteristics including religion and sexual orientation, and it is this legislation that prevents organizations like the NHS discriminating against LGBT people. A religious organization can be exempted from this law if it can demonstrate that such an exemption is necessary because of its religious aims. For me, as an employee of the NHS and a chaplaincy manager, I must abide by this legislation when recruiting and managing staff. I cannot restrict recruitment of staff due to, for example, characteristics of gender, religious affiliation or sexual orientation, and I myself cannot be discriminated against for any of these reasons either. This particular aspect of NHS healthcare chaplaincy had a significant impact on my own ministerial journey and exemplifies the ways expectations of denomination and organization can sometimes be in conflict. To illustrate this, what follows is a personal reflection on my own journey to healthcare chaplaincy and how it was impacted by the organizational context and expectations.

The relationship between denominational governance and chaplaincy within the NHS – a personal reflection

The status of healthcare chaplaincy has changed much over the years that I have been an accredited Baptist minister – that is, since 1999. Initially, chaplaincy was regarded as a post to which ministers could be 'seconded'. Then, it was regarded as a 'sector' ministry. Now it is simply seen as a 'qualifying office' within which a Baptist minister can serve and maintain their status on the accredited list of ministers. My NHS contract specifies that I need to be a faith leader who has accredited status within my belief group, which is why it is important that I retain my accredited status with the Baptist Union. The Ministerial Recognition Rules govern my current accreditation as a Baptist minister (Ministries Team, Baptist Union of Great Britain, 2022). They affirm that I have had my call to serve as a minister tested by the wider Church and undergone a period of formation at a Baptist college, before being commended to ministry in the churches of the Baptist Union. They set out various criteria for remaining on the list; these include serving within a qualifying office and not having been found guilty of gross misconduct, which would necessitate removal from the accredited list. One area, for example, where the Recognition Rules conflict with general employment practice within the NHS is over the definition of marriage. As a gay man, I would like to be able to marry my partner; however, the Recognition Rules in Appendix 4 offer an example of gross misconduct as sexual misconduct (that is, actions that are of a sexual nature or are sexually motivated) that brings the Church and ministry into disrepute. This specifically includes sexual intercourse and other genital sexual activity outside of marriage (as defined exclusively as between a man and a woman). While being married would not be an issue within the NHS – in fact, if it were an issue, this could be construed as unlawful discrimination – within my faith denomination this is prohibited.

There is a precedent in the CofE with Andrew Foreshew-Cain, who was the first CofE vicar to enter a same-sex marriage in 2014. He was able to keep his post but was prevented from taking up any new post and eventually resigned as a priest in 2017. He was eventually able to take up the post of chaplain of Lady Margaret Hall in Oxford in 2019 because Oxford college appointments are outside of the control of the CofE and, despite opposition from the Church, they were not able to block it. This precedent and informal conversations that I have had with senior managers suggest that, even if I were to be removed from the accredited list of Baptist ministers, the Trust would not want me to leave my job. But this is a precarious place to be in.

The situation I find myself in now is the culmination of a long journey of faith, discernment and discovery, which is still continuing! I came into NHS chaplaincy in August 2019 following a relatively long period in Baptist ministry, which began with my ministerial formation in 1995. After that period of initial ministerial formation was completed in 1998, I worked for Ordnance Survey for six months in the marketing communications department. In this role, whenever we began a project, we had to 'start a file', a physical card folder with paper notes in it. This file would hold all the documentation about the job that we were doing at that time. It was drummed into me that, 'If you get hit by a bus on the way home, can somebody else pick up the work that you have been doing?' This question had a profound impact on the way that I approached and undertook ministry in the following years, particularly in the completion, management and storage of important documentation. It is part of the reasoning behind, for example, SOPs in my current hospital setting. After this job, I went on to serve as a minister in churches in Oxfordshire and Staffordshire, getting married along the way. Life, certainly from the outside, looked settled and comfortable.

In August 2018, however, it felt very much like I had been 'hit by a bus'. Although I married in the year 2000 and my wife and I had two children, I had for some time been struggling with my sexual identity. Following a long period of self-reflection and theological reading and study, I finally acknowledged to myself that I was gay. For the following 12 months or so I wrestled internally with what this might mean for my marriage and my ministry. It was a very uncomfortable period of my life. I did not discuss this with my wife until a crisis moment came on our summer holiday in 2018 when we had a confrontation. The stress finally overwhelmed me and I broke down and told her I was gay. This led to extremely difficult and painful conversations and a very dark time for both of us. When we returned home, I met with the church leadership and told them that I was resigning from the Church as I was going to separate from my wife because I was gay.

As far as I am aware, although the Church needed to contact me about a few things, the affairs of the Church were in good order and well documented, and they were quite able to pick up the ongoing projects and bring them to completion. This meant that my immediate priority was to find another job so that I would be able to pay rent for a place to live. I found a job working as a gas and electric meter reader for small businesses in Staffordshire. I did not know where I could find employment again that related to my ministerial formation. I was aware at that time that no gay minister could get a job in Baptist churches.

At one point in this incredibly difficult time, I resigned from my accreditation. Trusted colleagues asked me to withdraw that resignation because, I was told, separation and divorce (and 'homosexual orientation') did not necessarily mean resigning from Baptist accredited ministry. This had been a result of a change to the Ministerial Recognition rules in the summer of 2018. Instead, I was advised it was best to keep my options open, and that there might be a future for me, for example, in chaplaincy. Until this point, I had never considered chaplaincy as an option, particularly hospital chaplaincy! When I was at a Baptist college in the 1990s, I accompanied a minister on hospital visits and ended up leaving the bedside in a great hurry as being there had made me very nauseated. Over many years of church ministry, perhaps helped by being married to a hospital doctor, I had managed to get over some of this and had got used to visiting people in the hospital – but it was certainly not my favourite thing to do. This, I believed, was the weakest part of my ministry.

In the situation I found myself, facing the possibility of having to leave ministry behind me, a good friend encouraged me to reconsider hospital chaplaincy. She had been with me in the church and thought I had skills that would transfer well to a hospital context. She pointed out that I was at my best talking to people and giving them support when they were in crisis, and that this was one of the main features of hospital chaplaincy. She encouraged me to look for, and apply for, hospital chaplaincy jobs, which I duly did. On my second attempt, I was appointed as a chaplain in a large acute NHS Trust and, much to my surprise, I enjoyed the work. I found it vastly rewarding to visit patients who were in crisis moments, whether that was because of surgery, illness or even death. More than this, I had found a place that would employ me as a gay man who was also a minister. My sexuality was not only tolerated but celebrated in the NHS, in stark contrast to my accrediting denomination.

This is where legislation like the Equality Act comes in. The result of this law, and the ability for religious organizations to be exempt, is that comments and actions that might be acceptable in a church or a denomination are not acceptable within secular organizations such as the NHS. In my experience, the contrast has been stark. In the city in which my Trust is based, there is a large LGBT population and a strong emphasis has been placed on showing that healthcare is open to all. The Trust's equality policy states that, 'You are required to take steps to eradicate any homophobic, biphobic or inappropriate attitudes in relation to the sexual orientation or perceived sexual orientation of people in the workplace' (Khan, 2022). The Trust's Equality and Diversity Strategy aimed for our Trust to be the first Acute Trust in the country to achieve the LGBT Foundation Pride in Practice accreditation. In 2021, the Trust was successful in gaining bronze accreditation under the Rainbow Badge accreditation scheme, developed in collaboration with the LGBT Foundation, Stonewall, the LGBT Consortium, Brighton & Hove LGBT Switchboard and GLADD (the Association of LGBT Doctors and Dentists).

When I joined the Trust, I joined the LGBT staff network and from this was asked to be on a staff committee that reported to the group HR committee looking specifically at the needs of LGBT staff during the Covid pandemic. This was quickly changed from a time-limited group for the pandemic into a group that would be available to feed into Trust initiatives more widely. We have contributed to campaigns such as the International Day against Homophobia and the Trust's entry into the annual Pride parade. This means that as a gay member of staff, the Trust considers that I have a vital contribution to the way that the Trust celebrates LGBT staff and shows to the local LGBT population that it can be a supportive place to work, as well as a supportive place to receive healthcare. As I write this, I am considering ways to improve the chaplaincy and spiritual care service so that it is more positive towards LGBT staff and patients, as the Trust works towards the silver standard in the Rainbow Badge accreditation scheme for NHS Trusts. This has already included a prominent display of posters showing faith support groups for LGBT persons as well as information about language, specifically gender pronouns. I have also rewritten our inclusion statement to make it more positive and obviously inclusive. It now says, 'The Spiritual Care Team is committed to creating a safe and inclusive space for everyone, respecting their beliefs, sexual orientation and gender identity.' As there is a belief that organized religions are not sympathetic towards LGBT people, I believe it is more important that the chaplaincy service is explicit about its inclusion and non-discrimination.

It is interesting to reflect on the various power dynamics at play here. Within chaplaincy, as a manager, I have relatively more influence than the other chaplains, so I am able to insist that our service reflects the inclusion of LGBT patients and staff. There may be chaplains who have very fixed views about LGBT issues that they would have complete freedom to express in their faith communities, where they have the power to do so, but in NHS chaplaincy they are constrained by Trust policies and their position within the hierarchy. As a member of the staff LGBT workforce group, I have an influence on Trust HR policy that is perhaps disproportionate to my 'banding'.

Concluding thoughts

Throughout this chapter, I have illustrated how the various governance arrangements that apply to my status as minister and chaplain overlap, interface and are at odds with one another on occasion. I have given an overview of the governance frameworks that have grown up around healthcare chaplaincy, particularly since nationalization in 1948 and more recently with professionalization, and I have reflected on what that means for healthcare chaplaincy in general, but also what it has meant for me as a gay Baptist minister. I have been able to practise a ministry that, at one point, I thought I would have to walk away from completely. Yet while my NHS employer's stated ambition is to make the workforce more reflective of the diversity of our city, I feel unable to marry my partner in view of the possible recriminations by my denomination, which could then put my employment at risk.

The landscape of LGBT inclusion is in a state of change and review, as tensions around LGBT rights, enshrined in English law, are being exposed within faith denominations. The UKBHC has begun to recognize this, following the CofE's recent decision to authorize prayers for same-sex blessings; a decision that is, at the time of writing, mired in continued debate. In light of this, the Chair of UKBHC sent a letter to all on the UKBHC register, recognizing that the decision may be difficult for some, presumably those who especially wished that the decision had gone further. As the Chair recounted a story of supporting two women in an emergency wedding and being with them until the wife died, he wrote, 'UKBHC recognises that individuals may change over the years and their persuasions about faith may alter so they may not be in good standing as a voluntary act whilst seeking another faith group to affiliate with, or for other reasons' (personal correspondence).

As our religious institutions in the UK continue to struggle to engage with the legal expectations and developments in society, chaplaincy is often a safe haven for those who no longer 'fit' within the structures of our historic denominations. More than that, chaplaincy can offer new opportunities for ministry and the chance to thrive in institutions that are often safer, more affirming and nurturing of a diverse range of staff. The denominations' losses are very often to the gain of the NHS and other chaplaincy contexts.

Bibliography

Khan, A. (2022), *Equality and Diversity in Employment Policy*, MFT Intranet, available at https://extranet.mft.nhs.uk/documents/policies/1064 (this document is only available to staff) (accessed 7.07.2024).

Ministries Team, Baptist Union of Great Britain (2022), Ministerial Recognition Rules, 12 October, available at https://www.baptist.org.uk/Publisher/File.aspx?ID=180015&view=browser (accessed 7.07.2024).

NHS England (2023), NHS Chaplaincy Guidelines 2023, available at https://www.england.nhs.uk/wp-content/uploads/2023/08/B1073i-nhs-chaplaincy-guidelines-for-nhs-managers-on-pastoral-spiritual-and-religious-care-august-23.pdf (accessed 7.07.2024).

Swift, C. (2014), *Hospital Chaplaincy in the Twenty-first Century*, 2nd edn, Farnham: Ashgate.
UKBHC (2014), Code of Conduct for Healthcare Chaplains, available at https://www.ukbhc.org.uk/wp-content/uploads/2019/12/Encl-4-ukbhc_code_of_conduct_2010_revised_2014_0.pdf (accessed 7.07.2024).
UKBHC (n.d.), available at https://www.ukbhc.org.uk/for-professionals/registration/registration-criteria/ (accessed 7.07.2024).
Van Dijk, L. (2021), 'Humanist Chaplains Entering Traditionally Faith-Based NHS Chaplaincy Teams', *Religions* 12(9), p. 744.

2

Trans-Atlantic Concepts for University Chaplaincy

IAN DELINGER

The background to this chapter is that I was born, raised and educated in the USA, yet trained for ordination at a Church of England theological college in Cambridge, UK, in my thirties. After being ordained and completing my training curacy, I served for eight years as chaplain to a university campus that was remote from its main campus and to a large faculty that included nursing, midwifery and social work. I am now rector of an Episcopal church parish in California in a small city with a university and a community college. My role requires me to work closely with the chaplain whom the local Episcopal churches financially support to provide campus ministries. These ministries are external to either institution.

As a UK higher education chaplain, I was tasked with starting the university chaplaincy ministry from scratch. As I did so, I relied heavily on my CofE ethos and experience of 'cure of all souls' and my dedication to the American ethos of liberal arts education fostered by my own time at Truman State University. In conversation with a friend and teacher in a university in the USA, I began to consider how my experience translated back to colleges and universities in the USA that had long since abandoned their church foundations. I thought that re-establishing chaplaincy in the originally church-founded institutions of the USA could add an element of engagement in the post-postmodern world in ways that would benefit students and staff (academic and support alike) to live out the core values of a liberal arts education.

What I discovered was that this blending of the liberal arts model of higher education and the cure of all souls fits the modern university landscape in both countries. The liberal arts ethos tempers the 'kingdom'-building tendency of the CofE parish system and transforms it into a sense of responsibility to each member of the institution for the benefit of their holistic growth.

The cure of all souls finds a way into the rigid separation of Church and state mindset that rejects or fears anything resembling religion. The blending of the two ethoses goes a long way to stave off the attitude of 'religion has no place on a modern university campus' which is dominant in both countries. It also aligns with the CofE's recent assertion 'that higher education is about seeking and celebrating wisdom, which is multi-faceted knowledge pursued and used well' (CofE, 2020, p. 3).

My experience was within a CofE foundation university, which was state-funded, unlike church universities in the USA. The chaplaincy was privileged to be a stand-alone department offering a ministry to the entire institution. However, the principles laid out in this chapter could be applied, in whole or in part, to chaplaincies that are not part of an institution, funded independently, and seeking pathways to stronger engagement across the institution they wish to serve.

Defining a chaplaincy's mission

Aside from the call to 'seek and serve Christ in all persons, loving your neighbour as yourself' in the Baptismal covenant of the Episcopal Church (1979, pp. 304–5), a chaplaincy must have a mission. That mission should align with both the mission of the Church and the mission, vision and core values of the university. If the mission is counter to the university, then a chaplain will find it difficult to make the case for continued and deepened engagement.

As with the various elements of the liberal arts ethos, chaplaincy can enable students and staff to reflect on the contemporary key issues in society and in their own lives in ways that shape their personal core values. Chaplaincy can become an integral part of nurturing students and staff and the whole institution in their commitment to key liberal arts ideals of free thinking, research and experimentation, self-expression, commitment to the immediate and wider communities, and breadth of study. All these are collaborative and dynamic. 'Moral awareness' in productive and engaged citizens creates respect for different viewpoints and an equilibrium of respect and inspiration between staff and student (Wellesley College, n.d.; Eisgruber, 2013; Roth, 2008; Truman State University, n.d.).

Given the flexibility to work among all members of the institution and within all areas as appropriate, chaplaincy can work both within established structures and in the interstices between all the other departments, in order to foster the vision and core values of the institution. Chaplaincy can encourage movement towards clarity in grey areas and gather disparate parts of the institution to help build a stronger, more cohesive and positive community, as a manifestation of the Christian faith and of shared humanitarian values (Adrian, 2003). In this way, strong leadership in chaplaincy can strengthen a university's ambition, for example, 'to cultivate in its students intellectual integrity, and courageous aspiration toward the best for oneself, one's family, one's society, and the world' (Truman State University, n.d.).

Chaplaincy can serve as a means by which to achieve the goals and values of a university within both the formal structures that purposefully enrich the lives of students and staff, and the interstices where unseen opportunities can be realized and fostered (Adrian, 2003).

Core principles

A chaplaincy must be founded on principles that shape the ministry of those involved and vice versa. Principles for a new chaplaincy could stem from the examples found in the Bible and the work of God in creation:

- Each person is unique and equal (Genesis 1.27).
- All persons are included; exclusion is by opting out (Galatians 3.28–29).
- All are sincerely welcomed (Mark 2.13–17); views may be respectfully challenged (Matthew 5.44–48).
- Each person will be met on his/her terms and brought along his/her own journey, which naturally intersects with the journeys of others (John 4.1–29).
- All persons form and live within the community (1 Corinthians 12.14–26).

The CofE's cure of all souls is shifted away from its rights and towards its responsibilities when underpinned by scriptures such as these within a university where the chaplain takes seriously the mandate to minister to every person in the institution, regardless of faith. Almost all universities in both countries now find themselves in a secularized and pluralistic society. Any chaplain needs to understand how to engage with all students and staff, regardless of their religious beliefs. To do this with integrity as a Christian ordained minister, we can look at the examples of YHWH and the deeming of all of creation 'good' and of Christ who associated with people of all backgrounds and, in doing so, broke with social, cultural and religious norms in order to challenge elitism and to end the marginalization of certain groups.

Establishing priorities

Priorities for chaplaincy must be in line with the mission, vision and core values of the institution that it serves. Campus ministry offers a variety of ministerial modes and opportunities, which stem from the immense diversity – community and people, activities, opportunities for mission and teaching, expressions of faith, walks of life – that can be brought together for meaning-making and sharing understanding. To accomplish this, a chaplaincy could work under the following priorities:

- Fostering the spirituality and faith of every person by offering and providing for worship, spiritual growth and study.
- Building community, a peaceful space (physical and metaphorical) and a safe environment.
- Building relationships and networks with students, staff and the wider community.
- Offering genuine hospitality.

These four example priorities align with both a liberal arts education and the cure of all souls. They encourage personal growth through a deliberate confluence of education and experience beyond one's academic discipline or institutional department. They do not exclude anyone of any particular background and, at best, offer an open invitation and, at least, demonstrably leave the door open for those who may initially be sceptical. They also offer a wide latitude for one's level of engagement, which could be the result of a variety of factors, including level of interest or commitment, seasonal workflows and the natural turnover of students and staff in a university.

Each of the example priorities are opportunities both to meet individuals where they are – or on their terms – and to invite or bring them into the chaplain's realm. This entire chapter is less about what goes on in the chapel and more about finding opportunities in the gaps of a multifaceted educational experience and institution. For example, being involved in student projects, large and small, or commissioning student projects for chaplaincy and for the wider Church, provides opportunities for learning for students and relationship-building for the chaplain, and is most likely without preference for a particular religion. Such involvement supports liberal arts ideals, particularly expanding the world view of those engaged; not everything is for the market or for profit. Similarly, collaboration on campus-wide events for both students and for staff, endeavouring to engage with the community as it exists, offering the gospel by both word and example, and fostering the mission, vision and core values of the university blend the liberal arts education with making provision for not just some, but all.

Fostering spirituality and faith

This priority comes with the assumption that all people have some sort of spirituality. There are many definitions of spirituality and there are many ancient and modern non-religious practices that would not be referred to by their adherents as spiritual but would be very familiar to people of faith as spiritual practices. This priority is not optional. If a chaplain fears that spirituality and faith will get in the way of student and staff engagement, then there are other professions to which they are better suited. Chaplaincy must endeavour to meet the spiritual needs of all persons by being the 'focal point for exploring faith, spirituality and worship, for those within and without the Christian community' (Heap, 2012). A person needs to have his/her physical, intellectual, emotional, social and spiritual dimensions nurtured. And a Christian can be a part of helping someone who is not a Christian nurture those dimensions while still demonstrably being a Christian; this is the foundation of the cure of all souls:

- A chaplain should foster the following among students and staff and help staff in their fostering of them in students (Heap, 2012):
  - Exploration and discovery of faith and spirituality.
  - Faith practice if that is wanted or needed.
  - Education for learning about other faiths.
  - Openness to constructive criticism and polite disagreement.
  - Challenging stereotypes and hostile attitudes.
  - Helping the institution 'deal properly and creatively with religion' [particularly in light of the rise of the religious right in national politics].
  - 'Building good relations with people of other faiths at a formative stage of life' [particularly amid increasing religious pluralism].

Chaplains, whether staff of the institution or external, serve to support the spiritual and pastoral needs of students and staff of all faiths, working among persons from different parts of the world who have different expressions of Christianity and different faiths. This could include ensuring that there is on-site provision for prayer for those of other faiths and seeking out places of worship and clerics of other faiths. In both countries, a Dean of Students would probably welcome someone who would take on that task and do it properly.

Building community

Building community within the diversity of a university requires immense creativity and flexibility and focused attention to the differing and changing needs of that community. Campus ministry ranges from highly individualized and personal, to open to all, and highly mission-focused 'community' can be both a committed, gathered congregation and a diverse community whose engagement and commitment are less defined. In building community, chaplaincy should bring the community together to:

- celebrate achievements;
- celebrate holidays (Christmas carol service, Easter, Passover, Eid al-Fitr, Diwali, Canadian and American Thanksgivings, International Coming Out Day, University Founders' Day, Graduation etc.);
- share and support one another in times of difficulty;
- offer pastoral care to students and staff;
- raise ethical issues with the institution and with individuals (Heap, 2012), and examine various points of view (Church of England, 2020, p. 9).

Community building is the focus of the majority of Christian ministries when stripped to their core: aside from our faith in Jesus Christ, everything from corporate worship to faith formation and discipleship have a fundamental community-building element. All the stories and letters in the New Testament are in the context of communities and strengthening them. So a university chaplain will already be equipped with community-building skills to some degree.

The events and activities that a chaplain might lead can be in the form of a programme specifically for the Christian community and those who choose to join in, or provision that fills gaps not filled by other organizations or departments. The openness of chaplaincy means that students and staff who would not otherwise encounter one another come together. Celebrating what the institution and individuals have achieved highlights the public service role of the chaplain and also emphasizes building community.

A less obvious element to building community is advocacy. All institutions, corporations, offices and organizations have a culture specific to them. Within a university, there could be a culture of the whole institution and subcultures within different departments and faculties, and staff and students can and do fall outside of those cultures. This often leads to not being heard, or needs and concerns not being addressed, sometimes intentionally and sometimes as something simply overlooked. Chaplains who are on the periphery of the culture of the institution or department can be well positioned to recognize needs that are not being addressed.

To be an effective advocate, the chaplain must have good relationships within the institution and be trusted. Advocacy can emerge from having built community and it can lead to forging a stronger community. It can emerge from having strong networks and it can facilitate networking. It also requires careful discernment in order to be effective and not to backfire. There are two distinct types of opportunities for advocacy to consider. The first is probably familiar to all chaplains: the same concern is mentioned by several people over a period of time. The first instance may seem as if it is an isolated one, and the person – staff or student – may appear to be fine with moving on after having someone trusted to share it with. As similar instances arise in pastoral contexts, it becomes clear that there is a problem that is not being addressed. A person who feels that their voice is not being heard will not take the necessary steps to address the situation. Perhaps they have tried but have been gaslit or suffered retribution. Students often feel that they do not have a voice. Even student unions can feel powerless when facing the authority of the institution.

The second type of opportunity for advocacy is when the institution clearly fails to live up to its mission, vision and core values, its policies or laws. This is difficult to address since it usually means confronting the most powerful individuals within the institution. However, we have many biblical examples of advocates who confronted what seemed impossible. The advocacy I am pointing towards here is the type that is discovered in the pastoral realm, in the gaps of provision, with seemingly no one obvious to take the lead. Chaplains internal to the institutions they serve will have a very different path to navigate than chaplains outside the institution. It cannot be overemphasized that advocacy requires discernment and must be rooted in pastoral care.

Pastoral work will typically be very casual. For example, stopping by staff offices or having coffee with a student or staff member, through which one-to-one relationships emerge, resulting in the confidence to share pastoral issues. For students this is key, as they are often unwilling to use the support services provided or may wish to share outside formal structures. Pastoral work can also be deliberate, especially when relationships have been built. This work can be a result of student support services needing additional help and seeing the chaplain as worthy of referrals. It can also come in the form of a crisis when there is not a department or staff member who feels that it is within their skill set to address the crisis and to hold the community in its pain and grief, yet who acknowledge that this is needed. This all circles back to fostering spirituality and faith and leads on to the next priority of building networks.

Building relationships, networking with leadership collaboration

In order to be effective throughout the organization, a chaplain must work among all levels of staff and with all students. This engenders trust at all institutional levels (management, administrative and services staff) through considering the person with whom s/he is speaking as a colleague. The chaplain can then collaborate with others to fulfil the mission of the university in unique ways. A well-networked chaplain might also facilitate collaborations between persons who may not otherwise have connections with one another. This mindset fits squarely in both the liberal arts ethos (interdepartmental and whole person) and the cure of all souls ethos (all are a part of the one).

Working with staff at all levels to develop strategic relationships, from student support to academic departments, results in opportunities to work with students and staff to utilize their skills, to encourage their development, and to benefit internal and external stakeholders. It results in a team of people who want to use their individual skills towards a common goal, who welcome open and honest dialogue, and who have the personal integrity to be accountable for their own mistakes. One example of this was when I was asked to host a weekly show for the university's radio station, produced by students. This unique chance was an opportunity to engage with students at their level in their context. Furthermore, the guests on the show included students and staff from across the four campuses, building new networks and opportunities. All of this led to the development of interpersonal and professional relationships, as well as mutual learning and greater understanding of both the world and individuals, all within an academic radio production programme.

Offering genuine hospitality

Christianity, along with its foundations in Judaism, has a long tradition of hospitality (Genesis 18.1–8). Chaplaincy should be the one place where each person knows they are welcome (friend or stranger) and will be cared for, regardless of that person's background or circumstances (Matthew 11.28–30). The chaplain and his or her team must be given the proper resources to offer genuine hospitality but must also possess the inherent traits and skills from which hospitality naturally emerges (3 John 5–8).

For me, hospitality is not only an inherent feature of Christian ministry, but it has proven invaluable as a means of connecting with people while establishing these new ministries. Genuine and generous hospitality helped engage with staff and students from across the university, meet them where they are on their terms, and find opportunities to engage with them in their contexts.

Measurable goals

Churches of all denominations have tried to fit their ministry into business principles and have failed (Swinton, 2001). The two are not wholly incompatible but must be woven together in a way that maintains the integrity of the primary principles of Christian ministry. The success of a ministry is difficult to measure. In a new chaplaincy, achievements could be measured by the extent to which chaplaincy is engaged with work across the university, through those who wish to identify their work as something they do as committed members of the chaplaincy community.

The way forward

Many colleges and universities in the USA have abandoned their church foundations and, along with that, their chaplaincies. Establishing a new chaplaincy within a previously secular campus has shown that, manifested in a twenty-first-century way, in line with both Christian and liberal arts ideals, a chaplain can play a key role in helping students and staff 'Fac[e] big questions about meaning and purpose, in life, about what it is to be human and what it is to be a good individual and community, in a place which helps to shape individuals and communities' (Heap, 2012) in a post-postmodern world (Adrian, 2003). Establishing a chaplaincy with a chaplain who is sensitive to the needs of the community, whose main focus is to serve the entire community, and who comes with a clear vision and sense of purpose seems a clear way forward for the modern liberal arts-based institution.

Bibliography

Adrian, W. (2003), 'Christian Universities, A Historical Perspective', *Christian Higher Education* 2(1), pp. 15–33.
Church of England Education Office (2020), *Faith in Higher Education: A Church of England Vision*, March, available at www.churchofengland.org/sites/default/files/2020-03///10929acfaith-in-higher-education-report_web.pdf (accessed 7.07.2024).
Eisgruber, C. L. (2013), 'Speeches and Writings (Princeton University)', *Presidential Installation: The Ideal of a Liberal Arts University*, available at http://www.princeton.edu/president/eisgruber/speeches-writings/archive/?id=11053 (accessed 7.07.2024).

Episcopal Church (1979), *The Book of Common Prayer and Administration of the Sacraments and other Rites and Ceremonies of the Church: Together with the Psalter or Psalms of David according to the Use of the Episcopal Church*, New York: Seabury Press.

Heap, S. (2012), 'Why Chaplaincy Matters', August, circulated paper arising from discussion in the Chaplains National Executive, Church of England.

Roth, M. (2008), 'What's a Liberal Arts Education Good for?', *Huffington Post*, 1 December, available at http://www.huffingtonpost.com/michael-roth/whats-a-liberal-arts- educ_b_147584.html (accessed 7.07.2024).

Swinton, J. (2001), *Spirituality and Mental Health Care: Rediscovering a Forgotten Dimension*, London and Philadelphia, PA: Jessica Kingsley Publishers.

Truman State University (n.d.), Mission Statement, Truman State University, available at http://about.truman.edu/mission.asp (accessed 7.07.2024).

Wellesley College (n.d.), 'The Value of a Liberal Arts Education', *Wellesley College*, available at https://calendar.wellesley.edu/about/missionandvalues/valueliberalarts (accessed 7.07.2024).

3

Police Chaplaincy: Diversity, Inclusion and Welcome

MAY PRESTON

The foundations of police chaplaincy stem from a mixture of the pastoral and historical-parish models, where needs were met outside traditional parish boundaries to address the new and unique experience of police officers. Its earliest forms were established in the Police Bible Reading and Temperance societies. Both were established in the late nineteenth century to address alcoholism and high levels of suicide among police officers in a particularly violent era and one where their (relatively new) role was not well understood. Axcell explains how this approach was entirely Christian yet recognized the need for a holistic model of chaplaincy to address the needs of an illiterate and stigmatized workforce, who found themselves isolated from everyday parish life as a result of their vocation (Axcell, 2016, pp. 25–30). However, I see how this form of chaplaincy represented the views and needs of a white, Christian, male-dominated environment, which was to remain late into the twenty-first century.

This may have been the most appropriate model at the time, but today police chaplaincy is much less monoculturistic and operates as a multifaith entity. In my force, a chaplaincy provision was established in 2013 in accordance with College of Policing guidelines (Association of Chief Police Officers, 2013). The guidelines advocate for a multifaith model yet make little reference to faith. Instead, the document places impetus on pastoral care as the foremost concern of chaplaincy 'with a brief that focuses on spiritual and emotional needs, chaplaincy offers a complementary role to that of trained counsellors, occupational health and welfare units' (Association of Chief Police Officers, 2013, p. 4). Currently the chaplaincy sits under the Equality, Diversity and Human Rights (EDHR) team while finding its activities ever-increasingly aligned to the well-being programme. I consider that the drifting into other strategic areas represents a misalignment between where the chaplaincy is perceived as being and where it is actually found.

Changes in the demographic of the UK in recent times have required the police service to adapt in accordance with the process of secularization. Slater states that the Equality Act 2010 and a focus on human rights led to generic diversity provision becoming a prevailing public norm (Slater, 2015, p. 5). While true of policing, there were additional developments that led to an increased focus on diversity. The Stephen Lawrence enquiry is widely regarded as a watershed moment for British policing and led to numerous inspections and inquiries undertaken by the UK government and Her Majesty's Inspectorate of Constabulary and Fire and Rescue Services.

Subsequent outcomes and recommendations culminated in the *Diversity Matters* report in 2003. This report observes an institutional 'resistance to police chaplaincy based on the perception that chaplaincy is a uniquely Christian concept and that it is wrong to promote one faith at a time when it is perceived that policing must be more inclusive' (HMICFRS, 2003, p. 120). The report mandated that all forces move towards multifaith chaplaincies with a generic provision to staff. Threlfall-Holmes suggests that this secular 'diversity model' of chaplaincy is utilized by organizations striving to be seen as more inclusive and is typically driven by statutory implications (Threlfall-Holmes, 2011a, p. 124). However, it could also be a genuine attempt to embrace difference and an improved creativity.

I am based in a large metropolitan police force in the north of England. It currently has a multifaith chaplaincy team comprising around 13 chaplains; one lead and one per geographic district: four Anglican, two Catholic, two Baptist, two Muslim, one Sikh, one Jewish.

It appears that the majority of forces established their multifaith chaplaincies within EDHR teams as a result of recommendations made in *Diversity Matters* (HMICFRS, 2003) and this occurred in the absence of official direction for how chaplaincies were meant to function. The national ACPO guidance relating to the functions and terms of reference for chaplains was not published until ten years later (Association of Chief Police Officers, 2013). To this day, chaplains remain under EDHR teams rather than being better placed to support the workforce. However, I believe there is another aspect to this, which is alluded to by the tone of *Diversity Matters* (HMICFRS, 2003). Whipp states there is an institutional wariness towards chaplains based on presumptions about the intentions of religious representatives coming into organizations (Whipp, 2018, p. 102). This feels true of my force, which appears to prefer its commitment to secularity and diversity as a safer option.

In institutions where multifaith teams provide specific chaplains to counsel on matters related to a particular faith, I see how such an alignment makes sense. Ryan states that this is a common feature of multifaith chaplaincies, with chaplains diversifying from their core pastoral role and acting as subject-matter experts (Ryan, 2015, p. 34). This resource is valuable in a policing context, particularly where incidents occur that have the potential for a profound community impact – for example, a terrorism investigation involving a place of worship. However, in my force this diversification within the chaplaincy does not occur and instead appears to adhere rigidly to a model where every chaplain serves every member of staff regardless of their faith or other characteristics.

The role of the faith adviser is instead given to staff support networks, such as the Muslim Police Association and Catholic Police Guild. They are chaired by police officers and have been given specific authority to represent staff in various official proceedings. This may have contributed to the underuse of the chaplaincy team as faith issues are automatically referred to staff networks, which are more inclined to engage robustly with respect to their own traditions and beliefs. For example, the Christian network is open only to Christian police officers and the executive hold strong views on a range of issues, such as the use of a once-consecrated chapel for the training of rape investigators. I suggest that this shift occurred unconsciously, by a process of the accumulation of powers given to staff networks which, over time, has resulted in a loss of relevancy for the chaplaincy.

This is not necessarily a bad thing. Boyce states that by placing one's own religious agenda aside, chaplaincy teams are more likely to focus on building provision in relative harmony (Boyce, 2010, p. 40). It also frees the chaplaincy of the political wrangling I have observed between the staff networks and allows a sole focus on pastoral work, which is highlighted as one of the most important issues for my force at this time. A report commissioned by the Police Foundation in 2019 suggests a 35 per cent increase in police officers reporting sick as a result of psychological issues since 2010, and that the reason for this is under-resourcing and relentless societal and organizational change (Keiran Lewis, 2019).

Attempts to define multifaith chaplaincy often centre on a concept of a shared hospitality. Boyce states that hospitality is common to all world religions: 'Each world religion has honed its beliefs and practices, some over thousands of years, to provide a framework for human sustainability for their respective communities' (Boyce, 2010, p. 35). However, it could be argued that hospitality is not a religious trait as much as it is a human one. Humanists argue that what functions as chaplaincy has been monopolized by subjective religions and was, until recently, hostile towards the non-religious movements (Humanists UK, n.d.). However, Spencer states that humanism is itself incapable of neutrality, and it is precisely this misconception about faith that dominates the public sphere today. Instead, he suggests multifaith groups give space to others in the public sphere because of their traditions of hospitality: 'What the state sees as problematic (differences in religions) is actually the basis for a good society, tolerance, dialogue, and co-operation' (Spencer, 2006, pp. 64–5).

The multifaith model also relies on sharing resources, which Threlfall-Holmes observes as a potentially thorny issue (Threlfall-Holmes, 2011b, p. 133). However, I suggest this is highly context-dependent, as in my force there are no worship spaces and chaplains are spread out across a vast area, with few resources to manage in the first instance. For my force, chaplaincy is more 'embedded' (Ballard, 2009), with chaplains working within the culture of the organization to enable them to comprehend the issues that officers face and converse with them in a language they understand. Although there are dedicated prayer rooms (usually containing no more than a table, chairs, prayer mats, and void of any iconography) in each police building, they are rarely used by the chaplaincy team. Instead, chaplaincy occurs alongside officers and staff, in corridors, parade rooms or 'refs rooms', where officers occasionally eat and rest together. It also occurs off-site, at the scene of incidents, which can occur anywhere in the force area. In practical terms this means chaplains engage first and foremost where they are and act as representatives of hospitality, rather than being concerned with the rites and rituals of their traditions.

Although the original model of police chaplaincy fits the historical parish model that regards the workplace as a form of parish in its own right (Threlfall-Holmes, 2011a, p. 121), police chaplaincy today is less formal and more incarnational. Here, chaplaincy 'is something one is rather than something one does' (Threlfall-Holmes, 2011a, p. 120). In walking alongside officers, chaplains are a source of presence and I agree that 'presence precedes function' (Whipp, 2018, p. 104). It is this lingering presence that acts as a reminder to us and reveals the transformative power of God. However, Whipp also warns that too much embeddedness can undermine missional integrity: 'Chaplains must negotiate a subtle course between the twin poles of cosy assimilation and crude opposition in order to find true missional integrity' (Whipp, 2018, p. 105).

Another aspect of a police chaplain's duties includes presiding over ceremonial services at times of tragedy, memorial services, or force funerals when officers are killed on duty. This fits the 'traditional heritage model', where tradition is highly regarded, and chaplains provide 'civic' service (Threlfall-Holmes, 2011a, p. 124). Force events such as the Remembrance Sunday service are held in local cathedrals and are almost exclusively Anglican in nature. This is unsurprising as the British police service is a body of the Crown and allegiance to the state and the King is explicitly referred to in the attestation oath taken by officers upon appointment. However, this oath was introduced at a time when the

CofE held considerable influence over the everyday lives of many people, and long predates the development of a multifaith society.

Overall, I believe, the most pressing need for the chaplaincy team is to provide inclusive pastoral care to the workforce and the multifaith model best enables this. Threlfall-Holmes states that this form of chaplaincy is one where 'the task of ministry is seen primarily as one of sharing in God's love and care for all people, unconditionally and without demanding any response' (Threlfall-Holmes, 2011a, p. 120). This addresses the situation of many staff while also adhering to the mandate for a multifaith chaplaincy, one that is underpinned by diversity. Threlfall-Holmes suggests that in secular settings this risks the chaplain taking the place of counsellors and being perceived as 'the professional nice guy, there at times of crises' (Threlfall-Holmes, 2011a, p. 123).

However, the difference between the support offered by counsellors and the occupational health team is that this support takes place in liminal, informal settings. It occurs without threatening the chaplain's spiritual integrity, as I do not see highly contextual pastoral care as problematic when balanced against one's own faith. Torry suggests that workplace chaplaincy is inductive, 'starting with people's experience and then seeing whether biblical passages or theological themes shed light on them' (Torry, 2010, pp. 155–6). Pastoral care is also central to Christianity and in multifaith settings extends beyond it. Lyall suggests that while the parameters of pastoral care are difficult to define, its aim is to support and affirm in times of trouble, in community, being sensitive to the uniqueness of each individual, taking seriously the social and political context (Lyall, 2001, p. 11).

Slater states that chaplaincies are often an 'unconscious ecclesiastical adaption' in response to cultural contexts (Slater, 2015, p. 9). Police chaplaincy originally emerged as a result of a gap that left police officers marginalized from the Church; this was not only a result of geographic factors, but a contextual gap. To fill this gap, it is crucial that chaplains are embedded and concerned with the well-being of officers 'in the field', being shaped by their role in ways a church minister could not be. It gives Christian chaplains the 'missional significance' Slater describes (Slater, 2015, p. 9). Whereas the church minister is regarded as the host, the chaplain is the guest with an agenda.

Caperon regards chaplaincy as an integral mode of mission that is both 'inevitably responsive to context and also rooted in pastoral presence' (Caperon, 2018, p. 128). Caperon goes on to describe the *Missio Dei* as 'a divine movement impelling the world towards the Kingdom of God, with the Church being called to collaborate in that mission' (Caperon, 2018, p. 130). I suggest that a multifaith approach, focused on care for others, is entirely congruent with the Christian understanding of the *Missio Dei*.

From examining these issues, it appears that there can be a misalignment regarding where the chaplaincy sits; this is a result of a previous reactive drive to be perceived as more diverse, resulting in a multifaith model of chaplaincy for the police service. The chaplains are not operating as spiritual advisers; instead, they are first and foremost the providers of pastoral care. This does not prevent the chaplaincy from operating, but has the effect of isolating the chaplaincy team from strategic discussions that may affect how it supports the workforce. Instead, it may be better aligned to the occupational health and well-being team. This would raise the profile of the chaplaincy and ensure more staff in need of support are identified. It would also enable the chaplains to be more aware of where to signpost staff and access support for themselves if they needed it.

A multifaith approach is most appropriate both practically, and for reasons of religious and secular inclusivity, in an increasingly diverse workforce (Hales, 2020, p. 10). Whipp states that 'it is more important than ever for religious sponsors to embrace and articulate a theology of chaplaincy which is genuinely committed to service and acutely sensitive to the imperialistic overtones of missional discourse in our largely, and uncomfortably, post-Christian society' (Whipp, 2018, p. 102). Police chaplaincy can comprise a mixture of the secular-diversity, incarnational and pastoral models. Threlfall-Holmes suggests that where multiple models converge this can also be regarded as the 'secular meta-model' where chaplaincy is regarded as a specialist service and accessed according to need – an essentially 'passive, consumer demand-led view of chaplaincy' (Threlfall-Holmes, 2011a, p. 125). However, a model centred on personal autonomy is attentive and able to meet the needs of staff in the organization. Whipp states that there is little room for religious exclusivity in the public services and 'the only valid stance for an embedded chaplain is to welcome, in a totally disinterested way, any and every authentically human encounter' (Whipp, 2018, p. 115).

Bibliography

Association of Chief Police Officers (2013), *ACPO Guidelines & Principles on Chaplaincy in the Police Service*, ACPO.

Axcell, D. (2016), *Where Duty Calls*, London: Deax.

Ballard, P. (2009), 'Locating Chaplaincy: A Theological Note', *Crucible*, July–September, pp. 18–24.

Boyce, G. (2010), *An Improbable Feast: The Surprising Dynamic of Hospitality at the Heart of Multifaith Chaplaincy*, Morrisville, NC: Lulu.com.

Caperon, J. (2018), 'Chaplaincy and Traditional Church Structures', in J. Caperon, *A Christian Theology of Chaplaincy*, London: Jessica Kingsley Publishers, pp. 119–43.

Hales, G. (2020), *Diversity Uplift: The Police Foundation*, available at https://www.police-foundation.org.uk/wp-content/uploads/2010/10/perspectives_workforce_diversity.pdf (accessed 7.07.2024).

HMICFRS (2003), *Diversity Matters – Full Report*, available at https://www.justiceinspectorates.gov.uk/hmicfrs/publications/diversity-matters-full-report/ (accessed 7.07.2024).

Humanists UK (n.d.), *Campaigns*, available at https://humanists.org.uk/campaigns/human-rights-and-equality/chaplaincy-and-pastoral-support/ (accessed 7.07.2024).

Keiran Lewis, A. H. (2019), *Police Workforce Wellbeing and Organisational Development*, London: The Police Foundation, available at https://www.police-foundation.org.uk/wp-content/uploads/2019/02/organisational_development_report_final.pdf (accessed 7.07.2024).

Lyall, D. (2001), *The Integrity of Pastoral Care*, London: SPCK.

Ryan, B. (2015), *A Very Modern Ministry: Chaplaincy in the UK*, London: Theos.

Slater, V. (2015), *Chaplaincy Ministry and the Mission of the Church*, London: SCM Press.

Spencer, N. (2006), '"Doing God": A Future for Faith in the Public Square', London: Theos.

Threlfall-Holmes, M. (2011a), 'Exploring Models of Chaplaincy', in M. Threlfall-Holmes and M. Newitt (eds), *Being a Chaplain*, London: SPCK, pp. 116–26.

Threlfall-Holmes, M. (2011b), 'Values and Tensions', in M. Threlfall-Holmes and M. Newitt (eds), *Being a Chaplain*, London: SPCK, pp. 127–40.

Torry, M. (2010), *Bridgebuilders*, Norwich: Canterbury Press.

Whipp, M. (2018), 'Embedding Chaplaincy: Integrity and Presence', in J. Caperon, *A Christian Theology of Chaplaincy*, London: Jessica Kingsley Publishers, pp. 101–19.

4

The Place of Healthcare Chaplains in Hong Kong: Organization, Governance and the Emergence of an Unlikely Role in Suicide Prevention

TAK HANG ANGUS LIN

In 2022, I moved to the UK from Hong Kong, where I had been serving as a chaplain in private and public hospitals for eight years. This reflection aims to set out some of my observations on the differences between the two healthcare chaplaincy contexts. To help illustrate this, I will explore one particular aspect of Christian chaplaincy in Hong Kong, which involves the expectations placed upon healthcare chaplains to provide the necessary support to patients who are displaying suicidal ideations.

The historical development of chaplaincy in Hong Kong and the place of spirituality in contemporary culture

In the UK, one entry requirement for chaplains serving in the NHS is that they have to be accredited 'as leaders in a recognised faith community' (NHS, online, n.d.). Chaplains are often, therefore, supported by their denomination and depend on their endorsement in order to be employed as a chaplain in a healthcare institution. To become a chaplain in Hong Kong, in addition to accredited study at a divinity school, we are required to complete at least two units of Clinical Pastoral Education (CPE). One CPE unit amounts to 400 hours of intensive training alongside clinical placement, preparing theological students and ministers to be spiritual care professionals, mainly within a hospital setting. We are not required to maintain any endorsement with any church; our accreditation as a chaplain derives from the divinity school study and the number of CPE units completed.

Consequently, chaplains in healthcare settings in Hong Kong are typically only accountable to the hospital chaplaincy committee as an employee. They do not have the same denominational links that most chaplains must maintain in the UK. This link with denomination within the NHS arises from the historical position of the CofE, which was often the default provider of chaplains in settings such as healthcare, prison and education. Contemporary healthcare chaplaincy in the UK is more diverse, both in denomination and in the breadth of faiths that now make up chaplaincy departments, yet this duality of allegiance to both the NHS and the endorsing faith group remains part of the chaplaincy experience; the connection with a recognized faith institution is firmly embedded within the culture. The landscape in Hong Kong is different and this arises again through the historical development of the discipline as well as perceptions of spirituality that have afforded an ambiguous understanding of the purpose of healthcare chaplaincy.

Hong Kong largely perceives itself to be a secular state. Over 50 per cent of the population regard themselves as 'non-religious', with only 12 per cent identifying as Christian (Hong Kong Government, 2022). This figure reflects a stark difference from England and Wales, where the 2021 census data revealed that 46.2 per cent of the population stated they were Christian (ONS, 2021). However, despite identifying as a secular state, 'the unofficial cultural and religious practices idiosyncratic to Hong Kong Chinese popular or folk religion remain a significant influence on the day-to-day life of local residents' (Yih, 2022). Those prevalent folk religions combine Buddhism, Daoism and Confucianism and possibly contribute to a confused understanding of spirituality among ethnically Chinese people and within the Hong Kong Chinese culture at large. The Chinese translation of 'spirituality', which is usually adopted in academic reading or conversation, has various meanings, leading to confusion for the public (Niu, McSherry and Partridge, 2021).

Hong Kong healthcare chaplaincy development was built on the foundation of overseas Christian missionaries whose main aim centred around proselytizing and converting local people. This history is likely to be the reason behind the widespread notion in Hong Kong that a chaplain is a pastor who proselytizes which, in turn, has resulted in suspicion around the discipline and a reluctance to engage. It has obstructed the professionalization and position of chaplaincy, which is misunderstood by the public as 'missionary work' and 'superstitious', and therefore not relevant to the secular world – even one with profound spiritual undertones. Consequently, even though chaplaincy has been advocated as a 'spiritual care provider' within the healthcare industry, the role of the chaplain lacks recognition and understanding among many physicians, nurses and allied health professionals.

Chaplaincy within such a context is clearly challenging. In my own experience, when I talked to people in the hospital setting, many had no idea what chaplaincy is, let alone what the service could provide; many, when I tried to explain, thought it was a religious service that was irrelevant to them. Patients in Hong Kong who have little or no knowledge about Christianity are often confused by the role of a chaplain in the hospital and this is perpetuated by the fact that we do not have official staff status and are often not ordained or accredited by a specific church or denomination. In other words, most hospital patients in Hong Kong are likely to decline a visit from a chaplain with no fundamental understanding of what the chaplain may be able to offer. This is not wholly different from the UK context, however. Hurly (2018) highlights how, in the UK, many people perceive chaplaincy as a religious provision that is, therefore, not relevant to them; yet evidence suggests that people in the UK displayed an openness to seeking someone to talk to about pastoral or spiritual matters in times of crisis (Humanists UK, online, n.d.). This is where, I would argue, the fundamental difference in chaplaincy reception lies between the UK and Hong Kong contexts: in the recognition and understanding of spiritual support. As Niu, McSherry and Partridge (2021) point out, when it comes to advocating for the advancement of spiritual care in healthcare, basic recognition of the importance of spirituality in Chinese culture is not widespread.

Government-owned hospitals in Hong Kong, as in the UK, are secular organizations, their main priority being to provide professional medical services that meet local citizens' needs, often with very limited resources. The ambiguous nature of spiritual care in Hong Kong means that chaplaincy development remains sluggish because patients, medical staff and even hospital managers neglect to attend to the pastoral and spiritual needs of patients and themselves. While the UK data suggest a decline in participation in forms of organized religion, its main institutions still recognize the importance of spiritual care. From my perspective as a chaplain who has come to the UK from Hong Kong, the place of chaplaincy in Hong Kong stands in contrast to the UK's Department of Health, which declared in 1948 that spiritual care is one of the responsibilities of every hospital (Snowden et al., 2020). This embeds spiritual care formally into the structure in a way that is completely absent from the structure in Hong Kong healthcare.

The organizational context of healthcare chaplains in Hong Kong

By the end of 2021, 115 chaplains were serving in Hong Kong's public and private healthcare settings. In government hospitals, chaplains are not directly employed by the Hospital Authority (HA) and most are considered honorary staff providing pastoral and spiritual care to patients and staff. My previous honorary appointment letter issued by the chief executive of the HA stated that the chaplain endorsed was accountable to the general manager of Administrative Services but not the general manager of clinical services, implying that the chaplain was not part of the clinical team, a team that included all allied health specialists. Even more conspicuous than the standing in the organization structure was a section regarding public liability policies that stated, 'You may, however, wish to be separately represented in any medical cases, in which event we will have no liability whatsoever in connection therewith' (Hospital Authority, 2017), suggesting that the HA did not retain responsibility for any conflict or issues in clinical practices relating to chaplains and could terminate an appointment for any reason. The HA has the right to govern chaplaincy and chaplains are accountable to hospital management but they are not paid by the HA. Furthermore, the HA does not allocate any resources towards the professional development of chaplaincy while continually encouraging the Association of Hong Kong Hospital Christian Chaplaincy Ministry (AHKHCCM), which serves as a liaison organization promoting chaplaincy, and all chaplaincy committees, to achieve professionalization and ensure holistic care is being implemented in hospitals, but with their own resources.

As chaplains are not in the HA pay structure, over 20 chaplaincy committees have been established to cover all the public hospitals, funded by various churches and donations from the public. Those committees are self-financed and provide spiritual care services in affiliated hospitals with the endorsement of HA as a non-government organization. Most of the director boards governing those committees are the representatives of local churches in the regional district and medical staff of the affiliated hospital. Chaplains employed by committees must be accountable to the director board and therefore the model of chaplaincy and its mode of professionalization are inevitably shaped by the board director's vision.

As Christianity in Hong Kong was imported by overseas missionaries, Hong Kong churches inherited an evangelical missionary tradition, emphasizing spreading the gospel to unbelievers and understanding proclamation and conversion as being foundational to being a Christian. This is a cultural perspective that director boards have inherited, where chaplaincy is largely perceived as a proselytizing ministry in the secular healthcare industry. This is where some of the tension arises in chaplaincy practice. The healthcare chaplain is funded by a structure that views their role as primarily missionary, evangelical, and for the purpose of growing the number of Christians. The hospital chaplain is also accountable to the HA, where the understanding of chaplaincy is underdeveloped and therefore the role is not embedded within the allied health professionals' team. Finally, the chaplain operates within a secular context that views the chaplaincy role with suspicion and where conceptions of spirituality are fragmented and undervalued. As a result of operating within a paradigm constructed through historical perceptions of Christians, the status and professionalization of chaplaincy has been limited. Chaplains have been considered only to be gospel preachers in hospitals. Their professional development has been seen by board directors as irrelevant to Jesus' 'Great Commission' and unnecessary by hospital management, as neither have viewed the discipline as akin to other allied medical services.

Finally, it is important to make note of a specific point in Hong Kong's history and its relevance within the story of healthcare chaplaincy. The year of 1997 was significant for both Hong Kong and England. In May of that year, the UK underwent a government change; with this, chaplaincy in England became more focused on a multifaith approach (Swift, Cobb and Todd, 2015). On the first day of July, the UK handed Hong Kong to the People's Republic. As Hong Kong was a colony of the UK before 1997, the operation and funding model of Hong Kong's public medical services followed the NHS to a certain extent, with both systems being financed by their respective governments (Swift, Cobb and Todd, 2015). While 1997 heralded a new era for chaplaincy in England, the handover of governance appears to have signified a stagnation for healthcare chaplaincy in Hong Kong. After 1997, the Hong Kong government focused most on their economic development and political stability, rather than attending to the pastoral and spiritual needs and welfare of society. Today, the relationship between the hospital chaplaincy committees and the hospital organization remains one that is not bonded statutorily and, therefore, it can be deduced that the government does not regard chaplaincy services as essential. Yet by introducing chaplaincy services into the hospital and appointing chaplains as honorary staff who are partially integrated into the system, the hospital management can state that holistic care is emphasized and implemented in medical care, without allocating any resources to this themselves.

An unexpected role in suicide prevention

While the historical understanding of healthcare chaplaincy, which still persists in chaplaincy boards, is of an evangelical missionary form, theologically the Hong Kong healthcare chaplaincy service tends towards the 'exile' model, defined as 'operating away from the Church' (Ryan, 2018). Chaplains in Hong Kong hospitals do not have the same faith or denominational expectations that we may see in the UK. They are afforded considerable flexibility to develop their ministry to fit into the specific healthcare institution. This lack of formal role or recognition within many hospitals, despite the requirement to undertake CPE to become a chaplain, means that the chaplain's role is ill-defined within the organization. In my experience, this has led to a 'stopgap' approach, where chaplains are requested to address specific needs identified by hospital staff that they are unable to meet themselves, either as a result of a lack of staff or expertise. As is common across many healthcare environments, medical staff in the hospital I worked in were under tremendous pressure, with a high patient-to-staff ratio, which led inevitably to the prioritization of immediate medical needs over any form of more holistic care. Such aspects of patient care were often fully outsourced to chaplains. The remit for what was covered under this was broad and included requests for support in areas that, arguably, required a high level of professional competence and expertise. One aspect of care that demonstrates this clearly is in the care of patients with complex mental health needs.

I was a chaplain in a government hospital located at the centre of a highly populated district in Hong Kong, employed by a chaplaincy committee that provides pastoral and spiritual care for patients and staff on a voluntary basis. Being a volunteer chaplain, I had no official position in the hospital from an organizational perspective. When practising as a volunteer healthcare chaplain, I was frequently asked to visit patients displaying suicidal intention. Referrals to chaplains of this nature became commonplace within the hospital following an incident where a patient died by suicide in a ward. This was devastating for all concerned and led to a thorough review of practices and procedures at all levels. A policy was implemented that required medical staff to refer patients displaying any suicide ideation to the care of the chaplaincy team. This helped to ease the pressure placed upon medically trained staff by transferring the care of such complex patients to the responsibility of the healthcare chaplain. However, this opened up questions around accountability for chaplains who had no formally recognized position in the institution and no accreditation from a faith organization. It also brings into question the evangelical aspect of chaplaincy, held by the hospital chaplaincy governing boards.

As a hospital chaplain, I was more than willing to approach anyone in crisis at any point in their life. I was comfortable being called upon to support patients who had attempted suicide or expressed a desire to. The World Health Organization (WHO) defines suicide as something that happens 'impulsively in moments of crisis with a breakdown in the ability to deal with life stresses' (WHO, 2023). Being present with a patient facing an existential crisis was often profoundly challenging, such encounters being deeply meaningful and spiritual in nature. Dietrich Bonhoeffer's words influenced me a great deal. He wrote, 'If the pastor is called to a dying person's side, there is no reason by which he can excuse himself' (Bonhoeffer, 1985, p. 59). While this clearly related to care of the dying, care of someone intending to take their own life follows a similar vein. How could I decline a call to pastor to someone in such a position?

The structure of Hong Kong hospitals, and their position within a society that perceives itself to be secular, means that the focus becomes one of medical science, policy, successful governance and economic management. But patients do not fit neatly into scientific, rationalistic boxes and those in a critical mental health crisis ask questions of personhood and spirituality that cannot be simply quantified and rationalized by science and policy.

However, there are serious questions about accountability, training, supervision and support that are not – as yet – being addressed sufficiently by the governance structures in Hong Kong. From my short time here in the UK, it is clear that chaplains would not be asked to take sole responsibility of patients with severe mental health issues, and would only be permitted to support the patient if they had undergone suitable training and the patient had consented to chaplaincy support. This is in no small part because chaplains are governed by the hospital Trust and the spiritual care team is a recognized discipline within the NHS. In Hong Kong, a chaplain is not recognized as a statutory member of the healthcare team. They are accountable to the administrative lead and to the independently run chaplaincy boards. While they are required to undertake intensive Continuing Professional Development (CPD) training, this may not provide them with the necessary skills to independently support patients in crisis. My observations and experience in Hong Kong have noted that complex mental health cases require a lot of management by the healthcare team, who are often stretched to capacity. Under such circumstances, it is often preferable to shift the workload and responsibilities to chaplains with no official status in the organizational chart. This clearly has implications for the chaplain, who may find themselves vulnerable in a number of ways. Their funding board may not perceive this work to be of an evangelical nature and therefore may question whether chaplains should undertake such a role. On the other hand, the hospital, with their limited understanding of chaplaincy, may see this to be a way to 'fill a gap' in their provision. The chaplain may find themselves out of their depth and with no established structure of support.

There are potential benefits, however, if this area of care is managed well. As a healthcare chaplain, even though I was not officially on the staff body, I sought to establish myself as a part of the hospital team, willing to share the workload, challenge and responsibility that the team faced. It is a way of offering spiritual support and being present as a chaplain. With this model of co-working, strong professional and spiritual relationships between medical staff and chaplains can be forged and these can enhance the acceptance of chaplaincy services in the hospital.

In one incident, I was asked to visit a man who had attempted suicide the night before. When I arrived, I was told by the medical staff that the patient was distressed and angry and was causing difficulties for both the staff and the patients. The staff were overstretched, and I was able to spend time listening to the patient's anger and being present to his needs at that moment. After a while he calmed down and was able to articulate clearly and reflect upon the circumstances that had led to his suicide attempt. I could then communicate this to the medical staff, who were relieved to see the change in their patient. They appreciated that the chaplain could assist with their routine, share their workload and defuse a difficult situation.

One benefit of operation within an 'exile' chaplaincy model is that the chaplain is not attached to any church's tradition and dogma. In Hong Kong, there are some problematic theological understandings of suicide that place such acts, or attempts, within a remit of 'sin'. A chaplain associated with a faith tradition that holds such a view may find themselves in a place of conflict and tension if repeatedly required to offer pastoral care to patients who have attempted suicide or display such ideations. The 'exile' model allows chaplains to be free from specific denominational expectations and understandings and therefore it provides a level of flexibility in dealing with various complex healthcare situations.

Reflecting on my role 'in the gaps'

It is a challenge to a chaplain's 'sense of belonging' and vocation to occupy this space of the gaps. Despite the extensive training requirements, without formal recognition from the hospital authority and no denominational endorsement, chaplaincy in Hong Kong can be a lonely place with little respect and recognition. This calling can leave a bitter taste in your mouth. I think of the activity required to live continually in this gap in Hong Kong, which has a very different approach from the UK, as a form of spiritual suffering. I recognize that the term 'suffering' has many connotations but, in this case, the chaplain of the gap encounters suffering in the loss of a 'sense of belonging' and recognized 'calling'. As servants of God, chaplains are often ignored, refused or rejected in the medical environment in Hong Kong public hospitals, and most of the time it can feel as if chaplains are functionally redundant. When we are called to help, we are often called at the convenience of the healthcare staff, to plug a gap they cannot plug themselves and, in doing so, to place ourselves in positions of vulnerability. I have found the words of the prophet Isaiah resonant at times:

> After he has suffered,
> he will see the light of life and be satisfied;
> by his knowledge my righteous servant will justify many,
> and he will bear their iniquities. (Isaiah 53.11, NIV)

While the position of a healthcare chaplain in Hong Kong is difficult, with ambiguity about role and a sense of loss of calling, to be able to meet a patient's spiritual needs or walk through crises restores my sense of self and enables me to find my place once more. Hospitals are full of sorrow and frustration, but when chaplains who embody a sense of the 'wounded healer' are invited to step into these situations, fellowship and freedom can be found: 'Every Christian is constantly invited to overcome his neighbour's fear by entering into it with him, and to find in the fellowship of suffering the way to freedom' (Nouwen, 1971, p. 77).

Conclusion

Hong Kong was a colony of the UK and inherited many social cultures and statutory systems, legal, education and medical services, but not, it appears, the UK structures of healthcare chaplaincy. As Hong Kong Christian development was profoundly influenced by the overseas missionary movement, the development of its healthcare chaplaincy has gone its own way in the past decades as an adjunct service, rather than as a discipline of the healthcare system, as in the NHS.

Being a largely volunteer service, chaplaincy in Hong Kong has been self-funded and has operated without sufficient resources, causing the rate of development to progress at a slow pace. The scale of chaplain offices is relatively insignificant to the whole public medical system, which is bound up with lots of regulations and procedures. The healthcare chaplain within a Hong Kong hospital occupies a space that is not fully appreciated. Cultural influences of secularism and a largely unarticulated concept of spirituality contribute to the position chaplains find themselves in today. The advantage of a small provision with minimal governance is that healthcare chaplains are flexible in the services they can offer. However, this can lead to situations that, while profoundly restorative and spiritual, can leave chaplains vulnerable in terms of responsibility and reporting. In this chapter I have used suicidal cases as an example to elaborate on the extraordinary operation of the Hong Kong chaplaincy compared to the NHS in England. There is much potential for development in Hong Kong where, among the chaplains themselves, there is an energetic ambition to provide pastoral and spiritual care to the patients and staff. Healthcare chaplaincy in the UK is now well regulated and provides comprehensive spiritual care services. Governance is strong under the auspices of the United Kingdom Board of Healthcare Chaplains and roles are well defined and boundaried. This gives significant protection to chaplains but may also have the effect of restricting their roles. There is much to learn from both contexts, once closely joined but now – in so many ways – very far apart.

Bibliography

Bonhoeffer, D. (1985), *Spiritual Care*, Philadelphia PA: Fortress Press.
Hong Kong Government (2022), *The Facts: Religion and Custom*, available at https://www.gov.hk/en/about/abouthk/factsheets/docs/religion.pdf (accessed 7.07.2024).
Hospital Authority (2017), Honorary Appointment letter to Tak Hang LIN.
Humanists UK (n.d.), available at https://humanists.uk/campaigns/human-rights-and-equality/chaplaincy-and-pastoral-support (accessed 7.07.2024).
Hurly, R. (2018), 'Chaplaincy for the 21st Century, for People of All Religions and None', *British Medical Journal* 363.
NHS (n.d.), available at https://www.healthcareers.nhs.uk/explore-roles/wider-healthcare-team/roles-wider-healthcare-team/corporate-services/chaplain (accessed 7.07.2024).
Niu, Y., W. McSherry and M. Partridge (2021), 'Spirituality and Spiritual Care among Ethnic Chinese Residing in England: Implications for Nursing', *Religions* 12(10), p. 887.
Nouwen, H. (1971), *The Wounded Healer: Ministry in Contemporary Society*, New York: Doubleday.
ONS (Office for National Statistics) (2021), Census 2021, *Religion*, available at https://www.ons.gov.uk/peoplepopulationandcommunity/culturalidentity/religion (accessed 7.07.2024).
Ryan, B. (2018), 'Theology and Models of Chaplaincy', in J. Caperon, A. Todd and J. Walters (eds), *A Christian Theology of Chaplaincy*, London: Jessica Kingsley Publishers, pp. 79–100.
Snowden, A. et al. (2020), 'Why are Some Healthcare Chaplains Registered Professionals and Some are Not? A Survey of Healthcare Chaplains in Scotland', *Health and Social Care Chaplaincy* 8(1), pp. 45–69.
Swift, C., M. Cobb and A. Todd (eds) (2015), *A Handbook of Chaplaincy Studies: Understanding Spiritual Care in Public Places*, Farnham: Ashgate.
WHO (2023), *Suicide*, available at https://www.who.int/news-room/fact-sheets/detail/suicide (accessed 7.07.2024).
Yih, C. (2022), 'The Impact of Cultural Diversity on End-of-Life Care', *Religions* 13(7), p. 644.

PART TWO

Inhabiting Public Ministry

5

Exploring Hospice Chaplaincy Through a Christian Understanding of Mortality

ANDREW WEBSTER

Chaplaincy has always featured in hospices, and this is in part due to the prominence of organized religion in society when hospices began but also is an expression of the 'total pain' model (Blake, 2011). This model proposes that human beings are a combination of physical, psychological, social and spiritual dimensions and that each part ought to be considered during end-of-life care. Chaplaincy in hospices has long been associated with attending to the spiritual element of patients, carers and staff, though it has developed over the decades to reflect changes in society. A marked decrease in the influence of organized religion has led to an emphasis on spiritual as opposed to religious care. This reflects the insights offered by scholars such as Davie (2015), who contends that while participation in organized religion may have declined in Western Europe there has not been the large-scale decrease of interest in spirituality as predicted by secularization theories. The importance of spiritual care in contemporary society is articulated in guidelines produced by the NHS (2015), while Todd (2018) traces how a theology of chaplaincy has tracked these changes. The exploration of mortality outlined below is an example of the type of contribution chaplaincy, understood as spiritual care rooted in Christian theology, can make as it adds value to the aims of the wider organization. Collin and Thomas describe what they consider to be the unique role of a hospice chaplain when they write:

> While a counsellor or even a friend may offer a presence, a listening ear, acceptance, affirmation or a broader perspective, something of the total formation of the chaplain will provide a unique way of supporting an individual, interpreting their personal, unique story through a bigger narrative. (Collin and Thomas, 2017, p. 100)

A theologically informed understanding of mortality is part of such a larger narrative and can also play a role in the formation of a chaplain, better equipping them to support people as they approach the end of life. The spiritual care policy for the hospice where I serve understands spirituality as, in part, 'the story people live by'. In sharing an understanding of mortality, I can provide patients with a story to help them make sense of what they are going through, as well as better shaping myself and the quality of support I have to offer. I think such a narrative is necessary as an alternative to the dominant story in contemporary society regarding mortality.

Du Boulay and Rankin (2007) detail how, from the beginning of their modern revival, hospices have attempted to help people experience a 'good death'. This aspiration is hindered by a prevailing societal attitude that appears reluctant to accept mortality. An extreme example is given by Harris (2021), who reports on the era of 'immortalists', which involves billions of dollars invested in research aimed at extending by decades the lives of rich people. Another journalist, Sample (2022), describes how billionaires are trying to cheat ageing by utilizing 'cutting edge' technologies that seem fantastical but may soon be reality. On the more prosaic level, it is possible to see mortality avoidance in a society that implies we are in control of our destinies and anything is possible. Smith (2016) uses the term 'cultural liturgies' to describe rituals, words and patterns of behaviour that reinforce a particular world view. Smith points to the endlessly reinforced message of consumerism that almost extinguishes notions of frailty or limits and instead portrays a meaningful 'good life' as one that has no restrictions (Smith, 2016, p. 46). In this world view, mortality is seen as an impostor with only very limited space in public discourse or individual life narratives. Consequently, when a life-ending diagnosis is received it can make coming to terms with impending demise more difficult.

Writers such as Yalom (2008) support the assertion that contemporary society struggles with the idea of mortality. Drawing on experiences as a psychotherapist he claims that the lack of attention to the reality of death leads to death anxiety as an underlying condition assailing people's sense of well-being in Western societies. As a solution, he recommends recognizing the impact death anxiety can have on people and learning to live with the reality of one's mortality. This, he contends, can be a most liberating process that can release people to live more fully and face their inevitable demise with a certain equanimity. A further significant voice is Becker. First published in 1972, the cultural anthropologist won a Pulitzer Prize for his thesis that much of human culture functions to avoid the reality of our mortal limits: 'Culture is in its most intimate intent a heroic denial of creatureliness' (Becker, 2011, p. 159). While denying death is initially energizing, for Becker it is ultimately destructive when exhibited in communities that tend to become increasingly excluding of others rather than face their limitations. It is better to recognize restrictions and dependences brought by death than base society on denial.

An explanation for the current prevailing attitude towards mortality can be found in the phenomenon identified by population scientists as the 'Great Transition'. Carter (2014) points to the dramatic increase in life expectancy over the last century. In 1900, average life expectancy for men was 44 years and women 47 years. By 2010 it was 78.2 years and 82.3 years respectively (Carter, 2014, p. 9). There are a multitude of factors behind this increase, including improved food security and civic infrastructure such as housing and sewerage, as well as progress in medical science, including vaccines and antibiotics. Consequently, the experience of frailty, dying and death moved from being intertwined with daily life to the margins of most people's experience. Death became increasingly privatized, with most deaths occurring in hospital and the expanded professionalization of funeral direction leading to increased detachment from the process of handling deceased people. Opportunities for people to 'bump against' mortality were further reduced with the advent of 'Direct to Cremation' funerals whereby there is often no ceremony at all and never a body present. Sunlife report that from February 2020 to July 2021, 24 per cent of funerals followed this pattern (Sun Life, 2022).

Given the retreat of illness and death from daily life it is not surprising that society is increasingly mortality-denying. The dominance of a medical understanding of health, and the implication that all diseases are fixable, is especially significant. Gwande (2014), a former US Surgeon General, presents a compelling case that the medical establishment, for all its impressive and welcome progress, has colluded (and possibly helped) to give rise to a scenario where we have a distorted relationship with our mortality: 'The experiment of making mortality a medical experience is just decades old. It is young. And the evidence is it is failing' (Gwande, 2014, p. 9).

In a society where the prevailing attitude towards mortality is one of avoidance or even denial, it can be even more challenging to receive a terminal diagnosis. A chaplain can make a distinctive understanding of mortality available that can help a patient interpret their situation and help them come to terms with their dying. Hospice chaplaincy is a public ministry, which means while it draws on the resources of faith there needs to be sensitivity and translation skills in making insights available. For example, Billings (2020) is an interesting voice given that he is both a professional theologian and also terminally ill with cancer. His theological reflections are insightful and yet couched in the language of the Church; the remedies offered are clearly 'confessional'. The public nature of chaplaincy means it is usually inappropriate to 'preach', as Billings sometimes does. Chaplaincy exists in the space between worlds, and while insights such as those offered by Billings can be informative they cannot be transferred wholesale. This is an instance of the difference between spiritual care as permitted in a secular environment and religious care that often isn't and is something that can give rise to the certain tension that a chaplain must learn to work with, as explored by Whorton (2018).

Following Smith's presentation of 'cultural liturgies' as stories expressed in symbol, ritual and words, a theology of mortality can be seen represented in the worship liturgy for Ash Wednesday, in particular the words, 'From dust you have come, to dust you shall return ...' as the minister marks a person's forehead with ashes (Methodist Church, 1999, p. 146). This makes explicit, despite the denial outlined above, that humans will indeed die. The liturgy draws directly on scriptures such as Ecclesiastes 12.3, and others such as Job 8.9 and 1 Corinthians 15.22, that death is inevitable, inescapable and actually lends meaning to life. There is truth in the cliché, 'all good things come to an end', and the idea of something going on for ever is in some ways intolerable. The value of something – a work of art, a novel, film, play, sports match, journey – is diminished if there is no ending. In Psalm 90 we are told it is the fact that life will end (all being well, after 70–80 years or so!) that gives cause for humans to 'number our days, that we may gain a heart of wisdom' (v. 12), the implication being that finitude is a requisite for understanding life's value. This forms the beginning of an alternative narrative that, quite simply, the sooner we acknowledge the most universal of truths the better; it will help with our dying, and our living. As Moltmann says, 'To live as if there were no death is to live an illusion. Death acts as a catalyst to plunge us into more authentic life modes and it enhances our pleasure in the living of life' (Carter, 2016, p. 50).

A second component to a theology of mortality drawn from Scripture is that life is fleeting, a 'mere handbreadth' according to Psalm 39.5. Ideas of transience and impermanence arise in the Bible and ring true for people diagnosed with life-ending illnesses. This can be disconcerting for people shaped by a narrative of permanence and unhindered thriving. A chaplain is well placed to suggest that this is in fact part of life and they have not failed. During bouts of treatment, Billings describes how he is made to feel a failure when he is continually given messages that if only he tried more, fought harder, followed a better diet, tried every treatment, even prayed harder, he would recover. For him and other patients, it is a relief to be told that the transience is in fact part of what it is to be human (Billings, 2020, p. 132).

A further element of a theology of mortality is that life is limited, not only by death but throughout. A strong component of the story told by society is that there are no limits to life and that anything can be achieved. In reality, people experience limits throughout their lives and to recognize this could be helpful when facing the most decisive of boundaries. It is also important to state that not all limits should be considered a natural part of life and are more a function of injustice. History is littered with examples of artificial limitations placed on humans – for example, based on gender, race or sexuality – that require a justice-seeking response.

The notion of life as having limits throughout can help dying people to understand the final limitation of death as being part of an ongoing process rather than something distinctive to life endings, as being in continuity with their humanness. An aspect of limitation and a key feature of a theology of mortality is dependency. A major strand of the mortality-avoidance story is an emphasis on independence and control. Billings (2020, p. 35) highlights the influence of psychologists such as Duhigg, who have encouraged people to regard themselves as possessing an internal locus of control for their lives and as being strongly autonomous. It can be disorientating to discover the truth that we are not in control of much of our lives and need to be reliant on other people at a very deep level. This is the experience of people who, despite their best efforts to live healthy lives, are diagnosed with a terminal illness, and can be a source of distress for hospice patients.

The Ash Wednesday liturgy represents people as ultimately dependent on God's grace. This points to an inherent interdependency in life. Becker's (2011) notion of 'creatureliness' captures some of this exposure and is developed by Radner, who writes from a Christian point of view, presenting it as a motivator to seek connection to creation and other people, involving as it does reliance on nature and human community for our needs. Acceptance of death as part of creatureliness, for Radner, enables him to 'engage in those realities of life as a creature whose experiences turn me toward my creatureliness in God's hands' (Radner, 2016, p. 128). Furthermore, it is a source of gratitude to the creator for our existence (Radner, 2016, p. 37). A chaplain can help patients come to terms with this lack of control and the need to rely on other people by communicating the story that interdependence is part of what it is to be human and to be embraced, not least as it is the route to deeper connectivity with creation and human community. It is not necessary to believe in God for a patient to recognize how human life can be greatly enriched by recognition of our need for other people.

The Ash Wednesday service is shared with other people, and this highlights the importance of community as an aspect of mortality arising from this interdependence. The Christian story proclaims that people are made for relationship with one another, going so far as believing this to reflect the triune nature of God. Chaplains need not discuss ontology (unless the conversation is initiated by the patient) to emphasize to dying people the value of community. A precious part of my role is helping with day hospices during which patients gather to share experiences, build relationships, share creativity and eat together. Many times, people have expressed deep appreciation for being part of day hospice. This is not a surprise according to the Christian narrative of mortality, which sees death as unavoidable and illness as part of our journey – but we travel best when we travel in shared company. Radner is convincing when he highlights how a feature of creatureliness is the need to eat and that this can become a pleasurable, community-building experience and is at the heart of what it is to be a mortal person (Radner, 2016, p. 191). This insight concerning community resonates with the contribution of a leading public health expert. Writing from a US perspective, Murthy (2020) identifies loneliness as a major threat to good health and advocates community, such as that expressed in our day hospice, as a solution.

The emphasis in the Ash Wednesday service on 'returning to dust' encourages an understanding of life as existing as part of creation rather than separate, drawing as it does on Genesis chapter 2 and the myth of creation from the soil. This aspect of mortality encourages an attention to nature, the idea of rhythms and seasons, and the naturalness of dying as part of life. It is not unusual for patients to express appreciation of the natural world, noticing the beauty in the simplest of things far more than when they were well. It is possible to encourage people to see themselves as part of this beautiful world, and that in one way or another they always will be.

Reference in the liturgy to God's grace draws attention to gratuity. From the Christian point of view, part of mortality is the recognition that our existence is a gift and that so much we enjoy is beyond our deserving. Gratitude features in many spiritual care conversations when I ask patients what they are thankful for and what they have enjoyed. It is remarkable how such simple conversations can help bring perspective and comfort to even the bleakest of situations. There seems to be an element of 'reframing'. It is not necessary or always appropriate to pursue the question 'To whom are you thankful?' to see how that value of gratitude as part of a theology of mortality can help terminally ill people come to terms with their situation.

One important element of the Ash Wednesday service is showing how humility is a feature of a theology of mortality. A key theme is the aforementioned allusion to the Genesis myth of human creation from the earth. Abbot Jamison, a Benedictine monk, makes the linguistic point that humility as a word and concept is rooted in the Latin word for 'soil' – *humus*. This gives us some perspective on our place in the scheme of things and helps keep us all down to earth. Cherry has explored a theology of humility in depth and presents ideas salient to this argument. Not least is that humility involves a 'down to earth acceptance of reality' combined with an 'honest and informed self-awareness' (Cherry, 2011, p. 43). Humility counters pretence and illusions of control and engenders a healthy perception of our place in a wider story where we are not at the centre of things, as well as an honest understanding of restrictions and limitations. As such, humility equips people to live well and, I would suggest, die well, since it enables people 'to engage with life at its most raw and disorientating' (Cherry, 2011, p. 168).

An emphasis on humility draws attention away from theological flights of fancy or escapism towards human embodiment. Cherry draws attention to the uncomfortable truth that physical deterioration can be unpleasant and is frequently avoided or disguised (Cherry, 2011, p. 74). He goes so far as to admit it can be humiliating, especially in later stages of life where even the most basic bodily functions become a trial. Humility can enable the acceptance of limits and dependency, which can help with the humiliations some people experience. Many hospice patients are reluctant to face their demise since physical disintegration can indeed be humiliating and traumatic. People whose bodies are breaking down and 'failing' are at the forefront of our work, and to be able to give reverent attention to what this might mean for a patient is deeply precious; this is even more so as humans remain divine image-bearers despite, or maybe because of, our clear limitations (2 Corinthians 4).

Cherry is clear that humility is not currently fashionable (Cherry, 2011, p. 3), which is consistent with the twenty-first-century context detailed above and the resistance to mortality. If chaplains are to champion humility as helpful in the work of a hospice, there is a sense in which we will be a countercultural voice, something aligned with the image of chaplain prophet as presented by Threlfall-Holmes (2011, p. 122).

In introducing the idea of a 'bigger narrative', Collin and Thomas referred to the 'formation of the chaplain'. With regard to this they say, 'the ability of the chaplain to stay present ... is only possible because the chaplain has a story which has shaped his or her identity and this is how the chaplain connects with and holds the other' (Collin and Thomas, 2017, p. 101).

If we allow ourselves to be shaped by this understanding of mortality, then chaplains will be better equipped to support terminally ill people. Chaplains can represent this theological perspective in themselves and in so doing are more able to be present and supportive to patients. The role of humility as a feature of a theology of mortality is especially significant. In the face of mortality there can be an anxiety – a desire to fix things, to do something when nothing can be done. This can be revealed in displacement activities or an inability to provide the one thing many terminally ill people ask for, which is simply to provide companionship. After many years of working in a hospice, Cassidy writes:

> So the spirituality of those who care for the dying must be the spirituality of the companion, of the friend who walks alongside, helping. Sharing and sometimes just sitting, empty handed, when they would rather run away. It is a spirituality of presence, of being alongside, watchful, available; of being there. (Cassidy, 1988, p. 5)

'Just sitting' and 'being empty handed' can be hard; humility can help us accept our limitations, avoid trying too hard to justify ourselves, and free us to be present with another person at the most challenging of times.

A theology of mortality can enhance the public ministry of hospice chaplaincy. In contrast to a contemporary narrative that marginalizes mortality, a Christian view encourages an acceptance of death, transience, finitude, limits, need for others and thankfulness, all of which can help patients who are living with terminal illness. Furthermore, such a theology gives place to humility, which can be helpful in accepting certain realities of life. Embracing this theology of mortality can also help the formation of chaplains to be people equipped to be companions to dying people.

Bibliography

Becker, E. (2011), *The Denial of Death*, London: Souvenir Press.
Billings, J. T. (2020), *The End of the Christian Life: How Embracing our Mortality Frees Us to Truly Live*, Grand Rapids, MI: Brazos Press.
Blake, L. (2011), 'The Rowan's Hospice', in M. Threlfall-Holmes and M. Newitt (eds), *Being a Chaplain*, London: SPCK, pp. 39–42.
Carter, M. (2014), *Dying to Live: A Theological and Practical Workbook on Death, Dying and Bereavement*, London: SCM Press.
Carter, M. (2016), *Helping Children and Adolescents Think about Death, Dying and Bereavement*, London: Jessica Kingsley Publishers.
Cassidy, S. (1988), *Sharing the Darkness: The Spirituality of Caring*, London: Darton, Longman & Todd.
Cherry, S. (2011), *Barefoot Disciple: Walking the Way of Passionate Humility. The Archbishop of Canterbury's Lent Book 2011*, London: Continuum Publishing.
Collin, M. and J. Thomas (2017), 'Our Unique Role', in K. Murphy and B. Whorton (eds), *Chaplaincy in Hospice and Palliative Care*, London: Jessica Kingsley Publishers, pp. 96–108.
Davie, G. (2015), *Religion in Britain: A Persistent Paradox*, 2nd edn, Oxford and Sussex: Wiley-Blackwell.
Du Boulay, S. and M. Rankin (2007), *Cicely Saunders: The Founder of the Modern Hospice Movement*, London: SPCK.

Gwande, A. (2014), *Being Mortal, Illness, Medicine and What Matters in the End*, London: Profile Books.
Harris, J. (2021), 'Welcome to the Era of Immortalists', *The Observer*, 7 November.
Jamison, C. (2007), *Finding Sanctuary: Monastic Steps for Everyday Life*, London: Orion Books.
Methodist Church (1999), *The Methodist Worship Book*, Peterborough: Methodist Publishing.
Murthy, V. (2020), *Together: Loneliness, Health and What Happens When We Find Connection*, London: Wellcome Collection.
NHS England (2015), available at *NHS Chaplaincy Guidelines 2015: Promoting Excellence in Pastoral, Spiritual & Religious Care*, available at https://www.england.nhs.uk/wp-content/uploads/2015/03/nhs-chaplaincy-guidelines-2015.pdf (accessed 7.07.2024).
Radner, E. (2016), *A Time to Keep: Theology, Mortality and the Shape of a Human Life*, Waco, TX: Baylor University Press.
Sample, I. (2022), 'If they could Turn Back Time: How Tech Billionaires are Trying to Reverse the Ageing Process', *The Guardian*, 17 February, available at https://www.theguardian.com/science/2022/feb/17/if-they-could-turn-back-time-how-tech-billionaires-are-trying-to-reverse-the-ageing-process (accessed 9.07.2024).
Smith, J. K. (2016), *You Are What You Love: The Spiritual Power of Habit*, Grand Rapids, MI: Brazos Press.
SunLife (2022), *Cost of Dying 2022 Report* (SunLife.co.uk).
Threlfall-Holmes, M. (2011), 'Exploring Models of Chaplaincy', in M. Threlfall-Holmes and M. Newitt (eds), *Being a Chaplain*, London: SPCK, pp. 116–26.
Todd, A. (2018), 'A Theology of the World', in J. Caperon, A. Todd and J. Walters (eds), *A Christian Theology of Chaplaincy*, London: Jessica Kingsley Publishers, pp. 10–17.
Whorton, B. (2018), 'Working with the Tension of Spirituality and Religion: A Chaplain's Perspective', in A. Goodhead and H. Hartley (eds), *Spirituality in Hospice Care: How Staff and Volunteers Can Support the Dying and Their Families*, London: Jessica Kingsley Publishers, pp. 163–84.
Yalom, I. D. (2008), *Staring at the Sun: Being at Peace with Your Own Mortality*, London: Piatkus Books.

6

The Prison Chaplain as a Pastoral Prophetic Presence: Perspectives from a Prison Chaplain in Nigeria

BASIL ODENORE

This is a personal reflection rooted in my experience. It is presented to inform, to provoke, to stimulate and to inspire but, more than this, I tell this story simply because I feel it is a story that needs to be told.

In many parts of the world, prison populations are stigmatized. As a result, inmates are often abandoned to a life of exclusion, with ideals of societal reintegration and rehabilitation coming a far second to notions of punishment. This was the story I found myself witnessing long before I took up a prison chaplaincy role. For most of my adult life, I have lived about a five-minute walk from the local prison. For many years, I watched as newly released inmates passed by my home towards the nearby market where they would beg for money. When I asked some of them why they did this, their answer was always the same: having been incarcerated for a long period of time, they had lost all contact with family members and help networks and had no other way to support themselves. It was encounters such as these that shaped my vision as I entered the prison as a chaplain with the Nigerian-based Christian organization called the Catholic World Evangelical Outreach.

Alan Baker defines chaplaincy as 'delivering a "ministry of presence" to people outside of a church' (Baker, 2021, p. 1). Such ministry has the potential to enable, empower and equip people most marginalized, by being present to their stories and paying attention to their needs. Being present to the narratives that people hold is a practice reflected in the many stories Jesus both told and heard. If chaplaincy is a 'ministry of presence', then maybe in this context such presence involves a pastoral response that enables inmates to retain their sense of humanity, as image-bearers of God, and a political and prophetic response that seeks to challenge some of the injustices that lead to losses of dignity and self-worth and hinder rehabilitation. In this chapter I will explore what this ministry of presence means for my practice as a prison chaplain and how it requires me to be present and active in places and arenas beyond the prison as the bearer of prison-inmate life stories.

My chaplaincy context

For the past 20 years, I have been serving as counsellor, preacher, teacher and healing minister at the Catholic Association of Friends United in Christ, a subsidiary of the Catholic World Evangelical Outreach. Part of my role is to act as chaplain to a local prison in Warri, a cosmopolitan Nigerian city. Warri was under British Empire rule from the mid-1800s until Nigeria gained independence in 1960. It was during colonial rule that the Warri prison was built, originally as a centre for the slave trade. The Portuguese traded slaves in the facility, holding them within the compound before transporting them to Portugal and other parts of Europe where they had their landing points. Though the slave trade was abolished at the international level in the 1880s, it was not until the 1940s that it was completely abolished in Nigeria. It was at this point that the building was converted from a centre for slave trade into the prison facility that exists today.

There remains a perception within mainstream Nigerian culture that prisons house people of 'no worth', and the conditions at Warri prison are challenging. Facilities are basic and congestion is significant, with occupation standing at three times its original capacity. This story is repeated throughout the Nigerian prison system, with reports that an estimated 70 per cent of inmates are awaiting trial and have not yet been convicted of a crime, with some waiting for trial for over a decade (Campbell, 2019). Prisoners are routinely deprived of basic amenities such as food, water, sanitation and healthcare. Once I had been assigned to the prison, I became concerned that many inmates were awaiting trial with no adequate legal representation and with nothing in the offing to address their squalid living conditions. Inmates awaiting trial often faced multiple indignities and were subjected to actions designed to increase their humiliation and sense of shame. Some encountered systemic abuse, exploitation and sexual abuse. Corruption within the system is rife, severely limiting the amount of funding available to improve conditions.

It is feasible to suggest that the landscape is changing, albeit very slowly. There has been growing recognition of the substandard nature of Nigerian prisons, and incidents of delayed justice and excessively congested, neglected environments have been well documented (Ezelio and Akinseye-George, 2020). In a bid to elevate a more compassionate and rehabilitative stance, the Nigerian Prisons Service underwent a reformation in 2019 through the Nigerian Correctional Service Act, which was signed into law that year, guided by the presidency of General Mohammadu Buhari. The name of the prison service was changed to the Nigerian Correctional Service to reflect the new approach. While a seemingly small change, the change of name indicated a potential change of attitude. Under its former name, the focus was on the labelling of inmates as prisoners, adding to a culture that sought to dehumanize them. This contributed to a system that entrenched the inmates, serving to detach them from any sense of worth, and facilitating a cycle of reoffending and re-incarceration. The new name focuses instead on the facilities themselves, reframing them as correctional and putting the emphasis on rehabilitation rather than incarceration.

The bill was devised to take the actions required to address situations where prison provision was inadequate. Section 2(1)(a) of the Act set out that its primary objective was for the Nigerian Correctional Service to comply fully with international – namely UN-human rights standards. The implication was that conventions such as the Universal Declaration of Human Rights applied to prisoners just as much as to anyone else. The reforms proposed were wide, ranging from replacing prison time with measures like community service for certain minor offences and granting prison authorities powers to reject prisoners when their prisons are at capacity (Campbell, 2019). Considering the challenges prior to the introduction and passing of the bill in 2019 and, in particular, the cultural and societal views towards those imprisoned, it is probably not surprising that the prison facility provision across Nigeria is yet to meet the minimum standards recommended by the UN. Indeed, it is apparent that progress is slow and prisoners continue to suffer. Implementation and culture change remain significant barriers to progress (Campbell, 2019). For example, in the provision, state controllers are mandated to notify the relevant agencies about any facility that has exceeded its capacity within a week. The agencies, upon receiving the report of congestion, are expected to swing into action to correct the anomalies by decongesting the facility within a three-month time frame. Unfortunately, at the time of writing, this is evidently not being put into effective practice as the problem of congestion remains a cause of significant concern. While legislation now exists, it is proving ineffective in changing the hearts, minds and actions of a system entrenched in a culture of contempt for peoples incarcerated. In the meantime, those housed in Nigerian prisons continue to live in crowded, dehumanizing environments, where hope is an elusive concept. What implications does this have for a 'ministry of presence' chaplaincy model?

Presence as acting 'with' and acting 'for'

The prison, as I see it, is a place for reflection and rehabilitation, where inmates can be helped to re-enter society as community citizens. The majority of the Nigerian population believe in a transcendent being and, in the prison where I work, most people seldom reject an opportunity to be prayed for once they are in difficulties. I see part of my chaplaincy role as being a pastor and preacher of the gospel and, with this, I understand that God wants those of us in such positions to do whatever is possible to help. Jesus calls us to be his hands and feet as we extend a warm hand of love to these people: 'By this all will know that you are My disciples, if you have love for one another' (John 13.35, NKJV). Beyond the call of the gospel of Christ, I speak out frequently about prison conditions because the culture means that both prison officers – and, indeed, faith leaders here in Nigeria – can miss out on the place of compassion because they see these inmates as the problem of society rather than victims of failed systems.

Jesus was concerned that many people were not just trapped by the state, but by what they may be going through. The prophet Isaiah prophesied of what would become part of Jesus' ministry – 'To open blind eyes, To bring out prisoners from the prison, Those who sit in darkness from the prison house' (Isaiah 42.7, NKJV). Jesus wanted freedom for all so that people might realize their full potential as God's children. In Luke's Gospel, when Jesus was called to read from the scroll of Isaiah, he announced to the congregation that the very words that Isaiah prophesied centuries before him were being fulfilled in his ministry. In another instance, before he breathed his last on the cross, Jesus extended his love to the prisoner who was nailed alongside him so that what could have become both a physical and spiritual death for the criminal changed to the restoration of grace, hope and faith. Similarly, the visit Jesus made to the spirit world, between his death and resurrection, was a clear testimony of his desire to create the opportunity for people to be free: 'by whom also He went and preached to the spirits in prison' (1 Peter 3.19, NKJV). Jesus modelled a ministry of presence.

Within the framework of 'presence ministry', I have come to appreciate this part of the ministry of Christ, which positions me, as the chaplain, to act as Christ would, to be *in persona Christi*, to restore dignity and bring hope. Presence means more here than simply being with and listening to those who are incarcerated. Presence, in an ideal situation, would be a way of 'acting with'; this is a principle discussed, for example, by Sam Wells, who argues that Jesus spent 90 per cent of his life being with people (Wells, 2015). As Tim Baker explains, this 'withness' involves listening to the stories of people and working with them to enable them to reach their full potential (Baker, 2022). This is certainly my vision, yet in the context of a closed prison environment where the voices of those inside are shunned by society, the ministry of presence that the chaplain inhabits – themselves on the edge of the two worlds – can be also to 'act for' and 'on the behalf of' those they minister to within the prison walls: to take their stories and needs to places that they themselves cannot access in order to facilitate better long-term outcomes for them. This is reminiscent of some Gospel scenes where people 'act for' others who cannot take their stories to the places they need to be heard. In Matthew 15, for example, we encounter a Canaanite woman who approaches Jesus on behalf of her sick daughter, who presumably cannot make the journey herself. Another example is found in Luke 7, where a Roman centurion petitions Jesus, again on behalf of his sick servant. As a prison chaplain operating from a 'ministry of presence' model, my role is to enable the stories and needs of the inmates to be present in the places that the inmates themselves cannot access.

In order to engender spaces of hope and rehabilitation, people's socialization needs and sense of self-worth are key considerations. My job as a chaplain with a ministry of presence concentrates largely on establishing a suitable programme of support for people who are in prison. Apart from a programme of pastoral care that seeks to address inmates' spiritual, mental and psychological needs, I have coordinated projects such as the commissioning and drilling of a water bore hole to provide better access to clean water (under the Catholic World Evangelical Outreach) and, together with other teams, I have aided the establishment of a library and the introduction of formal education in the prison. This has enabled inmates to participate in the West African Examination Council paper inside the prison for the first time.

Here, therefore, I both 'act with' and 'act for' those within my pastoral care. This vividly illustrates two significant parts of a chaplaincy 'ministry of presence' model. First, here in Nigeria, an often challenging social context, the role of taking on the *persona Christi* becomes central, alongside a second aspect of this approach – namely, acknowledging explicitly the inherent dignity of a person and upholding this in the lives of those whose self-worth has been denigrated.

In persona Christi

In my experience, I have encountered many prisoners who seek a loving non-judgemental being who would be sympathetic to their plights: Jesus is that being, and we represent him in how deeply we present his face as the God who holds every life as sacred. To be *in persona Christi* is to present ourselves as the face of the invisible Christ who loves unreservedly, who loves everyone no matter their social or economic status and who gave his life for the salvation of all.

The secular and/or faith-based community, to which we answer as stewards or pastors, entrusts us to help people strengthen while looking to a higher being for succour and help for their challenges. We receive training on how to be present, to listen, to be sympathetic, to respond empathetically, make fair and non-judgemental assessments, and provide what is necessary for people who seek help from us. This training shapes our lives and thought processes to make us the face of God to those who wish to find God in or through us.

The dignity of the human being

On the sixth day, according to the creation poem in Genesis 1, God created humans and declared them good. People are made in the image of God, and with this comes the recognition of the profound dignity of the human condition. Human rights are important as expressed in the value that is given to human dignity. Therefore, it is reasonable to postulate that human dignity is the root of human rights. The fight against poverty in all spheres of the globe, discrimination, inhumane treatments, persecution, torture and injustice is justified on the conception of human dignity. In a global economy where distinction between rights and responsibilities creates divides, I as a chaplain represent the Church, which upholds the protection of human dignity, calling for responsibilities and the building of a healthy community premised on the protection of human rights.

Jesus' ministry did not seek to be comfortable or politically correct, but rather he repeatedly sought to minister to people who were excluded and worn down by societal expectations. This was a ministry that was more than a passive presence but, instead, worked to actively uphold the dignity of humanity by improving people's conditions through healing, understanding, and shattering some of the long-held cultural beliefs. It is this understanding of my role, as a chaplain with a ministry of presence who is called to 'act for' people in the realm of my pastoral care, that rationalizes the actions that I take in improving the lives and circumstances of the prison inmates.

Engaging with story in prophetic presence

My encounter with inmates provides me with the opportunity to hear their own side of the story. Most inmates in Nigerian prisons struggle to have access to justice and, therefore, the opportunity to have their story heard.

The power dynamics in many situations of justice are heavily weighted against the person being accused. Sometimes, those accused may not have people to advocate on their behalf and incarceration is all but inevitable. In the UK, the state makes legal provisions for chaplains – it is enshrined in law that each prison should have an Anglican chaplain, according to the Prison Act of 1952. However, in the Nigerian Correctional Service, faith-based organizations have to request to collaborate with the system in order to have access to inmates. This changes the dynamic. Chaplains are not perceived as integral to the prison organization, and this contributes to the picture of a system that is not invested in the welfare of the majority of people within it. Prison chaplains occupy a space in the organization that is on the edge between the 'outside' and the 'inside'. This is a place of opportunity and prophetic response.

A case that deeply affected me involved an encounter with an elderly woman in prison who was brought there after her son was accused of theft and subsequently disappeared. When the search for him proved fruitless, the local authorities decided to imprison his mother instead. My role here was primarily to care for her, listen to her story and pray with her, but my role as chaplain was also to share her story, highlight such injustices, and influence national policy so that these incidents are not repeated.

The German sociologist, historian and political economist Max Weber discussed two distinct but separate kinds of prophet. One kind, according to him, has an ethical duty to proclaim the truth; the other is called to be an exemplar and live the truth (Adair-Toteff, 2016). While these are viewed as two separate models of prophecy, together, I think, they can shape a framework for prison chaplaincy practice. Amid abuses, discrimination, corruption and the failure of the state to ameliorate the conditions of those who need care, the chaplain in a Nigerian prison is often the most accessible and powerful representative that prisoners have. What does it mean to act as a prophetic presence and 'proclaim the truth' in my context? The majority of politicians in Africa may have no direct experience of prison life in any form and may never visit prisons to see the conditions that inmates live in. It is my role, therefore, to tell the stories of the people I encounter, to use my position to influence those in authority and inform the decisions they make.

Conclusion

No two people are the same, and not everybody experiences the same background in the same way. My lived experience is a product of a particular shaping, theology, culture and upbringing. I cannot impose or impress it on another. However, our stories, and the stories of those we encounter, can be places of growth and learning, renewed understanding and challenge. A ministry of presence is a ministry rooted in being present to the stories of those I encounter. But presence is not passive. As a chaplain I am not simply there to be a vessel to be filled up by the narratives of others. Stories are vehicles for transformation both of the storyteller and those privileged to be in the audience. They must be handled with care, respect and honour. Storytelling is a tool for transformation. Telling my story here has enabled me to see chaplaincy again in a new light and to re-evaluate my practice. When I shared part of my story as a prison chaplain in a presentation to other students in a postgraduate chaplaincy course, it led to fruitful conversations about practice, responsibility and the position of chaplain as a pastoral prophetic presence. This was the kernel that led to the reflection I present here.

The story of Warri prison, a building that has been linked inextricably to stigma, exclusion, neglect and misuse of power for centuries, is one that continues to propagate some of the miseries that it has inflicted on vulnerable people throughout its life. I entered the building with my own stories, stories of personal faith and understanding and stories of encounters with people who had recently left the system. The 'ministry of presence' model refers not only to being present to those we meet, but also to our own experiences. It is in the light of my own experiences, placed alongside the stories that I have heard from those I have ministered to, that I have shaped, and continue to shape, my own chaplaincy practice. This is a practice that seeks to act with, and act for, and continually strive to live out the call for true justice, human dignity and compassion.

Bibliography

Adair-Toteff, C. (2016), 'The Theological Context for Weber's Two Types of Ethics', *Revue internationale de philosophie* 276(2), pp. 231–51.
Baker, A. (2021), *Foundations of Chaplaincy: A Practical Guide*, New York: Eerdmans.
Baker, T. (2022), *Witness*, available at https://theologyeverywhere.org/2022/08/08/withness (accessed 7.07.2024).
Campbell, J. (2019), *Beyond the Nigerian Corrections Act*, available at https://www.cfr.org/blog/beyond-nigerian-correctional-services-act (accessed 7.07.2024).
Ezeilo, C. and P. Akinseye-George (2020), 'A Review of the Nigerian Correctional Service Act 2019', *Unilag Law Review* 4(1), pp. 138–47.
Wells, S. (2015), *A Nazareth Manifesto*, London: Wiley.

7

Pioneering Community Chaplaincy

HEATHER FARROW

This chapter critically examines the position of chaplain as 'guest' in community contexts. Through examining power dynamics in pastoral care and trauma theory, it demonstrates how the model is apt for, and shaped by, context. This theological model is best understood as a guest/host dynamic expressed through a countercultural use of power, where encounter, experienced through reciprocal guest and host exchange, forms Christ. This in turn forms humans to be more truly themselves, the kind of liberation every one of us needs.

Being a 'guest'

I write as a practitioner in a part-time ecumenical community pioneer role, in the north-east of England. One unique feature of this pioneering role is its rootedness in a local and well-established community centre. While I receive support, supervision and training from the church institutions, all my day-to-day encounters occur in the community setting that is my base. It is this feature that has led me to explore the work through a chaplaincy lens, recognizing that I am a pioneer in job title but perhaps also a chaplain in terms of the relationship I have with my host space (Whipp, 2018, p. 110).

My early months in the role were defined by a continual sense of newness. I spent a lot of time asking questions about what was happening, finding out about people's lives, the events taking place, how they were organized, and observing who seemed to be responsible for what. All routine procedures for getting to grips with a new environment. The job description for community pioneer included exploring ways of supporting/nurturing Christian community; however, the emphasis I felt was more appropriately focused on presence and trust.

The Chaplaincy Essentials course run by the Methodist Church explores the idea of chaplains as guests, rooting the theological dimension of the model in Jesus as a guest, particularly as envisioned through the

Gospel of Luke (Methodist Church, n.d.; Byrne, 2000; Bertschmann, 2017). It also has touching points with incarnational and pastoral care models (Threlfall-Holmes, 2011, pp. 116–37; Ryan, 2018, pp. 79–99). A guest can be defined as 'someone who receives hospitality at the home of another' (Oxford Dictionary, n.d.). A guest is often – although not always – invited, often – although not always – welcomed, and often – although not always – provided for. Hosts, on the other hand, might be identified as those who more readily inhabit the role of provider. Hosts may provide entertainment, food and rest among other things; they are the ones who 'receive' the guests (Bertschmann, 2017, pp. 33–4). In searching for a model to help explore my work in context, I found 'guest' to be a very resonant starting point. This chapter offers a contextual examination of 'guest' and asks what this might mean for the identity and development of chaplain(cy) in the community.

I paid close attention to my 'guest behaviours' (Methodist Church, n.d.). Asking questions, noticing, learning, figuring out and doing my best to abide by the house rules, offering to help, expressing gratitude and showing interest in people all formed the basis of my interactions with the staff and rhythms of the community centre. It could be argued that these behaviours do not need to be named, that they often form the foundation of interactions when one is in a new context or even familiar one. What I am proposing here, however, is that in paying close attention to and embodying these behaviours, a posture can be nurtured, with intent. In doing so, in context, I noticed more and more of my time was given over to going with the flow of the work around me, joining in with the hosts or, as Ryan says, 'learning the language of the setting' (Ryan, 2018, p. 82).

Chaplaincy is well documented as a ministry responsive to, and formed, where people are (Ryan, 2018, p. 79). It is possible to nurture this responsiveness through paying close attention to the obvious and more subtle dynamics at work *in situ*. I propose that inhabiting the role of guest is helpful and at times necessary for developing and deepening an understanding and awareness of context, both interpersonal and organizational.

An essential component of chaplaincy as summarized by a participant in Slater's research is 'accepting people for who they are and not who you want them to be' (Slater, 2015, p. 58). Inhabiting the guest role, consciously choosing it as a model, may guide the practice of accepting people for who they are and can help to create an environment where people share this, as they are able, within the unique dynamics of the context. A belief in being accepted is the foundation for healthy and potentially transformative encounters, and I suggest that the model of guest offers a framework for nurturing acceptance.

Notions of relinquishing some control in relationship was a recurring theme through Slater's research with chaplains. She cites Steddon, who summarizes the approach of the guest in the form of a question, 'Please can I come to your place and be part of what you do?' (Slater, 2015, pp. 11–12). This does not imply passivity; rather, it suggests setting aside an agenda, laying down the need for a particular outcome, and approaching encounters with an openness. These are guest behaviours that enable the chaplain to learn, to become a safe person in the context, and to build a picture of what is important for both the community and for individuals.

In her exploration of 'presence', Whipp uses the phrase 'exquisite attentiveness', which undoubtedly has a more poetic ring to it, yet I believe describes something akin to the intentional inhabiting of guest:

> being attentive requires a quality of calmness and stillness, even countercultural leisure, which the chaplain preserves amid the frenetic busyness of hard-working communities. Taking the time to listen, and to attend deeply, will hone her keenest skills of spiritual discernment and authentic compassion. (Whipp, 2018, pp. 109–10)

Harrison (2019, p. 21) highlights some discomfort with the idea of chaplain(cy) as guest. He views the guest as an outsider who can only come through invitation. The word does suppose a potentially more distant and temporary relationship with the host organization, which might be at odds with other 'presence' models such as Whipp's Embedded Presence (Whipp, 2018, pp. 101–17). However, what I am exploring is how that outsider status and invitation-only presence can be understood in a different way. Ryan's point that many chaplains and lay workers work part-time and cannot be a constant presence is noted and relevant (Ryan, 2018, p. 91). This pushes me to reflect on another dimension of guest behaviour.

Being a guest means being able to come and go. Given the part-time hours of work and my visitor status in the community, 'leaving' forms a significant part of the role. I have the capacity and need to leave. For the lone worker, learning the language of the host environment can mean using distance as a useful tool for safe practice. 'Leaving' means that my presence as a guest may well be perceived as setting 'powerful boundaries of availability' (Whipp, 2018, p. 106) and, while necessary and wise, has the potential to offset some of the desired and possible benefits of nurturing my attentiveness. One step forward, two steps back maybe? Whipp (2018, p. 104) raises the important question that I believe speaks to this point, asking how to maintain the balance between 'cosy assimilation and crude opposition'. There is a chance that 'leaving' might be interpreted as crude opposition simply because my identity may be viewed as ambiguous; it is neither one of local service user/paying visitor nor is it one of being at home.

Strong ties and deep family and historical connections in local communities can create an insular focus. My outsider status is regularly affirmed, my guest behaviour helps others remain comfortable in their host status. I have become aware of the careful balance it is wise to keep. Timing is everything: offers of help, asking the right question at the right time, drawing attention to an event, situation, difficulty, are all done with care. I am struck by Whipp's comment and find deep resonance with the reality that 'intrusiveness [can] destroy ... delicate trust'; the task is to 'watch ceaselessly ... without startling or disrupting' (Whipp, 2018, p. 109). Undoubtedly, some will view my 'leaving' as disregard, a lack of commitment; it could cause a 'disruption' or, as mentioned above, be interpreted as crude opposition. I paid close attention to the impact of my 'coming and going' behaviour, which is strongly associated with being a guest. Again, drawing on Whipp's observation that faithful presence matters, it is essential to get the balance of time spent *in situ* with time away, to prevent 'ministry on the margins ... being irrelevant' (Whipp, 2018, p. 104). On a more strategic note, I suggest that an awareness of this dynamic could inform the establishment of community posts. Part-time hours bring certain challenges, which are often unattended to. My reflections led me to conclude that leaving must be enacted with as much care as staying.

A possible strength associated with the guest behaviour of leaving is the ability to nurture relationships in other host organizations. Where time allowed, I had the capacity to become a guest (perhaps a different type of guest) in other gathering spaces in the community. Viewing my work through the model of guest in other contexts enabled me to recognize different host behaviours, hone my skills of paying attention, create opportunities for safe encounters, and ask relevant questions to build a picture of how the wider community functions. Kennedy and Stirling (2020, p. 290) describe micro and meso levels of functioning. 'Meso' can be understood in sociological terms to be about collectiveness, about connections between and across different groups and the characteristics of wider networks. Operating as a guest across several different spaces has raised my awareness of meso functioning and the possibilities this opens up for further developing chaplaincy in the community. The model of guest, understood as both exquisite attentiveness and a corresponding careful leaving, enables tentative bridge-building and deepens context-specific knowledge.

So far, I have explored how the model of guest alerts me, as a practitioner in a host environment, to interpersonal and organizational dynamics. I have examined how, in the context of being a lone worker, the model of guest has been both appropriate and revealing. I will now turn to discussing how robust it might be for developing as a chaplain.

Chaplain formation

The formation of a chaplain includes both the development of skills and the development of the person. In critiquing several models, Ryan highlights that some of them 'focus too much on the identity of the chaplain and too little on their methodology', while Harrison is convinced that more needs to be made of the services of chaplaincy rather than a focus on the individual (Ryan, 2018, p. 91; Harrison, 2019, p. 23). This leads me to ask whether the model of guest is a model of the chaplain's identity or a model of chaplaincy per se, exposing it as less robust for the development of a certain chaplaincy methodology but more able to form the identity of the chaplain.

A reflection on power

Kelly (2020, p. 291) describes the intentional use of self as a core skill of chaplaincy, rooted in and developed from self-awareness. I propose that the intentional use of self in pastoral care can develop through an understanding of power in relationship and learning how to hold that power. Following a brief review of some theory, I will make connections with the model of guest.

Doehring (2016, p. 43) asserts that 'power is always a feature of relationships' and that in most pastoral care situations there will be a 'difference in power'. Doehring also describes power dynamics in relational terms as 'an interchange of influence involving agential and receptive power', proposing that both types of power are present in each person in any relationship. Where there is balance or 'ebb and flow' of agential and receptive power, relationships can be safe and life-giving. Inflation of agential power, which can happen momentarily and build up over a sustained period, can lead to a diminishing and dehumanizing experience. This dynamic can become established very quickly and erode life-giving qualities in relationship. I suggest that an all-too-common tendency towards this imbalance, lack of ebb and flow, and possible rigidity of agential and receptive power impinges on the creation of safety. The dynamic might be subtle or obvious, but I propose the skill of the chaplain is attuned to the established pattern, recognizing the interchange, learning how to harness it to create safety. As acknowledged by Doehring, then, the chaplain has both agential and receptive power, activated to initiate encounter and to establish the beginning of a safe relationship for spiritual care (Doehring, 2016, p. 45). This statement highlights one way a chaplain might demonstrate an intentional use of self for the development of safe and good relationships. Developing the knowledge and skill to, as Doehring (Doehring, 2016, p. 47) puts it, 'counteract tendencies to maintain agential power in order to receive the mystery of the other' is at the heart of the chaplaincy encounter.

To see the relevance of this in the context and in relation to the model of guest it is first necessary to examine some deeper aspects of the context through the lens of trauma theory.

A reflection on trauma

Statistics and government Indices of Deprivation measure some aspects of life in urban communities. Added to them, among other things, are tribalism; a high incidence of drug-related crime; loss of employment opportunities following decades of post-industrial change; low-quality housing managed by an increasingly detached and poorly invested provider; high numbers of asylum seekers and refugees in overcrowded housing; high numbers of children, young people and families who need support to cope with/live well with neurodiversity; and lack of community facilities such as libraries, sports facilities, meeting spaces and safe outdoor play areas. What lies beneath this surface picture, however, are communities of people who have lived near one another for generations, have strong bonds of connection, love their neighbourhood, contribute in many ways to making it a safe place to live, look out for one another, share their resources and stories, and fight for their right to be heard, valued and have access to the services they want and need.

It is not possible to work in a community as I have described above and not hear, see and feel the effects of trauma. Trauma is now more widely understood to have lasting and deep psychological effects, which are caused by one-off events or even a series of overwhelming events. Bessel van der Kolk and Gabor Mate are two, among many, renowned trauma practitioners who have contributed much to this perspective (Kolk, 2015; Mate, 2022). I will draw predominantly from the work of Judith Herman, Shelly Rambo, Serene Jones and Karen O'Donnell, four key feminist practitioners and theologians working in the area, touching only briefly on theory as space permits. Their work resonates and speaks powerfully to the stories of women I have encountered who carry individual, ancestral and collective trauma. Herman states that 'traumatic events are extraordinary, not because they happen rarely, but rather because they overwhelm the ordinary human adaptations to life' (Herman, 1992, p. 33). Jones helpfully describes some general features of trauma that include, but are not limited to, hyperarousal, hypervigilance, numbness and dissociation, intrusive memories, diminishment in memory and language use, a sense of powerlessness, loss of hope, isolation (Jones, 2009, pp. 12–18). Many people I have encountered and listened to are held by their trauma in a 'loss of sense of self, a breakdown in normal knowing and feeling and a paralysing lack of agency' (Jones, 2009, p. 15). While trauma theory is widely recognized and understood in certain circles, and while there is an increase in access to specialist services for both treatment and support, finding ways of connecting this fast-paced development with grassroots organizations and communities seems more challenging. I believe it is essential, therefore, to explore how the model of chaplaincy as guest might help to make some kind of connection in context, bearing in mind that the chaplain is not trained in psychotherapeutic or counselling techniques.

O'Donnell and Cross (O'Donnell and Cross, 2022, p. xxi) highlight that 'critical attention to questions of power' will form a necessary foundation to any work with women who are living with trauma. Collins, drawing on Herman, proposes a three-part structure for growth following trauma that includes establishing safety, reconstructing the trauma story and restoring connection between survivors and their community (Collins, 2020, p. 201). Community centres can be places of healing, where people can gather, share their stories and connect with their community. There is great potential for individuals to experience growth through their involvement with such places. This is, of course, influenced by a wide range of factors beyond the interpersonal relationship with a chaplain. In his exploration of power, Kelly's typology reminds us to be attentive to the layers of exploitative, manipulative and competitive power that often operate (Kelly, 2012, p. 144). These can be manifest across close-knit communities where tribalism and deep, historical divisions dictate current realities. They can also be manifest in how centres themselves operate, complicated by pressures of reduced resources played out in the very real struggle to keep going. A challenge, as I see it, for chaplaincy in the community is to balance the recognition of the wider reality of power, the agenda of the host environment working under very real pressures, and the needs of individuals and communities for post-traumatic growth (Crisp, 2016).

Chaplaincy, as guest in the middle of this, has the potential to offer individuals an element of safety that is essential for the process of recovery and growth. It could be argued that incarnational or pastor models of chaplaincy might also facilitate safety; however, bringing context to bear, I believe that the setting aside of personal agenda so inherent in guest is essential here. I am likening the ideal guest to the one who knows how to carefully handle agential and receptive power in such a way as to create space for others to pay attention to their own use of power. My experience suggests that many relationships in community spaces do not find an ebb and flow of agential and receptive power, and so do not find the life-giving qualities needed for growth and recovery. In relating to the host environment and the wider community, chaplain as guest models a way of being that is countercultural. Chaplain as guest has the potential to give critical attention to the questions of power across interpersonal and community dynamics, so essential for the creation of spaces where a lingering lack of agency and powerlessness is often reinforced through inattention.

While I have only touched briefly here on trauma theory, I believe it is a context-specific skill required for community chaplaincy. I have highlighted the connection between this growing area of knowledge with an understanding of power dynamics based on Doehring's typology and have shown how guest as a model of practice can be understood as a countercultural use of power in response to the organization and to individuals seeking safety. I have also shown some ways the model of guest provides a lens through which to analyse and learn from context-specific encounters to nurture the formation of the chaplain.

A creative response using 'guest'?

I have previously highlighted the benefits and challenges of the 'coming and going' aspects of guest as a model for practice in context. I will now return to explore this further, using the work of Kennedy and Stirling to highlight some broader perspectives for chaplaincy in community settings.

From Person-centred to People-centred Spiritual Care (Kennedy and Stirling, 2020, pp. 258–71) describes a model for chaplaincy that resonates deeply with the idea of coming and going across different community spaces. Kennedy and Stirling propose an asset-based approach to chaplaincy that seeks to meet the needs of communities rather than just individuals. While this work is rooted in a healthcare framework, I believe it is highly relevant for exploring how communities move towards being safe and welcoming. The work involves bridge-building across community groups, working with health and social care practitioners and faith groups, to address issues related to spiritual health. In the model described by Stirling and Kennedy, individual work is still highly relevant but I am persuaded by the emphasis on 'organizational interventions to create the conditions for spiritual care: environment, ethos, character, and values' (Kennedy and Stirling, 2020, p. 260). I believe they are equally necessary for nurturing the conditions for post-traumatic growth in the community setting. While some might see this as a step too far for a chaplain, my experience in context leads me to believe that where these key components of environment, ethos, character and value are not addressed, individuals find it harder to flourish. However, according to Kennedy and Stirling, the chaplain cannot do this alone; but when connections are made and working relationships established across the boundaries of organizations, it is possible to work towards the creation of safe spaces. While spiritual health means something different for everyone, in the context of this discussion, I propose it incorporates the three non-linear steps for trauma recovery noted above: safety, reconstructing of story and reconnecting with community. Kennedy and Stirling's model draws a connecting line between the chaplain's use of self on an interpersonal level as discussed above, and the development of the chaplaincy in the wider community context.

In context, my approach to each community organization I have encountered has always been as a guest. I have asked 'What is going on and can I join in?' I resonate with the authors who state that they '[rely] less on [their] own interventions [and] now work with, and through, others to build spiritual health' (Kennedy and Stirling, 2020, p. 269). Some may fear the loss of unique identity in working like this, however my argument proposes that, in adopting the model of guest, the chaplain is well placed to not only read the signs of welcome and non-welcome but also to work interpersonally and across organizations towards the creation of safety. I suggest that there is a way of working that embraces chaplaincy as guest in individual, organizational and community-wide encounters and concur with the authors' observations that the 'social and spiritual health and well-being of the community grows as I diminish self and focus on others and their inner resilience and innate assets' (Kennedy and Stirling, 2020, p. 269). I believe this posture resonates with the model of guest I am proposing as a framework for the development of chaplaincy in the community.

Does guest have a theological grounding?

I have argued that guest is a model that prioritizes relationship. It relies on the chaplain's intentional use of self and points to the centrality of relationship, always enacting a countercultural use of power through noticing and adjusting the ebb and flow where the all-too-common tendency for the excess use of agential power is manifest. I have shown the relevance of developing these skills in relation to a trauma-infused context. I have also suggested that guest is a model that can guide wider organizational connections and nurture the development of community chaplaincy. It could still be argued that these tenets alone do not set chaplaincy apart from other caring and listening roles or indeed other health and social care or third-sector roles. In the following section I propose that the model of chaplain(cy) as guest is most thoroughly theologically grounded when understood through the guest/host dynamic. I turn now to explore this idea before offering final conclusions as to how the model might shape chaplaincy.

As already noted, guest shares a theological grounding akin to an incarnational model. Ryan suggests that encounter and presence together provide some theological weight, while also recognizing that context shapes the outworking of this (Ryan, 2018, p. 91). Whipp adds depth to this through her work on presence, referenced previously. She also calls for 'a depth of moral and spiritual generosity which reflects the kenotic quality of the incarnation' (Whipp, 2018, p. 110). The scope of this chapter does not permit an examination of the doctrine of kenosis; however, Whipp describes the kenotic quality as 'disinterested', which I take to mean, for the purposes of this discussion, holding at a distance from self, without an agenda for change and without wielding power over (Whipp, 2018, p. 115). I suggest that the model of guest as I have been exploring it has this kenotic quality.

Byrne points out that hospitality forms a notable frame of reference for the ministry of Jesus (Byrne, 2000, p. 4). The Gospel of Luke contains many stories of shared meals and visits. Luke emphasizes the itinerant nature of Jesus' life and narratively explores the many encounters around the table where Jesus has been invited by friend, enemy and enquirer alike (Bertschmann, 2017, p. 34). Of course, Jesus can be a 'difficult' guest, outspoken, disruptive and transgressing conventions. One such story is in Luke 7.36–50, when Jesus is a guest in the home of Simon the Pharisee and an uninvited woman creates a scene through her lavish display of love, welcome and confession.

There is no doubt that Jesus extends an inclusive grace to the woman: he certainly draws her from her marginal status and transforms her into an honoured guest. Jesus can be interpreted as the strong agent, the resourceful one offering something to the under-resourced (Bertschmann, 2017, pp. 44–5). All this is revealing of the nature of Jesus and his ministry, and potentially offers a way of viewing the outworking of Christian chaplaincy, ministry and mission. The illuminating reality presented to Simon the Pharisee, however, that 'his proper recognition of Jesus ... must come about through a proper recognition of the woman as a resourceful, loving host' (Bertschmann, 2017, p. 46), reveals another dimension that sheds light on the model of guest under discussion. Jesus' encounter with the woman and the subsequent parable exposes Simon's need for control, ownership and status. The exploration of the type of hospitality both central characters offered is used as a vehicle for exploring how each saw themselves in relation to Jesus and in relation to each other and, if we look, redirects our attention from Jesus as the resourcing agent of change. The key point to note is that Simon's own encounter with Jesus will be all the richer when he can see the woman as an equal host. Simon is not denied an encounter with Jesus, but I wonder if his capacity to receive the depths and richness of it is connected to his ability to see the woman through different eyes. The challenge for Simon is to let go of the control as the ideal host, stop thinking of himself and his reputation, and become able to see what the woman brings. I suggest that this parable illuminates the requirement to let go of hosting behaviour that hinders, and take up, with intent, the kind of guest behaviours I have been proposing. Put simply, the capacity to see others as hosts of Jesus' presence theologically grounds guest as a model of chaplaincy. Inhabiting guest leaves space for others to recognize their capacity to host.

Considering this conclusion, I propose that the model is best understood as both guest and host simultaneously. Luke's narrative reveals a reciprocal exchange during an encounter, adding layers of complexity and connection between Simon and the woman, their behaviour and response to each other, and therefore to Jesus. The chaplain, intentionally using self with the appropriate levels of agential and receptive power, opens the door for relationship, creates space and makes welcome. The chaplain as guest recognizes the other as host, which forms the basis for a safe and transformative encounter, crucially, for both parties. A transformative encounter ushers in the depth and richness of salvation as it did for the uninvited woman in Luke's narrative and, we might hope, for Simon the Pharisee, though that we are less sure of. I find Gruchy's depiction of salvation as 'the Christ who is formed in us always enhancing us as persons, making us not into someone else, but more truly ourselves' (Gruchy, 2006, p. 162) a beautiful description of the hidden and mysterious work of salvation that can occur through the kind of guest/host exchange described. I propose that chaplain(cy) as guest forms within us the awareness and capacity not only to see chaplain(cy) as a reciprocal encounter but to experience its power to form Christ around us and in us.

Bibliography

Bertschmann, D. H. (2017), 'Hosting Jesus: Revisiting Luke's "Sinful Woman" (Luke 7.36–50) as a Tale of Two Hosts', *Journal for the Study of the New Testament* 40(1), pp. 30–50.

Byrne, B. (2000), *The Hospitality of God: A Reading of Luke's Gospel*, Collegeville, MN: Liturgical Press.

Collins, N. (2020), 'Broken or Superpowered? Traumatized People, Toxic Double-think, and the Healing Potential of Evangelical Christian Communities', in K. O'Donnell and K. Cross (eds), *Feminist Trauma Theologies: Body, Scripture and Church in Critical Perspective*, London: SCM Press, pp. 195–214.

Crisp, K. (2016), 'Facilitating Growth in People After Trauma', conference paper, available at https://www.researchgate.net/publication/291166810_Facilitating_Growth_in_People_After_Trauma (accessed 7.07.2024).

Doehring, C. (2016), *The Practice of Pastoral Care: A Postmodern Approach*, Louisville, KY: Westminster John Knox Press.

Gruchy, John W. de (2006), *Being Human: Confessions of a Christian Humanist*, London: SCM Press.

Harrison, S. (2019), 'What is Mental Health Chaplaincy For?', in J. Fletcher (ed.), *Chaplaincy and Spiritual Care in Mental Health Settings*, London: Jessica Kingsley Publishers, pp. 19–30.

Herman, J. (1992), *Trauma and Recovery: The Aftermath of Violence – From Domestic Abuse to Political Terror*, New York: Basic Books.

Jones, S. (2009), *Trauma and Grace: Theology in a Ruptured World*, Louisville, KY: Westminster John Knox Press.

Kelly, E. (2012), *Personhood and Presence: Self as a Resource for Spiritual and Pastoral Care*, London: T&T Clark.

Kelly, E. (2020), 'Formation and the Intentional Use of Self: The Chaplain's Primary Resource', in E. Kelly and J. Swinton (eds), *Chaplaincy and the Soul of Health and Social Care: Fostering Spiritual Wellbeing in Emerging Paradigms of Care*, London: Jessica Kingsley Publishers, pp. 291–304.

Kennedy, J. and I. Stirling (2020), 'From Person-centred to People-centred Spiritual Care', in E. Kelly and J. Swinton (eds), *Chaplaincy and the Soul of Health and Social Care: Fostering Spiritual Wellbeing in Emerging Paradigms of Care*, London: Jessica Kingsley Publishers, pp. 258–71.

Kolk, B. van der (2015), *The Body Keeps the Score: Mind, Brain, and Body in the Transformation of Trauma*, London: Penguin Random House.

Mate, G. (2022), *The Myth of Normal: Trauma, Illness and Healing in a Toxic Culture*, London: Vermilion.

Methodist Church (n.d.), *Chaplaincy Essentials Course* (methodist.org.uk).

O'Donnell, K. and K. Cross (2022), 'Introduction', in K. O'Donnell and K. Cross (eds), *Feminist Trauma Theologies: Body, Scripture and Church in Critical Perspective*, London: SCM Press pp. xix–xxv.

O'Donnell, K. and K. Cross (eds) (2022), *Bearing Witness: Intersectional Perspectives on Trauma Theology*, London: SCM Press.

Ryan, B. (2018), 'Theology and Models of Chaplaincy', in J. Caperon, A. Todd and J. Walters (eds), *A Christian Theology of Chaplaincy*, London: Jessica Kingsley Publishers, pp. 79–99.

Slater, V. (2015), *Chaplaincy Ministry and the Mission of the Church*, London: SCM Press.

Threlfall-Holmes, M. (2011), 'Exploring Models of Chaplaincy', in M. Threlfall-Holmes and M. Newitt (eds), *Being a Chaplain*, London: SPCK, pp. 116–26.

Threlfall-Holmes, M. and M. Newitt (2011), 'Introduction', in M. Threlfall-Holmes and M. Newitt (eds), *Being a Chaplain*, London: SPCK, pp. xiii–xix.

Whipp, M. (2018), 'Embedding Presence: Integrity and Presence', in J. Caperon, A. Todd and J. Walters (eds), *A Christian Theology of Chaplaincy*, London: Jessica Kingsley Publishers, pp. 101–17.

8

Dementia, Social Care and Chaplaincy: Lessons Learned on One Lay Chaplain's Journey

ABIGAIL OGIER

For over 20 years I worked with young people, children and families in a variety of community settings as a qualified Youth and Community Worker, in both face-to-face and management roles. For most of those years, I was employed by a large children's charity, so it was something of a surprise to me to hear the whispers of a calling to ministry with older people, especially being rooted in a church that often seems fixated on attracting the young: the CofE's current national strategy and vision singles out 'younger' as a key element of its aim to become more diverse (Church of England, n.d., online). But this is where I find myself; perhaps that is one reason why I sometimes speak to my congregation in the care home where I am employed about my belief that God calls all of us in different ways at different points in our lives. My journey to this ministry was unexpected, but the sense of calling grew quickly from its germination in an experience during a placement while training as a Reader (licensed lay minister) in the CofE.

I started my training in 2016 and, in early 2017, went on placement alongside the rector in another parish who acted as my placement supervisor. The rector involved me in all kinds of aspects of ministry, but one of the most profound experiences during those months was a visit to a couple who had been part of the congregation at the parish church, but who now struggled to attend in person because of the wife's dementia. I'll call them Bill and Joyce. Joyce's dementia had progressed to a point where she had entirely lost her ability to speak. On the day we visited, we were to share communion with Bill and Joyce at home. My memory of our arrival is quite hazy – we had met at church and collected wafers and wine and walked to Bill and Joyce's house, where we were shown upstairs to a room at the back of the house. What I do remember clearly was being struck by a change in Joyce as my placement supervisor began the liturgy of communion in their home. She seemed to go from being disengaged, a bystander to the interactions between the rector, Bill and me, to being a genuine participant in what was happening. When we reached the point of sharing communion, I sensed a calm coming over her. At the end of the communion, I was asked if I would stay with Joyce while my supervisor and Bill washed up, and for those five or ten minutes as I spoke to Joyce about the view from the window, the church and my placement, I felt a connection that was undefinable but palpable.

Walking back afterwards, we reflected on the experience and my supervisor talked about the importance of avoiding an attitude that those living with dementia have 'already gone'. To my embarrassment, I recognized that this had been my unthinking attitude up until this point, but that meeting Joyce and sharing the sacrament with her had changed this for me – although I was not honest enough to say this at the time! My placement supervisor recommended reading John Swinton's (2012) book on dementia, which I subsequently borrowed from the college library and devoured. The book does not shy away from the awful impact of dementia, but did challenge my preconceptions, as well as introducing me to the deeply comforting reflection that, even if we forget God, God does not forget us.

Later, as changes to my working patterns did not ease the pressure of my job or the challenge of managing training alongside it, I started looking for part-time work. Still convinced of a call to work with older people, I considered moving into care work, but wasn't sure where to start. Then three different people from different areas of my life all sent me an advertisement for a role as community chaplain, working with people who had recently left prison. I applied and was offered the job. This was a wonderful role in a great small charity, and there is much else I could write about that work, but I will leave that to others. In terms of my own journey, it gave me the opportunity to test out my ministerial skills in a chaplaincy setting, and it also gave me a very positive experience of working with Methodist colleagues, as Greater Manchester Community Chaplaincy is based in Manchester's Methodist Central Hall. During that time, in July 2018, I was licensed at Manchester Cathedral, alongside three colleagues with whom I had trained, to be a Reader serving in the Wythenshawe team.

After about 12 months at Greater Manchester Community Chaplaincy, a clergy friend mentioned a job vacancy at MHA to me. MHA is a charity founded by the Methodist Church in 1943. Originally called Methodist Homes for the Aged, with the changing use of language today the organization simply goes by the initials MHA. They were seeking a chaplain at the local nursing home and on investigating this I was told by the chaplaincy adviser within MHA that this was one of two vacancies in the area. I visited both settings and, having a positive experience viewing each, applied for both roles. Following interviews, I was offered the post of chaplain at an 80-bed home that provided nursing care and specialist dementia care, and I began work there in June 2019.

The care home where I am based provides care to a wide range of individuals. There are a small number of people who receive residential care – their medical needs are not complex and they are not living with dementia, but they may have experienced falls at home or other experiences of frailty that have led them to choose to enter residential care. Some of these people had chosen this so as to be on hand for a spouse who was living with dementia and resident in one of the specialist dementia communities within the home. Others came into the home for nursing care, needing specialist care because of a range of medical conditions, or receiving end-of-life care for a terminal diagnosis. The largest number of residents, though, throughout my time there, have been people living with dementia. There are two dementia communities within the home, one providing residential dementia care and one dementia nursing, in addition to which some of the residents within the general nursing provision are in the latter stages of dementia, which is a terminal condition.

In my early months at the care home, I got to know the various residents as well as (slowly) finding my way around the building and getting to know staff members. The role of the chaplain within MHA homes is to look after the emotional and spiritual well-being of all residents, relatives and staff, whatever their religious and personal beliefs, as well as ensuring that there is regular Christian worship provided for residents, many of whom choose MHA homes because of their links to the Methodist Church or their desire for a home where they can continue to practise their Christian faith. When I started, there were several church groups already regularly visiting and providing services, so I only led worship myself once a month. My predecessor had been a Methodist presbyter and therefore able to lead services of Holy Communion himself. As an Anglican lay minister I could not do this, so I began the task of finding ordained ministers who could come in and help with this. I was able to put in place a system whereby the local Methodist minister visited three months in four, with the fourth Holy Communion being led by a priest from the CofE parish church. The local Roman Catholic church already had arrangements in place to send Eucharistic ministers after Sunday Mass fortnightly to see our Catholic residents. Other elements of my role involved individual visits, setting up a discussion/Bible study group, supporting music therapy provision, and being with those nearing the end of life along with their families.

I have always taken a broad definition of 'spiritual and emotional well-being' within all of this work. If staff are stretched and someone needs assistance to eat their pudding, my view is that pudding is good for the soul and I'll help out! I'm happy to be told why I'm wrong about religion by the occasional staunch atheist resident, just as I'm happy to explore a passage of Scripture alongside a group of folk in their eighties and nineties from various Christian backgrounds. I have found groupwork with this age group to be a deeply helpful and simultaneously challenging experience. They have deep and varied life experience, which they bring to their theological reflection, and are not afraid to say when they find something confusing or unsatisfactory, even if that something is generally held to be self-evident. But amid this wide range of work, I have to admit that my greatest passion remains ministry alongside people living with dementia.

Ever since that meeting with Bill and Joyce, I have pondered the way in which dementia is regarded by much of society, and have tried to respond to the challenge I felt that day. Over time, my sense that many of us have it all wrong about dementia has grown. My experience of walking alongside what has now been dozens of individuals living with dementia, including many in the very late stages of the disease, has been that although memories may be hard to get hold of, and behaviours may change, the underlying personality does not shift, and that people living with dementia at all stages are very capable of forming relationships and relating to others – both other people and God. This is affirmed by the conclusions of Christine Bryden, who herself lives with dementia, in chapter 7 of her book *Will I Still Be Me?* (2018, pp. 75–93).

An essential part a chaplain's role is to be present with people. Writing about chaplaincy within palliative care, Steve Nolan (2012) talks about chaplains as an 'evocative presence', an 'accompanying presence', a 'comforting presence' and ultimately a 'hopeful presence'. In one sense, the role of chaplain is all about being: being present, being empathetic, being aware. It is an unusual role in busy settings such as a care home, where most staff have a focus on 'doing', a very task-orientated approach. In this context, I have found that those who are able to express a view often comment on the high value they place on chaplains precisely because their role is to be available and present with people in the midst of life. Residents do not have to find an excuse to take some of the chaplain's time and this can be very different from their experience with carers or nurses, who come to perform a particular task and then leave.

From the chaplain's perspective, this 'being with' is what enables relationship to be built, regardless of the circumstances or diagnosis of the resident, but this presence becomes even more critical when ministering with people living with dementia. I have found during the past four years of ministry in a care home that time invested with those individuals is well spent and can result in deep and lasting connections. The resident may not remember me from one day to another in terms of my name or my job title, but positive interactions lead to a lasting relationship whereby they do retain a sense of relationship. One lady, who I will call Jean, loves to sing. When I first visited her and explained my role, she told me that she wasn't sure what she believed but that 'Of course when I was younger, we all went to church. I loved to sing hymns …', and then began singing 'Praise my Soul the King of Heaven'. We sang together and, more or less word perfect, she made it through all four verses. At future visits, rather than just inviting her to our services, I began to tell her what we would be singing; if she knew the hymn she would begin to sing it; if not, I would sing it to her. When, together with our activities coordinator during a period of vacancy in our music therapist post, we decided to set up our own 'choir', Jean was of course encouraged to come along and joined in enthusiastically. She has never retained my name, but now when she sees me at the start of a visit she will say 'I know you – you're the singing lady' or 'Are we singing today?' Just as Jean attributes an identity to me through our shared activities and time spent together, I hope that our interactions give her a sense of her own place in what I refer to as 'our community' – that is, the care-home setting.

The relationships formed between chaplain and resident are genuine and mutual, and I often find myself reflecting on how much I gain from them. A particular richness has been the way in which residents living with dementia have taught me to live in the present moment. This is a skill that I have always struggled with, being inclined either to analyse the past or daydream about the future, rather than fully experiencing the present. Those living with dementia find it harder to recall the past or to imagine the future, and so in my experience are very skilled at being in what Steven Sabat refers to as the 'personal present' (Sabat, 2001, p. 232). In order to successfully build understanding with them, I have found it necessary to get alongside them in that moment, to listen carefully and try to understand what is going on for them (this may be listening to their words, or watching their gestures, facial expressions and body language). It is then by remaining with them in that moment that relationship is built. The side effect of this for me has been that I have learned, by their example, how to be more mindful and present from moment to moment.

Where residents have progressed further with dementia and have very little or no verbal language, the role of the chaplain is equally valuable. Christine Bryden cites, but disagrees with, the assertion of W. S. Brown that 'language is essential in relationships' (Bryden, 2018, p. 86). She goes on to draw an analogy with newborn babies, who clearly build a relationship with their caregivers before they are able to express their needs verbally. In my practice, I find this analogy – although not perfect – is helpful. Just as a new parent needs to spend time with their baby making eye contact, touching or holding them and talking to them (even though the infant cannot participate fully in a conversation), similar strategies have enabled me to build relationships with residents who I have only known during the post-verbal stage of dementia. It is, of course, helpful when I have some background information, and so the relationship between chaplain and family members is an essential link within the triangle of care. This is a concept developed by Carers Trust Scotland (Martin, 2019), consisting of the person with dementia, their family and/or close friends, and professional care staff. With background information gleaned from family, I can speak to the resident about their earlier life, their family and their interests. Although I cannot know for certain what their perceptions of these seemingly one-sided conversations are, I draw encouragement from the responses I can observe – individuals becoming calmer or more settled, eye contact, smiles, a squeeze of my hand. I also remind myself that this not-knowing is as true in other relationships as in these; indeed, in some respects it is perhaps more possible for those with verbal communication skills to mislead me as to their perceptions of me or of our interactions. I am also aware of Bryden's comment that 'People with dementia need others to give [them] the benefit of the doubt' (Bryden, 2018, p. 88).

Since beginning this ministry, we have lived through the Covid-19 pandemic; an experience that itself heightened and changed many different aspects of ministry in social care. (For more information about chaplains' ministry during the height of the pandemic in care homes, see Siesage et al., 2023.) In terms of worship, an immediate impact was that visiting ministers and groups could not come into the premises for many months, as a result of a combination of government restrictions and organizational guidance at different points. However, in some respects we were in a better position than worshipping communities outside of care environments. When not in a period of an active outbreak, and subject to social distancing, small groups of residents could gather and worship within each individual area of the home – safeguarded by certain risk mitigations – for most of the period of nearly three years when we were under some form of restrictions. At various points we had to forgo Communion or singing and for much of the time we had to have smaller services in each of our four communities rather than gathering together, but worship continued. However, because of the restrictions on visitors I had to lead all of the worship, and so through this most challenging of situations I had the privilege of leading the residents in prayer and worship on a weekly basis.

Leading worship with people living with dementia can be challenging and needs adaptation some of the time and a willingness to incorporate the unexpected at all times. Interaction is to be encouraged, as an expectation of quiet and passive participation tends to lead to a large proportion of worshippers dozing off! This interaction is not always predictable or even helpful in a conventional sense, but it can be a source of both laughter and deep reflection. I think of the service in which I had chosen as the final hymn 'What a Friend We Have in Jesus', thinking it would appeal to the age group that would be gathering. As soon as we started singing, one lady shouted, 'What a load of rubbish – Jesus isn't your friend, you've never even met him!' This intervention, which in some settings might have been seen as unhelpful or disruptive, in the event led to a very interesting and deep conversation after the service with the lady in question and three other residents about what our relationship with God is like and whether it feels like a friendship or like something else.

I have noticed that most residents living with dementia choose to attend worship. This includes people like Mabel, whose daughter told me that she had never really been religious in earlier life but clearly found something from the services that appealed to her. During the services, she was quieter and calmer than in any other activities, and she joined in with the hymns and with responses to prayers. One study into the spirituality of children (Hay and Nye, 1998) observed that children have an innate spiritual awareness, and the authors reflected on whether this is trained out of young people in modern Western societies rather than, as is sometimes assumed, that moving away from this is a natural part of development. Reflecting on this, and seeing the way in which residents living with dementia engage with worship and spiritual input, has caused me to ask whether perhaps the decline of cognitive abilities might reverse some of this 'training out' and enable individuals to connect more easily with their spirituality, even as their intellectual capacity declines.

At the same time, the impact on concentration does require attention to how I make worship fully engaging, often in groups with a range of needs. Music is helpful to this, as is the use of familiar prayers and responses. A former colleague, Yvonne Myers, developed 'Biblical Yoga' (Myers, n.d., online) as a way of engaging the whole body with a passage of Scripture to enhance engagement. Speaking about biblical yoga, Yvonne recalls:

> It was like a miracle once I had discovered the combination. For weeks I couldn't quite believe we had moved from services where residents fell asleep in services and ten minutes later wouldn't remember they had been to a service ... to when we did Biblical Yoga and all the residents were engaged and talking about their personal faith and life journey and incredibly, even later in the day, remembered they had been to a service and would even remember parts of the scripture we had discussed. It was a magic combination that made the scripture so accessible and relatable to the residents. (Personal correspondence, 9 September 2023)

This approach has been very helpful with many residents as one technique of a 'toolbox' of methods and approaches. Familiar prayers and forms of worship can also help people living with dementia to participate fully, and I am careful to choose those that will be familiar to a wide range of Christians as my congregation is drawn from a variety of denominations. There are always Methodists, Anglicans and Roman Catholics present, and over the four years there have been members of the Baptist Church, the United Reformed Church, a Brethren congregation and independent Free Churches. The Lord's Prayer is of course a staple, and my experience is in line with that often reported: that people who are otherwise almost entirely non-verbal will join in when they hear the beginning of that familiar prayer. The opening response of 'The Lord be with you: and also with you' is often shared across many backgrounds, and we use this on Sundays and special days such as Christmas Day and Easter Sunday. I have found that open extemporary prayer works if each section is short, and we always use the response 'Lord, in your Mercy: hear our prayer'.

The final element that I have learned to be of value in leading worship is to incorporate visual clues to help residents identify when the lounge or dining room is being transformed into our church for the morning. Few of our homes in MHA are fortunate enough to have a chapel so, as in other care homes, worship tends to be held in whatever space is available. Setting up the room before I start assisting people into the space with a cross and a candle (battery operated) clearly visible, and some quiet music (either explicitly Christian or instrumental) playing, helps people to identify what is going to happen. This includes the atheist resident in our residential dementia unit, who then knows to avoid the particular space for the next half-hour. The candle is switched on while I pray our opening prayer, signalling the start of worship, and then switched off after I give the final blessing to indicate that this special time is drawing to a close. When I am away (on holiday or on occasional business elsewhere) I pre-record a service, which one of my activity co-ordinator colleagues puts on the television, and on these occasions she will take the cross and candle and take on the role of switching the candle on and off at the appropriate points.

It has been my experience that, together with music, worship is a powerful tool for finding a place of stillness and calm for many people living with dementia. Even residents who are generally vocal and unsettled often become quiet and calm during our short, simple services. One of the challenges is to highlight this effect to other staff. Sometimes well-meaning carers will start moving residents who have a tendency to be noisy out of the room ahead of worship, because they are having an unsettled day and the staff don't want them to upset the worship for others. But time and again, my experience has been that if they are encouraged to stay, they are able to participate and disruption to others is an unusual occurrence. Things that can trigger disruption or distress include any mistakes in the printed or projected hymn words or prayers, so proof reading material carefully is important. Those residents who follow the service in this way can find that any errors add confusion to their already confused world and make an otherwise calming experience unsettling. Less easy to prevent are the unknown associations that might come with a particular hymn or prayer, so I try to observe the reactions of different residents and note any that might lead me to avoid a certain hymn when they are present in the future, or to reword a particular prayer. It can be harder to judge which tears are helpful and cathartic and which are a sign of unnecessary distress, so sometimes, as well as spending time with the resident immediately after a service, I will discuss the reactions of an individual with a nurse or member of the care team, to help me assess how best to respond.

Another element of my role as chaplain has been providing end-of-life care, both to people living with dementia and to others in the final days of life. This is the part of the role that was entirely new to me and has been such a privilege. I have discovered that the skills and approaches that I have developed in other parts of the job are precisely those that are needed here. The ability to be present, to know when to share silence and when to speak, the availability to pray when this is appropriate and sensing when not to, and the willingness to support family members and friends as well as the resident, are all key.

At MHA, the chaplain in each residential setting is a key part of the care team. Their presence enables us to put in place appropriate care that meets spiritual as well as physical needs and that responds to the needs of every individual. It ensures that everyone is recognized as being a person with spiritual needs, not just those who have a formal, religious faith. Although increasingly people are entering care later in their journey and therefore staying for a shorter period, care homes remain a setting where chaplains can build a relationship with people over time, walking with them through this part of their life. MHA is unique among larger social care organizations in providing a paid chaplain in every setting; across the sector as a whole, the presence of a paid chaplain in dementia care is unusual. However, clergy and ministers with care homes within their parish have opportunities to put in place some elements of this kind of chaplaincy. Where chaplaincy is provided in care homes, it has been my experience that it is of great value, and this is articulated by residents and families. The 2022 Residents and Relatives survey (Hodgkinson, 2022) carried out within MHA found that 83 per cent of residents and 80 per cent of relatives who completed a survey said that provision of a chaplaincy and spirituality service was important. I believe chaplaincy makes a meaningful contribution for people in later life, and I hope that the personal story shared here will resonate with others and help to identify some of the ways we can both minister to, and be ministered to by, those in later life and people living with dementia wherever we encounter one another.

Bibliography

Bryden, C. (2018), *Will I Still Be Me?*, London: Jessica Kingsley Publishers.
Church of England (n.d.), *Vision and Strategy*, available at https://www.churchofengland.org/about/vision-and-strategy (accessed 7.07.2024).
Hay, D. and R. Nye (1998), *The Spirit of the Child*, Glasgow: HarperCollins.
Hodgkinson, J. (2022), 'Chaplaincy Summary – Care Homes Survey 2022', unpublished paper, MHA.
Martin, K. (2019), *The Triangle of Care: Carers Included: A Guide to Best Practice in Mental Health Care in Scotland*, Carers Trust Scotland.
Myers, Y. (n.d.), *Biblical Yoga*, available at https://biblicalyoga.weebly.com/; more information can be found at http://yvonnemyers.weebly.com/biblical-yoga.html (accessed 7.07.2024).
Nolan, S. (2012), *Spiritual Care at the End of Life: The Chaplain as a 'Hopeful Presence'*, London: Jessica Kingsley Publishers.
Sabat, S. (2001), *The Experience of Alzheimer's Disease: Life through a Tangled Veil*, Oxford: Blackwell Publishing.
Siesage, H. et al. (2023), 'Exploring the Changing Experiences of Chaplains Employed in Care and Residential Homes during the COVID-19 Pandemic', *Health and Social Care Chaplaincy* 11(2), available at https://journal.equinoxpub.com/HSCC/article/view/26645 downloaded 15/09/2023 (accessed 7.07.2024).
Swinton, J. (2012), *Dementia: Living in the Memories of God*, London: SCM Press.

PART THREE

Multifaith and Secular Dimensions

9

'How Shall I Sing the Lord's Song in a Strange Land?' Christian Biblical Perspectives on Theological Integrity in Inter- and Multifaith Chaplaincy

ANDREW JYOTHI ISAAC SUSAN

My reflection in this chapter arises from an occasion when I was asked to pray by a Muslim patient. I explained I was a Christian chaplain and offered referral to a Muslim chaplain, but the patient responded, 'It's OK. I just want you to pray for me.' I enthusiastically started the prayer, but halfway through a crisis struck me about how to end. Throughout my life, I had ended every single prayer 'In the name of Jesus. Amen'. What should I do?

I want to explain my positionality here as I believe that explains the reason why I was comfortable to start the prayer in the first place. My part of India has always been a place of harmonious religious coexistence. My father being a priest in the Church of South India, my family has always lived in vicarages, and my mother being a medical doctor had her private practice in the vicarages. So her patients of different faith backgrounds would come to the vicarage. I have seen many of them ask her for prayers, and she happily prays for them. In a very fluid way, at times the medical appointments would also involve pastoral care by my mother, ending with Christian prayers. If my father was at home, I have seen patients ask for a prayer from him. None of these patients – as far as I know – ever converted to Christianity. In fact, in return my mother received holy water from Mecca: 'Aravana Prasadam' offered in Sabarimala Temple, and 'Tirupati Laddu' offered in Tirumala Venkateswara Temple in Tirupati. Youngblood (2019, p. 8) speaks of cross-religious practice between different Chinese religions. One could argue that what is seen here is rather like such an inclusive syncretism. However, my family have always been practising Protestant Christians. This meant that the Bible has a primary position in faith life with daily reading at home. Therefore, I am not sure if I can theologically justify the religiosity involved here.

Raised in this 'special' context of being exposed to and living with other religious traditions while being Christian, I didn't hesitate when a Muslim patient asked for prayer. However, the NHS context is different. I cannot offer a prayer mediated through Jesus for a Muslim patient. I concluded with 'To God we pray' and both of us said 'Amen'.

Complexifying the event

This event of praying for a Muslim patient had a lasting impact on me. Did I betray my own faith? Did I do justice to the patient? Capps (as cited in Youngblood, 2019, pp. 5–6) proposes that pastoral actions are like texts that can initiate future hermeneutic reflection and re-reflection. As the interpretation is about something in the past, Ricoeur (cited in Youngblood, 2019, p. 6) suggests that this creates distanciation between persons and their actions, leading to 'reflection and re-reflection on the event in order to reveal new meanings'.

While the patient in my case did thank me for the prayer, it remained a concern for me and got me thinking about the theological dimensions and complexity of being a representative of one faith, in a secular setting, alongside representatives of other faith traditions, in a service (chaplaincy) that has faith(s) as an essential dimension. How can I sing 'the Lord's song' in a strange land?

Mohrmann (2008, p. 19) identifies the chaplain as a member of two professions. Normally, no religion ordains or commissions someone as a multifaith or interfaith chaplain (Aune, Guest and Law, 2019, p. 119). First, to be a chaplain one must be a recognized leader of a faith community. This means being commissioned or ordained to minister to the faith community (NHS Health Careers, n.d., online; Aune, Guest and Law, 2019, p. 119), and therefore called to sing the Lord's song, accepting the tenets of faith of the religion and denomination within the religion. Second, the chaplain is also a member of the profession of chaplaincy, which is located within a secular framework, outside the direct jurisdiction of religion. Hence, owing to 'dual professional allegiances' (Mohrmann, 2008, p. 20), chaplains may face contradictory moral demands (Mohrmann, 2008, p. 19). Baker terms this 'institutional duality' and suggests that it has been an 'enduring tension' from the early days of chaplaincy in secular settings, and that chaplains learn to negotiate this tension (Baker, 2021, p. 94).

In this chapter I explore this through the concept of 'theological integrity'. I argue that theological integrity is integral in the context of 'all faiths and none approach' in inter-/multifaith chaplaincy, and I shall explore this using selected biblical passages.

The concept of theological integrity in chaplaincy

Williams (2018, p. 60), in the context of the 'all faiths and none' framework of multifaith chaplaincy, says that 'Christian chaplains still need to find a way to articulate their role with a sense of personal and theological integrity drawn from their own tradition.' Drawing on this point, theological integrity in chaplaincy for me means that my actions as a chaplain should come out of my theological convictions, and those convictions need to be in alignment with the tenets of the faith that I represent.

I found this idea of theological integrity, in the context of chaplaincy, articulated in different ways in existing literature. For example, Aune, Guest and Law (2019, p. 36) write about the significance of 'Integrity of Faith' in chaplaincy, while Mohrmann (2008, p. 18) writes about 'Chaplaincy Ethics'. Fawcett and Noble (as cited in Liefbroer et al., 2017, p. 1777) engage with a similar tension in spiritual care provision by nurses to patients with different beliefs and hypothesize that it can be challenging for Christian nurses to maintain 'professional and religious integrity'. Pesut et al. (2012, p. 832), using the term 'brokering diversity', speak of chaplaincy as a space where chaplains negotiate their own truth claims with those of others. Similarly, Mellon (2003, p. 60) states that it is crucial for the chaplain to have a solid theological foundation and 'also be able to balance personal convictions with the orientation and faith of those receiving care'.

In this chapter, I am not attempting to propose a universal standard of theological integrity that applies to chaplains of all religious traditions. Mohrmann (2008, p. 19) argues that chaplaincy ethics owing to interfaith commitments cannot be founded on 'ethical frameworks of specific religious traditions'. Likewise, Williams (2018, p. 61) speaks of the impossibility to 'create one overarching theology of multifaith chaplaincy'. What I attempt to develop here is what I perceive to be a possible way forward given my own positionality. As a Christian, how can I serve in an inter-/multifaith setting for people of 'all faiths and none' with integrity to my own faith tradition? How can I sing the Lord's song in a strange land amid other songs? However, prior to presenting my argument, I want to critically engage with a few existing practical frameworks and approaches that address this tension.

Generic chaplaincy

The concept of generic chaplaincy focuses on spiritual care without religious specificity. In this framework, the chaplain – regardless of their religious adherence – is expected to provide spiritual care to all patients requesting it. This approach attempts to make chaplaincy a neutral space (MacLaren, 2021, p. 27). It is argued that this approach requires chaplains to be re-professionalized into trans-denominational and even trans-religious roles (Engelhardt, 1998, p. 232). It is also suggested that this approach developed as a result of the pattern of secularization in Scotland, while in England secularization led to the affirmation of different faith traditions in chaplaincy (Eccles, 2014, p. 2). Pattison (2001, p. 34) criticizes generic chaplaincy as a 'metaphysical marshmallow that is non-specific, unlocated, thin, uncritical, dull, and un-nutritious'. I share this view primarily because I doubt the integrity of this approach to chaplaincy. The chaplain is forced to sing the song set by the administrators of the strange land.

Code-switching and neutralization

Code-switching and neutralizing are two strategies used by chaplains in generic spiritual care (Youngblood, 2019, p. 7). In 'neutralization', chaplains use generic spiritual language rather than specific religious language and seek common aspects of the faith traditions of the people being provided with care. In 'code-switching', the faith-pattern and vocabulary of those receiving care are adopted by the chaplain during the time of providing care. The chaplain shall respond in the religious language of the person and may even participate in rituals (Cadge and Rambo, 2022, pp. 64, 80). Liefbroer et al. (2017, pp. 1788–9) recognizes these strategies as attempts to 'create a third, relational space, in-between two discourses'. These approaches are seen as useful by some scholars (Eccles, 2014, pp. 7–8). They are also valued as an important competence required in providing person-centred care. Cadge and Sigalow (2013, p. 153) found that while some chaplains in their study reported experiencing tensions in adopting these approaches, most were comfortable with them.

In my chaplaincy experiences, I have applied these approaches – for example, reading out a prayer that was mediated through a saint for a Catholic patient, something I was not used to as a Protestant Christian. Another time I affirmed a Hindu patient sharing about his pilgrimages to different temples, churches and mosques in India, as he spoke about his spirituality as universal, an idea that I personally do not hold. These events were mostly instinctive responses rather than learned skills.

However, these approaches leave me with some serious concerns. Youngblood (2019, p. 7) makes a significant critique about code-switching and neutralization in these approaches: 'the epistemological, anthropological, soteriological and – importantly – ethical norms are established from outside the religious language-systems meaningful to either the patient, chaplain, or both.' In code-switching, the religious patterns of the care seeker are uncritically adopted, and this may be a betrayal of the chaplain's own faith. In neutralizing, by taking generic spiritual languages and patterns, the very specific and concrete needs of the care seeker could be ignored (Youngblood, 2019, p. 7). Liefbroer et al. (2017, p. 1790) also asks how reasonable it is to expect all spiritual caregivers to have in-depth knowledge of all faith traditions. I am personally concerned about the appropriateness of these methods. For example, I cannot as a Christian recite the Shahada with integrity (Youngblood, 2019, p. 7).

For me, these approaches attempt to paint a picture that cross-religious spiritual care is straightforward if chaplains possess enough professionalized interfaith competencies, and to some extent trivialize unique faith traditions. In my experience, these methods could also be dangerous in chaplain–patient relationships. A few sessions after I supported the Catholic patient in prayer, I had to tell her that I was a Protestant. Her immediate response was, 'So you don't believe in saints.' For this patient, in a religious ritual such as reciting a prayer mediated through a saint, it was important that the person who recited the prayer shared her faith. Similarly, Cadge and Sigalow (2013, p. 155), in the study in which they expressly support code-switching and neutralizing, also report patients seeking specific religious services of their own faith leaders. For me, these strategies lack the element of integrity that gives the chaplain the freedom to sing the Lord's song and requires them to sing strange songs in strange settings.

Interfaith chaplaincy, multifaith chaplaincy, 'All faiths and none' approach

In chaplaincy, the terms 'interfaith' and 'multifaith' are understood both synonymously (Liefbroer et al., 2017, p. 1777) and in contrast to each other (Stewart-Darling, 2017, p. 68). When understood synonymously, they denote the presence of chaplains of different faith traditions while spiritual care can be across traditions. When understood as being in contrast to each other the term 'interfaith' is associated more with the concept of 'generic chaplaincy' and 'multifaith' is understood as denoting the presence of a plurality of faith traditions, meaning a team of chaplains who bring their distinctive religious expertise (Schipani, 2017, p. 76). Stewart-Darling (2017, p. 68) favours the concept of 'multifaith' over 'interfaith', as she observes that this approach helps the chaplain have more integrity to their own faith tradition.

In the NHS chaplaincy context where I worked, which follows the 'all faiths and none' approach, I have come across the terms 'multifaith' and 'interfaith' used both synonymously and distinctively. In this framework a major aspect is the distinctiveness of the concepts of 'spiritual care' and 'religious care' (UKBHC, 2020, pp. 2–3). While the chaplain is expected to provide spiritual care to patients of 'all faiths and none', they are valued for the distinct theology that they embody and they are not expected to provide religious care (that is, engage in rites or ceremonies from faiths or traditions that they do not follow), or to provide guidance that contradicts their own convictions (NHS England, 2023, online). I find this distinction helpful as it empowers the chaplain to be true to personal faith, while being able to serve the care seeker with integrity. Our team included humanist chaplains as well, to cater to the needs of persons who do not follow a particular faith. In this approach spirituality is seen as a universal phenomenon that could include organized religion but need not necessarily. In my opinion this framework of 'all faiths and none' takes seriously religious diversity and spirituality beyond the bounds of faith traditions. It also gives maximum possible space for chaplains to operate with integrity. In this approach, for me the chaplain comes with their own song of their own Lord, while acknowledging that several singers sing in different settings and music with their own adorations.

Now I want to engage on how this singing can happen. How will I sing my Lord's song, while there are other songs being sung around me? How can I negotiate the truth claims that I represent with that of others? I came across two paradigms for inter-/multifaith chaplaincy to operate in a healthy way. I present both here because one approach favours a priori truth and the other favours a posteriori truth.

Cooperative pluralism

Baker (2021, pp. 95–6), writing from the context of chaplaincy in the USA, develops the idea of 'cooperative pluralism', which he describes as 'the practice of sustaining acceptable and supportable coexistence between adherents of different religions'. Cooperative pluralism requires mutual respect, shared responsibility to relate to others, and amicable coexistence. Here the chaplain is welcome to share personal faith whenever invited, to bring 'healing and hope'. But it does not support proselytizing. For me this approach is more authentic than code-switching and neutralizing because I have had experiences where patients of other faith traditions ask me about my own understanding of healing, where I have shared from my faith. Here I see an effort to make meaning of the present experience of suffering drawing from other faith traditions.

It is significant that cooperative pluralism puts forward the idea of 'cooperation without compromise' (Baker, 2021, p. 96). This principle,

I believe, is helpful as it gives the chaplain a comfortable space to hold on to faith while respecting the faith of the care seeker and his/her/their colleagues, and actively reflect on one's faith when invited. An important aspect I identify in cooperative pluralism is that it privileges a priori truth. From my understanding of this approach, the expectation from the chaplain is that they respect other faith traditions, and a similar respect without challenge is available to the chaplain as well. I sing my song, while my colleague of a different tradition sings their song. But will my song be interrupted in the process? Or will there be new harmonies heard when different songs are sung together? The next approach I discuss is one that I believe addresses this aspect: an approach where a posteriori truth is valued.

Comparative theology and the paradigm of hospitality

Comparative theology can be described as an approach in which truth is seen as a posteriori through dialogue between contrasting faith traditions (Youngblood, 2019, p. 2). Williams (2018, pp. 62–3), focusing on the idea of 'transcendent otherness' and 'beyondness' in the Christian understanding of God, suggests that 'the unknowability and indefinability of the divine ... provides a potential lens' for exploring the differing perspectives on truth.

From a Christian vantage point, 'hospitality' is developed as an essential moral paradigm of comparative theology by several Christian scholars, such as Luke Bretherton and Marriane Moyaert (Youngblood, 2019, p. 2). In the context of interreligious relations, Moyaert proposes a linguistic approach to hospitality that transcends the limits of unfamiliarity that might constrain hospitality, by taking Ricoeur's idea of 'linguistic hospitality' (Youngblood, 2019, p. 4): a mediation between 'the peculiar and the foreign' (cited in Bredvik, 2021, p. 100). This perspective allows for the strangeness of the other language to challenge the translator. The act of translation inevitably brings some meanings that are different from the original language because, first, the translation must conform to another language and, second, the host language will be transformed by foreign concepts. This results in the development of a new world of meaning; while something is lost, something is also gained. Here, linguistic hospitality is taken as a hermeneutical concept – an ethic rooted in the philosophical concept of hospitality. Balancing between an 'openness for the other and preservation of [own] identity' is necessary for this hospitality (Bredvik, 2021, p. 101). Therefore, Moyaert suggests that comparative theology is done in a fragile hermeneutical space where tension exists between betrayal and faithfulness. The comparative theologian exposes their own faith system to that of a strange one, risking its transformation (Youngblood, 2019, p. 5).

When appropriated into the realm of interfaith chaplaincy, Youngblood (2019, p. 5) suggests that comparative theology and interreligious hospitality provide 'a practical hermeneutical ethic', and a reminder to 'take real religious differences seriously'. Williams (2018, p. 65) argues that interfaith chaplaincy 'effectively requires openness to the idea that truth is not the exclusive property of one faith, or of one tradition within one faith'. So I sing my Lord's song but I also listen to and appreciate other songs around me; sometimes this can be mutually interrupting and unsettling, and at other times new harmonies might come up when different songs are sung and listened to at the same time.

Truth-in-hand and truth-in-process

From my readings and my experience in a inter-/multifaith chaplaincy, I see both cooperative pluralism (Baker, 2021, p. 95) and hospitality (Youngblood, 2019, p. 5) as important. These concepts, when brought together, give the chaplain the space to preserve identity but also require them to be generous and respectful to, and be moved by, other faith traditions.

I also recognize a tension when these concepts are brought together. The idea of cooperative pluralism, and particularly the principle of 'cooperation without compromise', privileges a priori truth without any external challenge. The expectation here is mutual respect. However, comparative theology and the paradigm of hospitality favours a posteriori truth. This means that the theological and spiritual horizons of the chaplain could be challenged – and even potentially transformed – in the multifaith chaplaincy engagement.

I find the concept of 'two kinds of truth' by Graham Adams (2022, p. 37) helpful to creatively explore this tension. Drawing from the works of Andrew Shanks, he carves a distinction between two ideas – namely, truth-in-hand and truth-in-process. Truth-in-hand is 'the claim to possess a truth, as though by articulating it we grasp the very truth of something'; truth-in-process is being attentive 'to the "uncontainability" of truth; the appreciation that what we hold cannot be the whole story' (Adams, 2022, p. 41). While the author privileges truth-in-process, he also affirms that 'we always need some degree of [truth-in-hand] to articulate ideas about the world, and to build common cause with others'; truth-in-process relies on truth-in-hand (Adams, 2022, p. 39). Adams uses the analogy of a closed fist to represent truth-in-hand, and an open palm to represent truth-in-process (Adams, 2022, p. 39). Drawing from this, I argue that the chaplain is in a space of fluidity and movement, constantly opening and closing their palm. While affirming and representing the truth-in-hand – that is, the theological and moral convictions that they embody, hold preciously and represent – there is a need to be open to the possibility of the truth-in-process that could happen through the encounter in the inter-/multifaith chaplaincy.

Bretherton suggests (as cited in Youngblood, 2019, p. 2) that faith-groups need 'theologically-grounded practical-ethical paradigms' for the structuring of mutual relationships. This brings me to the final question. Can all this be done with theological integrity? Does my Christian faith allow me to have both truth-in-hand and truth-in-process? As a Christian chaplain, I want to appeal to the Bible.

A God of diversity – the Tower of Babel

The Tower of Babel narrative in Genesis 11 is, for me, God's affirmation of diversity. Moyaert theologically grounds the idea of linguistic hospitality on this passage (Bakker, 2011, p. 380). What is deconstructed in Babel is not unity of humanity, but instead the human quest for uniformity. The quest for a monolithic-totalitarian movement towards imposed homogeneity is thwarted by God (Held, 2017, pp. 12–13). Rabbi Naftali Tzvi Yehudah Berlin says that God found the unanimity alarming because it is a sign of totalitarian control. He suggests that the builders refuse to let anyone leave the city because that could cause the development of new thoughts and perspectives. Babel was trying to be the centre of ideological enforcement (cited in Held, 2017, pp. 12–13). Raimundo Panikkar (1979, p. 212) exposes how religions, particularly Christianity and Islam, have attempted to become Babel when they tried to become 'not just the number one religion, but ideally the one religion'. The climax of the Babel narrative has several implications, but particularly significant for me is how, amid multiple truths, my religious belief can be universally true (Feldmann-Kaye, 2020, p. 38). God's will in creation is diversity, and Babel represents a human attempt to undermine this will. Therefore, the multiplication of languages and dispersal of people can be argued as a restoration of God's blessings. For me, the resultant development of diverse faith traditions is also therefore God's blessing.

A God of all people – Amos 9.7

Amos offers me new lenses to understand God's relationship with people. It challenges the claims of exclusive relationship to God. Eidevall (2017, pp. 234–6) points out that there have been several contrasting scholarly opinions on why Cushites are mentioned in the rhetorical question at the beginning of the verse and suggests that this makes two points. First, Israel is like any other people to Yahweh and, second, this equal concern extends to even geographically distant and different people. This undermines any claim Israel has to uniqueness and specialness among the nations (Beck, 2008, online).

The second part of the verse draws from Israel's Exodus relationship with Yahweh, upon which the specialness and uniqueness is founded and something it held with privilege (Beck, 2008, online). Samartha (1994, p. 352) says that even in Christian faith the Exodus has been interpreted in an exclusive manner – in other words, that God's redemptive mission was revealed only in the history of Israel, and later in the Western Church. While the prophet does not refute the Exodus relationship, he explicitly deconstructs the notion of Yahweh's exclusive relationship with Israel (Beck, 2008, online). Even more, a similar relationship is established between Yahweh and Judah-Israel's arch enemies the Philistines and Arameans (Eidevall, 2017, p. 236). Drawing from the idea of the beyondness of God (Williams, 2018, pp. 62–3), I see this verse as giving me the space to accommodate and acknowledge with integrity the faith traditions that I personally do not follow, believing that there exists a divine relationship in these faith traditions that I may not comprehend.

Acknowledging and respecting diverse faith traditions – Micah 4.5

Micah 4.5 presents a unique profession of faith. Part of the oracle of salvation (Shaw, 1993, p. 102), this verse is a liturgical response of the congregation. Koyama (1988, p. 200) suggests that the presence and efficacy of other gods are acknowledged here. There is no condemnation of practising different faith traditions. Samartha (1981, p. 103) suggests 'There are different faiths, there are alternative ways of salvation, there are different hopes about human destiny, and there are different affirmations as to what happens in the end.' A vision of peaceful coexistence of different faith traditions, without threat, can be observed here (Groenwald, 2017, p. 61). This verse carries extra significance in the context of inter-/multifaith chaplaincy since it encourages people to stand steadfast in their religion while also recognizing the validity of other faiths.

Encounter with the Samaritan woman

Drawing from the narrative of Jesus' interaction with the Samaritan woman, Baker (2021, p. 14) describes what he terms as the three foundational pillars of chaplaincy. First, chaplaincy is about 'being intentional through movement and direction'. In the narrative Jesus moves away from the Jerusalem temple, which is the centre of religion for Jews, and enters a territory that is strange to Jews. Religious Jews avoided Samaria when travelling to Galilee, even though it is the shorter route. Victor (2016, p. 163) suggests that Jesus travelling through Samaria has both geographical as well as theological necessity. Jesus is not just hastily transiting through Samaria but is pausing and taking time to engage with people on whom the Jewish religion had ascribed pollution. I see here an intentional effort to meet the other in a strange land. This has a direct implication for chaplaincy. Chaplains meet people not in the convenient home ground of the church but in the inconvenient space of a secular setting. As Jesus chose to use the route usually avoided by Jewish clergy, chaplains chose to move out of centres of religious activity and convenient pathways, to secular uncomfortable spaces.

The second pillar of chaplaincy is 'embracing diversity through connection and compassion' (Baker, 2021, p. 16). Jesus asks for water and establishes a connection. Contrary to the traditional reasons ascribed to the woman coming to the well at noon, which usually focus on her moral status, Victor (2016, p. 168) suggests that it is possible that the woman made frequent trips to the well out of necessity to fetch more water. Midday, being the hottest time of the day in West Asia, when people prefer to stay indoors, this woman is out in the sun fetching water probably not by choice but by compulsion of fulfilling her duties. And Jesus encounters her breaking the human-made religious-cultural-ethnic-social barriers. Similarly, chaplains find people where they are, often in times of suffering, and create space for conversation. This surprises the woman as drinking water from her vessel is enough for a Jew to become polluted, but that starts a conversation. As with the differences between Jews and Samaritans, there exist theological differences between different faith traditions. Naseri (2015, p. 170) suggests there is, in the exchange between Jesus and the Samaritan woman, acknowledgement as well as mutual respect for the distinctiveness of their standpoints. Similarly, chaplains in a multifaith setting are committed to facilitate plurality and respect diversity.

Third, Jesus is 'seeking transformation through presence and service' (Baker, 2021, p. 18). Both Jesus and the Samaritan woman appreciate the conversation. In the context of chaplaincy this involves the chaplain being present through the uncomfortable and often painful moments of the person's life. Jesus addresses the deeper need of the Samaritan woman by asking what he can do, which leads her to asking Jesus for the living water. Baker (2021, p. 17) suggests that often people come to chaplains because they trust that they will be listened to and not judged.

For me, this emphasizes the importance of the ministry of presence by the chaplain while being willing to offer service when asked.

The walk to Emmaus

Fiona Stewart-Darling (2017, p. 108) uses Jesus' walk with the two disciples to Emmaus to explain the evangelistic dimension of chaplaincy. She draws out four stages in the journey, namely Listening, Answering Questions, Explaining and Choice. Jesus begins the encounter through listening to the concerns of the two disciples. Then he engages through conversation answering their questions. Third, he explains from the scriptures the events that had happened. Finally, when they had reached the village, the disciples chose to invite him to their home. Stewart-Darling says that the chaplain has the privilege to be part of someone's faith journey, often not knowing the outcome. Newitt (2011, p. 105) identifies attentive listening as an essential competency for effective chaplaincy, also stressing the importance of pastoral theological education to respond to people's concerns in a time of trouble as well as to give Christian explanations to their experiences. Finally, the choice rests with the care receiver to invite the chaplain to their space. Baker (2021, p. 17) suggests that without an invitation it is not appropriate for a chaplain to share their faith.

The Emmaus narrative also portrays the interchangeability of the host–guest roles in chaplaincy. Stewart-Darling (2017, p. 109) says that in any chaplaincy encounter the chaplain must be willing to practise both embassy and hospitality. Here Jesus receives hospitality when being invited to the disciples' home, but then becomes the host in the breaking of the bread.

Conclusion

In this chapter I have attempted to engage with the theological complexity that I experienced in inter-/multifaith chaplaincy. For me, chaplaincy is a strange land where the chaplain is called to sing the Lord's song amid a multitude of songs. The crux of what I wanted to explore is the reality of multiple truth claims and the chaplain's experience of complex negotiations between personally held truth and the truth that arises in chaplaincy encounters.

I have sought biblical explanations to substantiate the new understandings that came out of this process. Through my explorations and, given my positionality outlined in the introduction, I believe multiple truth claims arise out of the divine blessing of diversity. God, as I understand Her, relates with people who sing songs different from mine. I will sing the Lord's song while others sing the songs that came through their religious experiences or experiences that aren't necessarily religious. My calling as a chaplain is to be present, listening to and engaging with different songs, until finally I am called to sing the Lord's song while enjoying, encouraging and cherishing the multitude of songs.

Bibliography

Adams, G. (2022), *Holy Anarchy: Dismantling Domination, Embodying Community, Loving Strangeness*, London: SCM Press.

Aune, K., M. Guest and J. Law (2019), *Chaplains on Campus: Understanding Chaplaincy in UK Universities*, Coventry: Coventry University; Durham: Durham University; Canterbury: Canterbury Christ Church University.

Baker, A. T. (2021), *Foundations of Chaplaincy: A Practical Guide*, Grand Rapids, MI: Eerdmans.

Bakker, F. L. (2011), 'Fragile Identities: Towards a Theology of Interreligious Hospitality', *Exchange* 40(4), pp. 379–81.

Beck, R. (2008), 'Amos 9.7: "Exodus" in the Plural', *Experimental Theology*, 14 January, available at http://experimentaltheology.blogspot.com/2008/01/amos-97-exodus-in-plural.html (accessed 7.07.2024).

Bredvik, L. S. (2021), 'Linguistic Hospitality in Spiritual Care and Counselling', in L. S. Bredvik et al. (eds), *Care, Healing, and Human Well-being within Interreligious Discourses*, South Africa: African Sun Media, pp. 100–12.

Cadge, W. and E. Sigalow (2013), 'Negotiating Religious Differences: The Strategies of Interfaith Chaplains in Healthcare', *Journal for the Scientific Study of Religion* 52(1), pp. 146–58.

Cadge, W. and S. Rambo (2022), *Chaplaincy and Spiritual Care in the Twenty-first Century: An Introduction*, Chapel Hill, NC: University of North Carolina Press.

Eccles, J. B. (2014), 'The Chaplaincy Experience: Negotiating (Multi-Faith) Time and Space in a Northern English General Hospital', *Journal of Pastoral Care & Counseling* 68(3), pp. 1–12.

Eidevall, G. (2017), *Amos: A New Translation with Introduction and Commentary*, New Haven, CT: Yale University Press.

Engelhardt, H. T. (1998), 'Generic Chaplaincy: Providing Spiritual Care in a Post-Christian Age', *Christian Bioethics* 4(3), pp. 231–8.

Feldmann-Kaye, M. (2020), 'Multiple Truths and the Towers of Babel: Deconstructionism in Jewish Philosophy', *Tradition Journal* 52(4), pp. 37–43.

Groenwald, S. (2017), *Creating a Culture of Care for Students & Faculty: The Chamberlain University College of Nursing Model (NLN)*, Philadelphia, PA: Lippincott Williams and Wilkins.

Held, S. (2017), 'Tower of Uniformity: What Really Went Wrong at Babel', *The Christian Century* 134(23), pp. 12–13.

Koyama, K. (1988), *Three Mile an Hour God*, London: SCM Press.

Liefbroer, A. I. et al.(2017), 'Interfaith Spiritual Care: A Systematic Review', *Journal of Religion and Health* 56(5), pp. 1776–93.

MacLaren, D. (2021), 'All Things to All People? The Integrity of Spiritual Care in a Plural Health Service', *Health and Social Care Chaplaincy* 9(1), pp. 27–41.

Mellon, B. F. (2003), 'Faith-to-faith at the Bedside: Theological and Ethical Issues in Ecumenical Clinical Chaplaincy', *Christian Bioethics* 9(1), pp. 57–67.

Mohrmann, M. E. (2008), 'Ethical Grounding for a Profession of Hospital Chaplaincy', *The Hastings Center Report* 38(6), pp. 18–23, available at http://www.jstor.org/stable/25165385 (accessed 7.07.2024).

Naseri, C. (2015), 'The Encounter between Jesus and the Samaritan Woman in John 4:1–42: A Model for Christian Ecumenical Dialogue', in L. E. Ijezie, S. Audu and A. I. Acha (eds), *The Church in Nigeria and Ecumenical Question*, Lagos: Cathan Publications, pp. 170–95.

Newitt, M. (2011), 'The Role and Skills of a Chaplain', in M. Threlfall-Holmes and M. Newitt (eds), *Being a Chaplain*, London: SPCK, pp. 103–15.

NHS Health Careers (n.d.), *Chaplain*, available at https://www.healthcareers.nhs.uk/explore-roles/wider-healthcare-team/roles-wider-healthcare-team/corporate-services/chaplain (accessed 7.07.2024).

NHS England (2023), *NHS Chaplaincy – Guidelines for NHS Managers on Pastoral, Spiritual and Religious Care*, available at https://www.england.nhs.uk/long-read/nhs-chaplaincy-guidelines-for-nhs-managers-on-pastoral-spiritual-and-religious-care/ (accessed 7.07.2024).

Panikkar, R. (1979), 'The Myth of Pluralism: The Tower of Babel – A Meditation on Non-Violence', *Cross Currents* 29(2), pp. 197–230.

Pattison, S. (2001), 'Dumbing Down the Spirit', in H. Orchard (ed.), *Spirituality in Health Care Contexts*, London: Jessica Kingsley Publishers, pp. 33–47.

Pesut, B. et al. (2012), 'Hospitable Hospitals in a Diverse Society: From Chaplains to Spiritual Care Providers', *Journal of Religion and Health* 51(3), pp. 825–36.

Samartha, S. J. (1981), *Courage for Dialogue: Ecumenical Issues in Inter-religious Relationships*, Geneva, World Council of Churches; Maryknoll, NY: Orbis Books.

Samartha, S. J. (1994), 'Religion, Language and Reality', *Biblical Interpretation* 2(3), pp. 340–62.

Schipani, D. S. (2017), 'Many Faiths, One Human Spirit: A Christian Contribution to Spiritual Care in Multifaith Contexts', *Vision: A Journal for Church and Theology* 18(2), pp. 76–85.

Shaw, C. S. (1993), *Speeches of Micah: A Rhetorical-Historical Analysis*, Sheffield: JSOT Press.

Stewart-Darling, F. (2017), *Multifaith Chaplaincy in the Workplace: How Chaplains Can Support Organizations and their Employees*, London: Jessica Kingsley Publishers.

UKBHC (2020), *Spiritual Care Competencies for Healthcare Chaplains*, available at https://www.ukbhc.org.uk/wp-content/uploads/2020/10/UKBHC-CCs-180220.pdf (accessed 7.07.2024).

Victor, R. (2016), 'Jesus and the Samaritan Woman: Liberation of a Dalit', *Asia Journal of Theology* 30(2), pp. 160–76.

Williams, R. (2018), '"All Faiths and None?": Theological Issues in Multi-Faith Chaplaincy', in J. Caperon, A. Todd and J. Walters (eds), *A Christian Theology of Chaplaincy*, London: Jessica Kingsley Publishers, pp. 59–78.

Youngblood, P. W. (2019), 'Interfaith Chaplaincy as Interpretive Hospitality', *Religions* 10(3), p. 226, available at https://www.mdpi.com/2077-1444/10/3/226 (accessed 7.07.2024).

10

Baptist Prison Chaplaincy: A Divided Duty?

SIMON HOLLIS

Chaplaincy within prisons has existed in England for over 250 years. Uniquely within the prison context this faith-based role is enshrined in law, the legal requirement for the appointment of an Anglican chaplain dating back to 1773 (Phillips, 2013, p. 4). Since the latest iteration of this requirement in the Prison Act 1952, there have, however, been significant changes in the multicultural nature of English society (Welby, 2018, p. 253).

Commentators have noted two emerging themes regarding the expression of religious belief since the 1960s: a decline in those identifying as belonging to any defined Christian faith (Slater, 2015, p. 14), accompanied by a simultaneous burgeoning in the development of chaplaincy (Ryan, 2015, p. 6). From a societal perspective there has been an increased emphasis on an agenda of equality, diversity and inclusion in the contemporary public square. In the prison context, this has found expression over the last three decades in the development of Multifaith and Secular (hereafter MFS) chaplaincies. In this changed and changing social landscape, there are accordingly sensitivities as to the ongoing suitability of an inherited Christian model for chaplaincy and whether the Christian faith, let alone a single denomination, can with integrity facilitate a chaplaincy for all in MFS contexts.

Such societal changes might also seem to exacerbate a potentially pre-existing conflict for the individual Baptist chaplain between their denominational and institutional roles. Both the appointment of the prison chaplain and their terms of service are governed by statute law and binding government guidance. Endorsement of the chaplain by an approved Faith and Belief Adviser is an occupational requirement of prison chaplaincy. In describing their role, Prison Service Instructions (PSI) 5/2016 state that 'Chaplains and Chaplaincy Teams [are] appointed to meet the needs and reflect the faith make-up of the prison population' (His Majesty's Prison and Probation Service (HMPPS), 2023, p. 7). The chaplain accordingly works in a religiously diverse team, meeting both the faith and pastoral needs of those of differing religious beliefs and of none.

By contrast, however, the ordination vows upon which the Faith Adviser's endorsement of the Baptist chaplain is founded are explicitly Christian and church-based. They have an overtly missional agenda, the ordinand promising that 'as a disciple of Jesus Christ, I will call others to follow him' (Ellis and Blyth, 2005, p. 124). This accords with the third 'Declaration of Principle' of the Baptist Union of Great Britain (BUGB), which states that 'it is the duty of every disciple to bear personal witness to the Gospel of Jesus Christ, and to take part in the evangelisation of the world' (BUGB, n.d., online). At first sight, therefore, such promises might appear to contradict the legal proscription against proselytization in Section 10 of the Prison Act 1952. Is there, therefore, a dilemma for the Baptist chaplain? If there are potentially differing agendas between being a Baptist minister and chaplain in an MFS team, can these legitimately coexist, or are there fundamentally divided duties?

Volland notes the dangers of a Christian opportunistically accepting public funding to pursue a denominational missionary endeavour that conflicts with that of their host establishment (Volland, 2015, p. 52). This concern must be taken seriously where the chaplain may serve in a secular prison, funded by a secular government, potentially led by a chaplain who does not hold the Christian faith and where approximately a third of the prisoners may identify as being 'non-religious' (Sturge, 2022, p. 21). I explore whether a Baptist chaplain can minister with theological integrity in such a setting, both in the sense of implying an internal consistency between belief and action, and that of a theological honesty and sincerity in fulfilling the chaplain's role. I suggest that the existence of such integrity is not simply desirable from a personal perspective but is fundamental to the authenticity, trustworthiness, credibility, transparency and example of the chaplain (Lamb, 2006, pp. 13–34).

For the Baptist chaplain to achieve an integrity between their beliefs and actions in a MFS setting presupposes that an understanding of their role and context can in fact be achieved. Noting the sheer variety of different chaplaincy contexts that presently exist in England, Ryan states that 'depending on the field, organisation, belief, and specificity of the role in question there is very little consensus on how to define what a chaplain is' (Ryan, 2015, p. 10). In seeking to understand their place in the context of MFS chaplaincy, the prison chaplain might be assumed to be better served than chaplains in other arenas. They are bound by mandatory government guidance PSI 5/2016, which seeks to define what is understood by the role of chaplain and the key aspects of 20 major faiths and beliefs that they may encounter (HMPPS, 2023).

Even in such a relatively codified legal context, exact definitions of key concepts remain elusive. Mirroring concerns raised regarding prison chaplaincy by Humanists UK (2023, online), Bloom notes that even basic terms such as 'faith', 'belief' and 'religion' are often used by the state in ways that are inexact or inaccurate (Bloom, 2023, p. 48).

Precise language is, however, important in the chaplaincy context, both for achieving clear and respectful communication with different belief groups and stakeholders, and identifying what issues need to be addressed (Bloom, 2023, p. 48). A lack of clearly accepted definitions is likely to prove problematic not only in shaping national policy but also in establishing the agreed framework for dialogue with those of other faiths and beliefs that the Baptist chaplain will need in their daily practice.

What may present as challenges to the daily practice for the Baptist chaplain in MFS settings often prove to have their origins in wider underlying theological or ideological tensions. In this instance, for example, agreeing a consensus about the term 'religion' may prove problematic precisely because of the widely differing views about the existence and significance of a deity between the Abrahamic faiths, Buddhists, Hindus, Pagans and Humanists (Bloom, 2023, p. 47).

If the definition of individual chaplaincy roles and what constitutes a religion prove problematic, the challenges of reaching a settled understanding about the role of the MFS prison chaplain increase exponentially when considering multiple faiths and beliefs. The contemporary prison chaplaincy team is likely to be served by representatives of the major world faiths, including Christian, Muslim, Sikh, Buddhist and Pagan, as well as an increasing presence from Humanists.

A Baptist understanding?

I have suggested that the Baptist chaplain may struggle with the imprecise terminology describing the MFS setting, which may itself reflect that the rapid growth in chaplaincy over the last two decades has outstripped a matching theological reflection to underpin its practice (Slater, 2015, p. 7). Dixon suggests that chaplaincy research is often driven by the imperatives of the organization or context concerned and has accordingly developed in a reactive and piecemeal fashion in which, for example, healthcare has received considerably greater attention than the prison environment (Dixon, 2022, p. 15).

A Baptist chaplain may look to their denomination to assist in understanding a theology of MFS prison chaplaincy. The BUGB is held together by a three-part 'Declaration of Principle', encapsulating key aspects of Baptist belief. The Baptist emphasis upon the gathered, local church is expressed in the first of these three Declarations: namely 'that each Church has liberty, under the guidance of the Holy Spirit, to interpret and administer [Christ's] laws' (BUGB, n.d., online). This ecclesiology has two direct implications for the Baptist chaplain in an MFS setting. First, for Baptists, ordained ministry tends to be located within the local church context. The strength of this view is reflected in the fact that until 2002 a formal secondment from the accredited ministerial list was required to serve as a chaplain (Bowers, 2005, p. 6). Indeed, the ongoing use of the language of 'Sector Ministry' on the BUGB website suggests that the role of chaplaincy may still be perceived as peripheral, rather than central, to denominational life (Caperon, 2018, p. 17). A second corollary of this first Declaration is that, since Baptist theology is determined by the local church, there is not necessarily a distinctive and accepted denominational view relating to a specific issue (Fiddes, 2003, p. 3). The BUGB's 'Theology of Sector Ministry' is accordingly able to offer several differing, and mutually competing, ecclesiological rationales for chaplaincy, while also confirming that there is not a settled Baptist position (Bowers, 2005, pp. 11–14).

While liminality is often an inevitable feature of the chaplain's role, a practical outworking of marginalization in this church context is that research, training or equipping chaplains for MFS chaplaincy ministry are unlikely to be seen as denominational priorities (Slater, 2015, p. 6). It remains the case, for example, that neither chaplaincy ministry itself nor working in a MFS context form any mandatory part of Baptist ministerial formation.

Given the fluid and complex nature of MFS chaplaincy, this lack of a coherent and clearly communicated theology of chaplaincy is doubly unfortunate. First, as we have noted from Bloom, it is likely to make dialogue with the multiple stakeholders with whom the Baptist MFS chaplain engages more difficult (Bloom, 2023, p. 44). This may, in turn, make developing models of good practice more challenging to achieve (Hewson and Crompton, 2016, p. 131). Crucially, though, it may also leave the chaplain feeling unsupported by their denomination, hidden and disconnected from mainstream institutional church life (Todd, Slater and Dunlop, 2014, pp. 21–8).

Here, as with the definition of 'religion' above, I suggest we may usefully engage in what Swinton and Mowat describe as a process of 'complexification', reflecting upon the presenting issues to better understand the complications that may underlie them (Swinton and Mowat, 2016, p. 16). Slater, writing from an Anglican context, argues that the apparent local or denominational marginalization of the chaplain flows from a wider operant theology that tends to place the locus of mission primarily within the confines and activities of the established Church.

This understanding of missiology in turn shapes the institutional Church's ecclesiology and understanding of ministry, inevitably placing the chaplain on the periphery. Slater argues, however, that the chaplain shares in the *Missio Dei* (Slater, 2015, p. 95) which, following Bosch, is focused on serving God's mission in the world rather than viewing any individual church (or minister) as the 'author or bearer of mission' (Bosch, 1991, pp. 389–92). For such mission to be embraced by the Church may necessitate 'radical reformation' (Bradbury, 2000, p. 179), demanding that its understanding of missiology, and consequently its ecclesiology and expressions of ministry, are recalibrated (Slater, 2015, p. 116).

I suggest that Slater's observations are entirely applicable to a Baptist context, and that an important aspect of the Baptist chaplain's role may be to invite a reimagination of the scope of ministry and mission within the wider Baptist family. Such advocacy is needed not merely to make explicit the theological integrity of the chaplain's role; instead, it is to expand our vision of where and how God is active in the world, seeking to understand God's purposes more deeply and fitting ourselves better to share in God's work.

A community of learning

While change is awaited, the individual Baptist chaplain will need to find their own way of negotiating their role in their daily setting. The onus will be on them to be responsive, enquiring, proactive and eager to learn if they are to engage seriously with the presenting issues of MFS chaplaincy, rather than their being able to rely on accessing training already embedded in existing church structures.

Paradoxically, the Baptist chaplain may discover that it is within the context of the MFS chaplaincy itself (rather than through their denomination or the prison as an organization) that the deepest learning regarding other faiths and beliefs takes place (Boyce, 2010, p. 22). In a society where there continues to be a widespread lack of faith literacy (Bloom, 2023, p. 51), the MFS chaplaincy itself provides a natural forum for discussion and exploration of faith-related issues as they arise (Stewart-Darling, 2017, p. 64). Within this setting, world faiths may be encountered not as monolithic or static structures but that which is given expression in the lives of individuals (Schmidt-Leukel, 2009, p. 44). As Collicutt pithily describes the situation, drawing from her practice as a clinical psychologist, 'When we visit someone at home, we get a fuller picture of the whole person' (Collicutt, 2015, p. 160). This is not to argue for an uncritical naivety about other faiths and beliefs, disregarding the significant dangers of syncretism and relativism. Rather, it is to suggest that where serious critical appreciation is demanded, this may often more effectively take place through the lens of friendship and understanding (Schmidt-Leukel, 2009, p. 45).

In this relational setting, the chaplain may not only learn about other faiths and beliefs but also learn from them. A move may then take place from tolerance of other beliefs to appreciation of them (Schmidt-Leukel, 2009, pp. 30–45), providing a basis for the Baptist chaplain to test and sharpen the sufficiency of their own faith understanding (Newbigin, 2014, pp. 243–4). Indeed, Volf argues even further: that in reflecting the nature of the triune God, it is only as we encounter and embrace the 'other' that we are truly able to live authentically (Volf, 2003, p. 40).

Learning through shared community to deepen understanding of our own faith and the beliefs of those whom we live alongside not only creates the possibility of a greater intellectual integrity by better understanding Christian beliefs, but the learning process itself may embody and model integrity, as the Baptist chaplain seeks to practise their faith consistently when faced with the challenging realities of daily prison life.

Integrity in chaplaincy: truthfulness and honesty

I turn now to the second aspect of integrity I have identified – namely, that of truthfulness and honesty. In the secular context that has been described, can a Baptist chaplain properly continue in their role or is their position now an unjustifiable anachronism? Section 7 of the Prison Act 1952 still specifically requires the appointment of an Anglican chaplain, with section 10 then making provision for further ministers of other (unspecified) denominations (Prison Act, 1952). I suggest it is, therefore, helpful first to review how the CofE as a religion of the state has sought to develop a continued rationale for brokering faith and belief in the public square over recent decades.

In 1994 the then Prince Charles suggested that the monarch's role as head of the Church might better be expressed as 'Defender of Faith', rather than 'Defender of the Faith'. This, as Pepinster notes, appeared to imply that Anglicanism was concerned with only 'one particular interpretation of the Faith' (2022a, p. 270). However, in 2012, Queen Elizabeth II set out a subtly different understanding of the established Church's place in society, stating that its role 'is not to defend Anglicanism to the exclusion of other religions. Instead, the Church has a duty to protect the free practice of all faiths in this country … gently and assuredly, the CofE has created an environment for other faith communities, and indeed people of no faith, to live freely' (Queen Elizabeth II, 2012, online).

On his accession, the King pursued a similar theme when he spoke of the Church's

> duty to protect the diversity of our country, including by protecting the space for faith itself and its practice through the religions, cultures, traditions, and beliefs to which our hearts and minds direct us as individuals. This diversity is not just enshrined in the laws of our country, it is enjoined by my own faith. (King Charles III, 2022, online)

I suggest three important points can be drawn from this developing position that relate to the Baptist chaplain's understanding of integrity as truthfulness.

An intentional response

I have suggested that the Baptist chaplain's role has developed in ways that have often necessarily been reactive to others, and that have not always been matched with a considered response or overarching strategy at a denominational level. By contrast, the remarks of both monarchs demonstrate a conscious attempt to provide an adaptive and intentional response to a fluid situation, seeking, as part of their national church leadership role, to establish a reasoned basis for integrity of practice. Second, as they consider the Church's role in engaging with society, their analysis is noteworthy in its desire to embrace both their personal faith and the polity of the Church, connecting both with their relationship to the state.

Third, as I suggest above, such active and purposeful reflection at a national leadership level is helpful when seeking to ensure integrity as truthfulness in the public square and may lead to new theological understandings. In this instance, it is at least arguable that rather than simply clarifying the Church's role, both monarchs were fundamentally extending its remit to include a protective role for those with no defined faith, thereby reshaping its missiology and ecclesiology (Pepinster, 2022b, online).

A denominational hospitality

In terms of integrity, the monarchs reach a key conclusion whereby Anglicanism (and also potentially other Christians depending upon how the justification for this is established) can offer a form of denominational hospitality towards those of other faiths and none. Such a position appears felicitous both to the practice of MFS chaplaincy and the individual chaplain in interpreting their role. While defending conflicting and mutually exclusive faith positions may be neither practically nor theologically realistic, the chaplain can now advocate freedom to express individual belief while simultaneously raising awareness of the claims of the Christian faith (Pepinster, 2022a, p. 296).

I suggest that an ability to offer a denominational hospitality towards other faiths and none can perhaps more readily be detected from Baptist history than that of Anglicanism. Since the emergence of the Baptist denomination in the early seventeenth century, a concern and respect for those with differing beliefs has been embedded in the DNA of their belief. In what is reputedly the first English book on religious freedom, *A Short Declaration of the Mistery (sic) of Iniquity*, published in 1612, the leading Anabaptist Thomas Helwys argued for religious freedom not only for Christians but also, using the language of the time, for 'heretics, Turks and Jews' (Helwys, 1612, p. 69). In doing so he articulated views that were to prove fundamental to, and defining of, the dissenting nature of Baptist belief. Helwys's approach went far beyond the language of mere respect and protection for those of other faiths and none, to committed advocacy on their behalf. He modelled what were to become core baptistic concerns for justice and the championing of freedom of belief: values that helpfully serve the contemporary Baptist chaplain's ability to act with integrity in the MFS setting.

A secular context

Contemporary UK society has increasingly moved from reliance on a faith-based paradigm to a secularism inclined to accept only that which can be empirically proven (Bruce, 2002, pp. 60–73). As with other terminology considered above, however, secularism proves itself a 'slippery' concept (Williams, 2012, p. 2). Even in developed societies predominantly shaped by secular thinking, individuals have persistently remained aware of a spiritual or transcendent dimension to human existence: indeed, such consciousness may be increasing (Glasner, Schuhmann and Kruizinga, 2022, p. 139). Religious faith has endured, with the agenda of diversity and inclusion, including recognition of religion and belief, increasingly being recognized as being of importance in UK society (Stewart-Darling, 2017, p. 59). Schmid suggests that describing such a society as post-secular, in that it makes accommodation for such beliefs, may therefore more accurately define the context for contemporary chaplaincy (Schmid, 2020, p. 168).

It is such an approach, which Williams calls 'procedural secularism'

(Williams, 2012, p. 3), that facilitates the state providing for and funding MFS chaplaincy in prisons in England and Wales. It may be noted in passing that the choice of the UK government to adopt an MFS chaplaincy at all is indeed a conscious choice. Different jurisdictions, such as the USA and France, have adopted different approaches (Beckford, 2011, p. 59).

The very existence of the MFS chaplaincy may, however, provide a platform for the Baptist to serve with integrity, in the sense of the chaplain's role being consistent with, and truthful to, the expressed intentions of the employing organization. Also, as I have suggested above, a MFS model that employs faith-specific rather than generic chaplains is likely to allow individual team members to act with greater freedom and integrity rather than less (Stewart-Darling, 2017, pp. 62–3). The possibilities of this procedural secularism may indeed lead to a deeper level of integrity. Stewart-Darling suggests that any chaplaincy team needs to be attentive to, and to some extent reflect, the community being served (Stewart-Darling, 2017, p. 67). Such views are arguably only further reinforced where, as in the prison context, the chaplaincy is for a 'total institution' (see Hunt, 2012) that is publicly controlled and funded. Where the Baptist chaplain is able to work publicly and well in such an MFS prison setting, in a community that is often a microcosm of wider society, this may serve as a powerful witness. They may model integrity (in the sense of a deep truthfulness) both in the living out of their own faith and what it might mean to live and work well together with those of other faiths and beliefs (Todd and Tipton, 2011, p. 22).

A note of caution should, however, be sounded. As with other voices I consider that shape the nature of prison chaplaincy, the state will have its own agenda, driven by both pragmatism and ideology, which may in turn create challenges to the individual integrity of the chaplain. Beckford suggests that MFS prison chaplaincy has developed as it has in England and Wales because of an ideological commitment to religious diversity as an end in itself; this has subsequently been reframed within an overarching concern to maintain social cohesion (Beckford, 2011, p. 51). Such analysis is entirely consistent with the recently published (and government commissioned) Bloom report (2023). This scarcely mentions pastoral and faith-based support within MFS chaplaincy, but instead places extensive emphasis on the state's concerns regarding radicalization, extremism and forced conversion (Bloom, 2023, pp. 86–100). Over a decade ago, Todd and Tipton expressed concern regarding developments in this direction, noting that acting as an agent of the prison establishment in this way potentially compromised the neutrality of the chaplain that is fundamental to their role (Todd and Tipton, 2011, p. 4). In a situation that is constantly changing, the Baptist chaplain should therefore remain attentive to the developing agendas of both the state and other stakeholders, to ensure that their integrity is not compromised.

Integrity within the prison

One important aspect of integrity is how the Baptist chaplain should relate to those identifying as 'non-religious'. Even within the prison context, different types of establishments will present markedly different issues in terms of the interface between a faith and secular agenda (Dixon, 2022, p. 12). A prison exclusively holding people convicted of sexual offences will, for example, house a community serving longer sentences with a broader age demographic than, for example, in a remand prison. Noting Woodhead's findings that the likelihood of identifying as non-religious significantly decreases with the increasing age of cohort (Woodhead, 2017, p. 251), this profile will in turn affect the manner, urgency and extent to which issues of the faith/secular interface present themselves in this defined context. My experience is that older generations living within a prison are more likely to view the chaplaincy as embodying what Davie describes as a 'vicarious religion' (Davie, 2015, p. 88) whereby a non-practising community looks to church leaders to perform faith-based rituals, embody moral codes and offer space to debate unresolved issues within society on their behalf (Davie, 2015, p. 6).

In practice, therefore, identifying as 'non-religious' cannot be assumed to be synonymous with lacking any faith-based understanding of the chaplaincy role. Conversely, identifying as being of a specified religion is not necessarily definitive in a prison context. Alongside the already devout, and those who are converts or may be returning to faith from childhood, there will be the 'opportunist' and 'professional enquirer' (Todd and Tipton, 2011, p. 30). As Todd and Tipton note, defining the faith/secular interface is therefore considerably more nuanced than a 'believer-attendee versus non-believer-non-attendee dichotomy' (2011, p. 39).

Similarly, the way in which different beliefs interrelate and may present themselves to the Baptist chaplain have rapidly changed over the last decade and are likely to defy any neat categorization. As Woodhead notes, issues are now unlikely to present as debates between specifically defined faiths (such as Jews, Muslims, Sikhs or Buddhist) or, as per Berger, focused on either religious/secular or interreligious discourse (Berger, 2014). Rather, the Baptist chaplain is presented with a 'cultural super-diversity', whereby the individual prisoner may hold a complex variety of beliefs drawn from different faiths and traditions (Woodhead, 2017, p. 258). I am reminded of being asked as a Baptist minister to share the rosary with a prisoner identifying as Pagan.

The complex ways in which pluralism, and also the interrelationship between religious believing and belonging, present themselves to the chaplain may express ways that faith continues to endure in a post-secular society (Taylor, 2007). Both suggest the need for a pastoral approach attuned and sensitive to issues of faith. From a theological base respectful of religious freedom, I suggest that the Baptist chaplain is well equipped to explore with integrity these issues of belief with individual prisoners. Equally, that integrity will demand that where a prisoner is antithetical to religious belief or aligned to another faith, they should properly be referred to another member of the chaplaincy team.

I have suggested that the issues arising for the contemporary Baptist chaplain are complex and fluid, shaped by multiple stakeholders whose voices are not neutral, and that they result in challenges that are often both highly context-specific and contested. Against this unpromising background, I nevertheless suggest that the call of a Baptist minister to prison chaplaincy is one that can rightly be embraced with joy and full integrity, as a chaplain 'who, in partnership with God and others, challenges the status quo by energetically creating and innovating in order to shape something of kingdom value' (Volland, 2015, p. 32).

Bibliography

Beckford, J. A. (2011), 'Religion in Prisons and in Partnership with the State', in J. Barbalet, A. Possamai and B. S. Turner (eds), *Religion and the State: A Comparative Sociology*, London: Anthem Press, pp. 43–64.
Berger, P. L. (2014), *The Many Altars of Modernity: Toward a Paradigm for Religion in a Pluralist Age*, New York: De Gruyter.
Bloom, C. (2023), *The Bloom Review: Does Government 'do God?': An Independent Review into How Government Engages with Faith*, available at https://assets.publishing.service.gov.uk/government/uploads/system/uploads/attachment_data/file/1152684/The_Bloom_Review.pdf (accessed 7.07.2024).
Bosch, D. J. (1991), *Transforming Mission: Paradigm Shifts in Theology of Mission*, New York: Orbis Books.
Bowers, F. (2005), *Theology of Sector Ministry: A Document Outlining the Theology and Ecclesiology of Those Serving in Sector Ministry*, available at https://www.baptist.org.uk/Publisher/File.aspx?ID=111420&view=browser (accessed 7.07.2024).
Boyce, G. (2010), *An Improbable Feast: The Surprising Dynamic of Hospitality at the Heart of Multifaith Chaplaincy*, Morrisville, NC: Lulu.com.
Bradbury, N. (2000), 'Ecclesiology and Pastoral Theology', in J. Woodward and S. Pattison (eds), *The Blackwell Reader in Pastoral and Practical Theology*, Oxford: Blackwell Publishing, pp. 173–81.
Bruce, S. (2002), *God is Dead: Secularization in the West*, Oxford: Blackwell Publishing.
BUGB (Baptist Union of Great Britain) (n.d.), 'Declaration of Principle', available at

https://baptist.org.uk/Groups/220595/Declaration_of_Principle.aspx (accessed 7.07.2024).

Caperon, J. (2018), 'Introduction: The Age of Chaplaincy', in J. Caperon, A. Todd and J. Walters (eds), *A Christian Theology of Chaplaincy*, London: Jessica Kingsley Publishers, pp. 101–18.

Collicutt, J. (2015). *The Psychology of Christian Character Formation*, London: SCM Press.

Davie, G. (2015), *Religion in Britain: A Persistent Paradox*, 2nd edn, Oxford and Sussex: Wiley-Blackwell.

Dixon, T. M. (2022), 'Pastoral Care on Remand and the Role of the Prison Chaplain' (doctoral thesis, University of Durham, United Kingdom, available at http://etheses.dur.ac.uk/14705 (accessed 7.07.2024).

Ellis, C. J. and M. Blyth (eds) (2005), *Gathering for Worship: Patterns and Prayers for the Community of Disciples*, Norwich: Canterbury Press.

Fiddes, P. S. (2003), *Tracks and Traces: Baptist Identity in Church and Theology*, Eugene, OR: Wipf & Stock.

Glasner, T. J., C. Schuhmann and R. Kruizinga (2022), 'The Future of Chaplaincy in a Secularized Society: A Mixed-Methods Survey from the Netherlands', *Journal of Health Care Chaplaincy* 29(1), pp. 132–44.

Helwys, T. (1612), *A Short Declaration on the Mistery* (sic) *of Iniquity*, available at https://theangus.rpc.ox.ac.uk/wp-content/uploads/2016/02/FPC-D-50_02.pdf (accessed 7.07.2024).

Hewson, C. and A. Crompton (2016), 'Managing Multifaith Spaces: The Chaplain as Entrepreneur', in C. Swift, M. Cobb and A. Todd (eds), *A Handbook of Chaplaincy Studies: Understanding Spiritual Care in Public Places*, London: Routledge, pp. 123–36.

HMPPS (His Majesty's Prison and Probation Service) (2023), *Faith and Pastoral Care for Prisoners: Prison Service Instructions 5/2016*, available at https://www.gov.uk/government/publications/faith-and-pastoral-care-for-prisoners-psi-052016 (accessed 7.07.2024).

Humanists UK (2023), *Equal Access to Pastoral Support or Chaplaincy*, available at https://humanists.uk/campaigns/human-rights-and-equality/chaplaincy-and-pastoral-support/ (accessed 7.07.2024).

Hunt, S. J. (2012), 'Spirituality in UK Prisons: Prescription and Limitations of Chaplaincy Reform', in M. Fowler, J. D. Martin III and J. L. Hochheimer (eds), *Spirituality: Theory, Praxis and Pedagogy*, Leiden: Brill (e-book).

King Charles III (2022), *The King's Remarks to Faith Leaders*, available at https://www.royal.uk/kings-remarks-faith-leaders (accessed 7.07.2024).

Lamb, J. (2006), *Integrity: Leading with God Watching*, Nottingham: IVP.

Newbigin, L. (2014), *The Gospel in a Pluralist Society*, London: SPCK.

Nouwen, H. J. M. (1976), *Reaching Out: The Three Movements of the Spiritual Life*, Glasgow: William Collins Sons & Co.

Pepinster, C. (2022a), *Defenders of the Faith: The British Monarchy, Religion and the Next Coronation*, London: Hodder & Stoughton.

Pepinster, C. (2022b), *Platinum Jubilee: Queen's Firm Push to Interfaith Freedom*, available at https://www.churchtimes.co.uk/articles/2022/27-may3-june/features/features/queen-s-firm-push-to-interfaith-freedom (accessed 7.07.2024).

Phillips, P. (2013), 'Roles and Identities of the Anglican Chaplain: A Prison Ethnography' (doctoral thesis, University of Cardiff), available at https://orca.cardiff.ac.uk/id/eprint/59848/1/phillipspmlphd.pdf (accessed 7.07.2024).

Prison Act (1952), available at https://www.legislation.gov.uk/ukpga/Geo6and1 Eliz2/15-16/52/contents (accessed 7.07.2024).

Queen Elizabeth II (2012), *A Speech by The Queen at Lambeth Palace, 2012*, available at https://www.royal.uk/queens-speech-lambeth-palace-15-february-2012 (accessed 7.07.2024).

Ryan, B. (2015), *A Very Modern Ministry: Chaplaincy in the UK*, available at https://www.theosthinktank.co.uk/cmsfiles/archive/files/Modern%20Ministry%20combined.pdf (accessed 7.07.2024).

Schmid, H. (2020), 'Interfaith Chaplaincy in a Post-Secular Context', *Journal Studies in Interreligious Dialogue* 30(2), pp. 163–85.

Schmidt-Leukel, P. (2009), *Transformation by Integration: How Inter-faith Encounter Changes Christianity*, London: SCM Press.

Slater, V. (2015), *Chaplaincy Ministry and the Mission of the Church*, London: SCM Press.

Stewart-Darling, F. (2017), *Multi-Faith Chaplaincy in the Workplace: How Chaplains can Support Organisations and their Employees*, London: Jessica Kingsley Publishers.

Sturge, G. (2022), *House of Commons Library: UK Prison Statistics*, available at https://researchbriefings.files.parliament.uk/documents/SN04334/SN04334.pdf (accessed 7.07.2024).

Swinton, J. and H. Mowat (2016), *Practical Theology and Qualitative Research*, London: SCM Press.

Taylor, C. (2007), *A Secular Age*, Cambridge, MA: Harvard University Press.

Todd, A., V. Slater and S. Dunlop (2014), *The Church of England's Involvement in Chaplaincy*, Cardiff and Cuddesdon: Cardiff Centre for Chaplaincy Studies and Oxford Centre for Ecclesiology and Practical Theology, available at https://orca.cardiff.ac.uk/id/eprint/62257/1/Todd%2C%20Slater%20%26%20Dunlop%202014%20Report%20on%20Church%20of%20England%20Chaplaincy.pdf (accessed 7.07.2024).

Todd, A. and L. Tipton (2011), *The Role and Contribution of a Multi-Faith Prison Chaplaincy to the Contemporary Prison Service*, Cardiff Centre for Chaplaincy Studies, available at https://orca.cardiff.ac.uk/id/eprint/29120/1/Chaplaincy%20Report%20Final%20Draft%20(3).pdf (accessed 7.07.2024).

Volf, M. (2003), 'Exclusion and Embrace: Theological Reflections in the Wake of "Ethnic Cleansing"', in W. A. Dyrness (ed.), *Emerging Voices in Global Theology*, Eugene, OR: Wipf & Stock, pp. 19–46.

Volland, M. (2015), *The Minister as Entrepreneur: Leading and Growing the Church in an Age of Rapid Change*, London: SPCK.

Welby, J. (2018), *Reimagining Britain: Foundations for Hope*, London: Bloomsbury.

Williams, R. (2012), *Faith in the Public Square*, London: Bloomsbury.

Williams, R. (2018), '"All Faiths and None?": Theological Issues in Multi-Faith Chaplaincy', in J. Caperon, A. Todd and J. Walters (eds), *A Christian Theology of Chaplaincy*, London: Jessica Kingsley Publishers, pp. 59–78.

Woodhead, L. (2017), 'The Rise of "No Religion": Towards an Explanation', *Sociology of Religion: A Quarterly Review* 78(3), pp. 247–62. available at https://web-s-ebscohost-com.ezproxy2.commonawards.org/ehost/detail/detail?vid=3&sid=aef562c1-653a-49f3-8fe3-c1a8c57aff1b%40redis&bdata=JnNpdGU9ZWhvc3QtbGl2ZQ%3d%3d#AN=ATLAiGFE171030003054&db=rfh (accessed 7.07.2024).

11

'Do we really need 500 crosses?' Chaplaincy Administration

CAROL THORNE

When 500 palm crosses were ordered in time for the Holy Week commemorations, an email questioning the need for them was received from a member of the Senior Leadership Team (SLT). I understood that the thrust of the email was a result of the fact that the Trust was approaching the end of the financial year, and so spending was being closely monitored and the workforce was being advised to buy only essential items. The response to the email enquiry stated that the crosses were important not only to the Trust's patients and their carers who were observers of Easter but also to many, many members of Christian staff, for whom the crosses were of huge significance in the build-up to Easter.

The hospital chaplaincy service is situated within the Patients' Services division, and some senior leaders have in the past admitted to having little in the way of understanding about chaplaincy: what it is for; who 'uses' it; what is needed for it to function in a way that meets the needs of those requesting its support – patients, their families and friends, staff members and so on. The exchange concerning the palm crosses was, in my opinion, somewhat symbolic of the relative lack of knowledge regarding the importance of religious artefacts such as these, particularly in the context of having to closely monitor spending within the Trust in such difficult times.

Swinton and Kelly discuss this lack of understanding of chaplaincy and, indeed, the inability to appreciate the importance of one's spiritual well-being alongside one's physical health, being prevalent within the NHS, potentially within the ranks of its managers as well as clinical practitioners. They observe, 'the call to take spirituality seriously and to reframe our understandings of health and wellness is often neither obvious nor welcomed' (Swinton and Kelly, 2016, p. 175). I understand my role in chaplaincy through the model of deacon. This approach, of seeking to serve the totality of needs of the patient, the carer and the colleague, requires that attention is paid equally to the spiritual as well as the physical being. The provision of palm crosses at this particular time, especially in view of the difficulties people were experiencing in terms of the rise of the cost of living and the discontent within the NHS workforce related to pay, serves to bring comfort to believers that they are loved by the Christ they serve, and we have found this to be a unifying experience for people of all Christian denominations within the hospital.

My position of liminality within the health service means that I am conscience-bound to ensure that person-centred spiritual care, the care of the client as a whole, is at the forefront of the support I offer. This requires me to be of service not simply to the patient-client but additionally to the clinician-client as well as the manager-client in educating and advising them regarding the importance of this need. This can be understood as a 'bilingual ministry' – that is, a ministry that speaks not solely the semantics of a religion-based ministry but also language that is specific to the context of the settings in which chaplains are sited (Ryan, 2018, p. 82). So I am challenged to ensure that my working ethos and motivation reference the Trust's values and visions as well as my own deacon-based intent to serve others and, in so doing, serve my Christ.

As someone who works within this deacon model of ministry, I am tasked to 'be an agent of God's purpose, walking alongside', as described by Norma Higgott in her blog (2020). It is part of my role, therefore, to accompany managers and senior leaders on their voyage of discovery about the multi-faceted nature of the chaplaincy and spiritual care service and what it does on a spiritual, pastoral and religious level to help support those who are struggling with the big issues of life, including family fallings-out, mistrust of medical personnel, sickness and death.

In 1 Corinthians 9.19–23, Paul essentially makes himself a slave to everyone, limiting his own civil liberties and autonomies in order to reach those whom he serves. Paul makes this commitment regardless of the cost to himself and without ill-feeling or mistrust of those whom he is called to serve. This helps as a standard for me to aspire to in my own practice, where walking alongside the SLT, chaplaincy and clinical colleagues enables us all to support one another in supporting the patients, carers and other staff members when at their most vulnerable. When this is achieved, the core (Trust) values of working together and being honest and open are more likely to be met, enabling us to be better placed to reach the ideal which demonstrates that everyone matters. The end result may not necessarily be the winning of others for Christ, but that my faith (Christ) is seen in me, whether the person I am serving is of my own tradition, a follower of a different religion or someone without any faith at all; their being recipients of my servanthood serves to affirm that my faith has propelled me to serve them, even though they may have a different viewpoint.

My resolve to serve others in my role as secretary to the Chaplaincy and Spiritual Care team is enhanced, I think, by my black African-Caribbean (Jamaican) heritage, a culture full of hospitality, laughter and warmth. My Pentecostal tradition is one that may have had the reputation of being somewhat insular in the past, but I am excited to be part of the movement of healthcare chaplaincy from its traditional white Anglican, male, middle-class origins to a place where chaplains of a variety of heritages are welcomed and indeed embraced. The opportunity to work with chaplains from Orthodox, Anglican, Catholic, Muslim, Baptist, Jewish as well as Pentecostal backgrounds is one that I find incredibly fulfilling and rewarding. Working within a large inner city with an incredibly diverse population, our presence reaffirms the value of our servitude to those from the communities we represent, further reinforcing my approach in working within the deacon model of chaplaincy. Whether this is achieved by welcoming visitors with the offer of a cup of coffee and a biscuit or offering the use of the quiet space for much needed alone time, or liaising with staff to organize a baby blessing, emergency wedding or a memorial for a much respected and loved staff member, I seek to serve to the very best of my calling and ability.

Bibliography

Higgott, N. (2020), 'Reflection by a Deacon Hospice Chaplain' (blog), Deacon: CofE Network of Distinctive Deacons, available at https://cofedeacons.org/2020/12/23/reflection-by-a-deacon-chaplain/ (accessed 7.07.2024).

Ryan, B. (2018), 'Theology and Models of Chaplaincy', in J. Caperon, A. Todd and J. Walters (eds), *A Christian Theology of Chaplaincy*, London: Jessica Kingsley Publishers, pp. 79–100.

Swinton, J. and E. Kelly (2016), 'Contextual Issues: Health and Healing', in C. Swift, M. Cobb and A. Todd (eds), *A Handbook of Chaplaincy Studies: Understanding Spiritual Care in Public Places*, London: Routledge, pp. 175–86.

12

Identity, Ministry and Healthcare Chaplaincy: Reflections From a Black, Female, Assemblies of God Minister

AGATHA NGAMBI

A chaplain is a valuable member of the healthcare sector workforce, providing spiritual, pastoral and religious care to patients, families and the healthcare team. Yet the identity of the chaplain, and the contribution a chaplain brings to the health sector, is often misunderstood. Repeatedly, as I've walked down the corridors of the hospital where I work, I have been asked, 'What does a chaplain do?' Even though I wear a badge denoting my place as part of the healthcare professional team, my identity and place within the NHS are often unclear.

This chapter is the culmination of my personal exploration of navigating faith, identity, gender and vocation between my chaplaincy and denominational positions. It asks questions that I still have to answer. However, what I hope to draw out in this personal narrative is the impact on identity and experience when holding a multiplicity of roles – the intersections, the differences and the varying expectations – and working in diverse environments.

The many layers of my identity

Guala and Mittone affirm that we show up as we are (Guala and Mittone, 2010), which relies on us having a good understanding of who we are. However, what happens when our understanding of who we are is denied or challenged? I am a black woman, a healthcare chaplain in an inner-city hospital Trust, and an ordained Assemblies of God minister. Sometimes these roles have seemed incompatible – either to myself or to others, and this has prompted considerable reflection on what is important to me in terms of understanding and living out my own identity and calling.

Our identity plays a significant role in our decision-making. Ewan Kelly, former doctor and now healthcare chaplain, points out that our identity is what we are left with when all else is stripped away (Kelly, 2012, p. 2) and it is formed by our life stories. Identity is a complex concept that shifts with the times, as we move, grow and change. I was born in Zambia, where I spent my childhood and early adulthood. During my formative years, going to the Roman Catholic church with my parents, I had the desire to serve God as a nun. I discussed this with my priest back then and he was very encouraging; however, my parents thought I was too young to decide. After my secondary education, I trained to be a nurse, got married and had three children. I began worshipping in a Pentecostal Assemblies of God (AoG) church, and my childhood thoughts of serving God as a nun were far behind me.

After migrating to England in 2006, there was a further shift in my faith, identity and priorities. The passion I had to serve God was reignited and this time it was very strong. I understood my identity as that of a missionary, moving from a familiar homeland to a foreign land, and I began to explore ordination.

Called to ministry as a black woman

My journey to ordination wasn't easy; it was faced with resistance within myself. Questions about my ability, my call and whether I could leave nursing all surfaced. My identity as a black woman in ministry, however, was not an issue at this point, and both my husband and my lead pastor were very encouraging and supportive. Having completed a degree in theology and biblical studies alongside a Christian leadership and minister-in-training course, I was ordained as a fully accredited Assemblies of God minister in May 2017.

Most Pentecostal denominations who accept the ministry of women point to the fulfilment of prophecy in Joel 2.28–29, referenced in Acts 2.16–18 (NIV): 'Your sons and daughters will prophesy ... Even on my servants, both men and women, I will pour out my Spirit in those days.' The understanding is that the outpouring of the Holy Spirit that the AoG believe began in the early twentieth century was a fulfilment of these two scriptures and that the text is suggestive of an inclusion of both women and men in ministry in the new age. This theological view is core to the history of women who successfully pioneered and directed a wide spectrum of ministries in the AoG in the early twentieth century.

In practice, however, I have experienced challenge and tension between this scriptural understanding of the acceptance of women in ministry and the reality of our involvement in that role. Even though I am privileged to be part of an organization that supports and encourages women's leadership, there is a resistance from some leaders and members in churches to accept and engage with women in ministry. Following my ordination, I was assigned to a church as a resident pastor. I was the first woman, and the first black person, to serve as pastor in that congregation, and some members of the congregation struggled with my appointment. One of the parishioners invited me to their house for dinner just to find out what made me 'so bold and confident' to lead their church as a woman. Her questioning was based on her interpretation of Scripture, particularly the assertion in the letter to Timothy that no woman should be permitted to have authority over a man (1 Timothy 2.12), reiterated in the letter to the Corinthians (1 Corinthians 14.34–35). This lady understood that the woman's place in the church was that of support and not leadership. I empathized with where she was coming from because I used to think that way myself, and we talked about how the call of God had been so great that I'd had to wrestle with what Scripture and vocation meant in my life. At the end of the evening, the lady said, 'I am convinced of your calling because you carry a unique authority that can only come from the Holy Spirit.'

While I expected some resistance to my ordination, it was initially surprising for me to discover that it was not just some men in my denomination, but also some women who were not ready to accept and support fellow women in leadership. Initially I felt rejected and let down by my fellow women, who I expected support from. However, I realized that the reasons behind resistance were often complex and nuanced, based on issues about their own identity and confidence and their experiences and influences growing up. It could be said that it is from the place of self-confidence and belief in one's identity that we are able to place equal value on what women do.

Ministry in the NHS

When I transferred ministry from a church-based setting to a healthcare chaplaincy role, it was immediately apparent that I was now working within a different paradigm of operation when it came to issues such as gender inclusion. The hospital Trust, in line with all NHS bodies, operates under the Equality Act of 2010, which legislates clearly that discrimination against the specified 'protected characteristics' is prohibited by law. This meant that I could not be excluded because of my gender.

However, in practice this is a far more complex issue. While my employer cannot discriminate against me as a woman, because my role is a faith-based one, some patients still find it difficult to accept my ministry as a female chaplain – particularly around the undertaking of specific religious rites or rituals. I had an encounter with a female patient who identified as Anglo-Catholic and believed that communion should only be done by a male priest. This made me realize that, in this space, my role was that of an invited guest. The patient was the host and I was the invited guest in their space. It is important to acknowledge that a patient should have power in their space and a choice concerning what care is given to them.

The most recently published NHS chaplaincy guidelines define healthcare chaplaincy as a service and profession that is focused on ensuring that all people, religious or not, have the opportunity to access pastoral, spiritual and religious support when they need it (NHS England, 2023, p. 5). The role of chaplaincy in healthcare is regulated by both NHS policies, local and national, and the UK Board of Healthcare Chaplaincy (UKBHC), but fundamental in determining the identity and location of chaplains in healthcare is acknowledging their place within multiple communities at the same time (Cobb, 2013). How can a chaplain operate with the understanding that they are accountable to multiple communities who often have competing and divergent expectations?

From my perspective, I was ordained with the understanding that I have a divine call to serve the people within the Church. Though to an extent the role of a minister in the Church has a degree of professionalism, the healthcare chaplain is serving in a secular arena where he or she is expected to work alongside other health professionals in meeting the requirements of the organization. My sponsoring denomination views chaplaincy in the light of missions and evangelism, with the vision of bringing a Christian view to the people chaplains meet. This vision influenced my initial understanding of a healthcare chaplain but, as I grew in experience, I began to see that there is often a difference between what the individual chaplain thinks they are for and what the host institution thinks the chaplain is for. This is where guidelines, policies and procedures can play a part in defining roles and generating levels of understanding across the disciplines.

The guidelines for a minister in church ministry are often very different from those of a healthcare chaplain. While a minister has an obligatory relationship with the sponsoring denomination or community, which often provides the initial training and accreditation or ordination, the registration and accreditation of healthcare chaplains held by the UKBHC gives them an opportunity to raise their professional profile within the NHS, by being recognized as allied health professionals (Harrison, 2019, p. 22). Even though healthcare chaplains work within a legal framework that is permissive rather than prescriptive (Cranmer, 2016, p. 79), it can be difficult for a chaplain not to view the requirements of the employing institution as prescriptive. One way in which tension can arise is in the expectation of access to people within the context of the ministry.

Local NHS policies often expand upon the guidelines set in the UKBHC, making specific reference to the way in which hospital visits are conducted, drawing on the General Data Protection Regulation (GDPR), for example, which can limit the access chaplains have to patient records. Chaplains, therefore, cannot simply search for patients who identify with a particular religion, and instead must wait for patient referrals. In church ministry, visiting a church member could be viewed either as a requirement or an expectation on their minister. The expectation is often implied rather than directly articulated. It is not unusual for a minister from my tradition to take the initiative and 'pop round' to a congregation member or person associated with the Church. In a hospital setting, however, a patient visit must be requested, and is by referral only. Operating in both positions, or moving from one setting to the other, can cause some confusion over role, vocation and, ultimately, identity.

A further example relates to my theological understanding on baptism, arising from my sponsoring denomination, which is that it is the first step of obedience taken by a person who has truly repented and believed in Jesus Christ as the Lord and Saviour of their lives. The notion here is that a person should have the ability to receive God's word and understand it (see, for example, Acts 2.41; 8.12 and Mark 16.15–16), and therefore infants, who are not able to accept and understand the word in this way, are to be dedicated to God and not baptized. As a healthcare chaplain, I am often required to conduct the baptism of babies within the hospital Trust. I recall an encounter when I was called on to support a family whose baby had just died, and they requested for their baby to be baptized and named. The mother was from the CofE and the father had no faith affiliation. They were desperate to have their baby baptized and blessed. While my compassionate self was willing to support the family, my passionate Pentecostal minister self was not prepared to undo my theology. Nevertheless, my role and the requirements of my employer meant that, at this time, it was pastorally appropriate, and fully expected of me to answer the call of duty and give the parents the support they needed. They were grateful for the support and requested prayer for the other two children at home. Even though the encounter resulted in meeting the parents' religious and spiritual needs, there was some tension in me. The Revd Tony Kyriakides, the Bishop of London's adviser for healthcare chaplaincy, once said 'as I journey into the wilderness of ill-health, broken bodies and terminal illness where God is ready to be found and experienced ... I have needed to be flexible, adaptable, ready to learn and apply the language of healthcare, and to be supportive of colleagues of whom so much is asked and required' (Kyriakides, n.d.). These words helpfully articulate the path I often take in healthcare chaplaincy. Flexibility and adaptability are key components of the role yet sometimes it is inevitable that tensions arise and, when they do, these tensions often remain unspoken and unacknowledged even though they can be difficult to live with.

Conclusion

It could be said that when we are telling our stories we find ourselves in the stories we tell, and discover our weaknesses, our strength and our passions. Ultimately, knowing our true self gives us the ability to work on these weaknesses, utilize our strengths and develop our passion.

I am of the understanding that identity is a complex concept. Over the years my identity has shifted as I have moved, grown and changed in my journey from wanting to become a Roman Catholic nun, to pursuing a nursing carer, being ordained as AoG minister, doing full-time ministry in the parish and now working as healthcare chaplain. Often I have navigated my identity in various roles and contexts, with the understanding that the view of who I am and what I stand for could ultimately affect how I carry out my roles both as a healthcare chaplain and ordained minister who is still actively involved in church ministry. It is no doubt that the power I carry as a minister in the local church is not exerted the same in my chaplaincy role because my employing organization determines my responsibilities. Sometimes it could be confusing to navigate responsibility in both roles, but self-awareness of my environment has been instrumental.

Understanding our identity at every given time and place is key to our effectiveness. It is from a place of self-knowledge of our ability and identity that we can respect and value the difference in other people and deliver a competent service. Knowing my identity has given me the ability to approach various encounters with confidence, even in the midst of tension. It is from the place of self-confidence in our distinctiveness that we can make a positive impact upon the people we encounter, especially in complex situations. My self-confidence is not based on my gender, ethnicity, intellect or competence but recognizing the call of God that is irresistible and is the driving force. In times of challenges my strength and assurance come from the fact that I am fulfilling the will of God for my life, which gives me joy and satisfaction.

As Frederick Buechner says, 'The place God calls you to is the place where your deep gladness and the world's deep hunger meet' (Buechner, 1973, pp. 118–19).

Bibliography

Buechner, F. (1973), *Wishful Thinking: A Seeker's ABC*, London: HarperOne.

Cobb, M. (2013), 'Change and Challenge: The Dynamic of Chaplaincy', *Health and Social Care Chaplaincy* 10(1), 10.1558/hscc.v10i1.4.

Cranmer, F. (2016), 'Chaplaincy and the Law', in C. Swift, M. Cobb and A. Todd, *A Handbook of Chaplaincy Studies: Understanding Spiritual Care in Public Places*, London: Routledge.

Guala, F. and L. Mittone (2010), 'Paradigmatic Experiments: The Dictator Game', *The Journal of Socio-Economics* 39(5), pp. 578–84, available at https://doi.org/10.1016/j.socec.2009.05.007.

Harrison, S. (2019), 'What is a Mental Health Chaplain For?', in J. Fletcher (ed.), *Chaplaincy and Spiritual Care in Mental Health Settings*, London: Jessica Kingsley Publishers.

Kelly, E. (2012), *Personhood and Presence*, London: Bloomsbury.

Kyriakides, T. (n.d.), 'Introducing Healthcare Chaplaincy: A Personal Perspective', available at https://www.churchofengland.org/node/26749/printable/print (accessed 7.07.2024).

NHS England (2023), *NHS Chaplaincy: Guidelines for NHS Managers on Pastoral, Spiritual and Religious Care*, available at https://www.england.nhs.uk/wp-content/uploads/2023/08/B1073i-nhs-chaplaincy-guidelines-for-nhs-managers-on-pastoral-spiritual-and-religious-care-august-23.pdf (accessed 7.07.2024).

13

Mystic Sweat: Unveiling Spiritual Dimensions of Music-infused Workout Classes and Their Implications for Chaplaincy

AREK MALECKI

Individuals often come to gyms at times of emotional distress, deeply wounded or dissatisfied with their life situation. Drawing from my own experience as a group exercise instructor as well as a Unitarian minister, I am aware that the instructor–participant connection, albeit brief, can be intense. It taps deeper than rationality.

The heightened emotional experience that occurs during group exercise, fuelled by adrenaline and endorphin rush, often leads participants to confide to their 'fitness pastors'. My class attendees have spoken to me about poor mental health, self-harm, relationship problems, illness in family, addiction and bereavement. Admittedly, as someone who started his fitness journey at his lowest point in life, I cannot deny its salvific qualities. It would not be an exaggeration to say that it was the gym that kept me going when I was prepared to give up.

This can be problematic, since group exercise instructors are not typically trained as pastoral carers, mental health professionals or chaplains. Consequently, they may lack the necessary skills to hold space for individuals in difficult life circumstances. Yet the environment and the immersive experience they create attract vulnerable people, and often induce the 'pastoral' conversations I recognize as a Unitarian minister. Raphael notes that gyms, in contrast to religions, have not had centuries to develop frameworks that help to manage difficult life situations and crises, or mark life's milestones. While fitness leaders can become central figures within their communities – 'evangelists on a transcendent bike' (Raphael, 2023, p. 98) – they are often ill-prepared to care spiritually or emotionally for their 'congregants'. This led me to explore the existing provision for spiritual care at fitness centres and wonder whether there is a call for gym chaplains.

Sports Chaplaincy UK has a branch of gym chaplaincy, but it appears to be an underdeveloped provision (Sports Chaplaincy UK, 2023, online). There are currently six Faith RXD 'chapters' meeting in the UK (Faith RXD, 2023). Although not explicitly a form of chaplaincy, it is worth noting that these chapter groups organize activities that combine faith and fitness with explicit discussion of faith and a clear statement of belief underpinning their activities, available on their website. The RXD website reflects the integration of individual and communal aspects that I found of central significance in my research but in a way that is explicitly Christian, though open to all. In wider literature, there is almost nothing written about gym chaplaincy, the only connections usually made being between chaplaincy and the gym in prison contexts.

From my perspective as a Unitarian, there has been relatively little emphasis on chaplaincy within our movement and it remains a developing field. However, the Unitarian College has recently started offering a chaplaincy course and a small number of active ministers have undertaken specific chaplaincy roles, including in universities, among paramedics and with the police. Chaplaincy roles fit well with the commitment within the constitution to 'recognising the worth and dignity of all people and their freedom to believe as their consciences dictate' (The Unitarians, 2023), and from my own experience it seems that gym chaplaincy is an area in need of attuned and open ministry and support, which Unitarians, by our constitution, are well suited to offer.

Coincidentally, it was as I began my research in January 2023 that Rina Raphael's *The Gospel of Wellness: Gyms, Gurus, Goop and the False Promise of Self-Care* was published. It is an intriguing analysis of the booming wellness industry, examining the ways in which it has become a dominant force in contemporary culture, resembling a religious phenomenon. It scrutinizes the industry's underlying assumptions and values, while acknowledging its capacity to provide a sense of meaning, purpose and community for its followers – much like spirituality.

In her critique of commodified fitness, Raphael distinguishes between 'wellness' and 'wealthness'. While acknowledging that something of a spiritual nature takes place at exercise classes, she provides a critical evaluation of its commercial and exclusionary dimensions: 'While the upper class perfects their downward dog, the communities most in need of physical exercise profoundly lack it' (Raphael, 2023, p. 277). She argues that the industry's focus on well-being of the individual can obscure the structural and economic factors that contribute to social disparities. This finding is backed by a comprehensive 15-year study by Lancet Global Health, which revealed that over a quarter of the global population lacks adequate physical activity (Guthold et al., 2018, online). Disappointingly, the volume appears to focus primarily on the binary of exclusive 'wealthness', where memberships of elite clubs with renowned superstar instructors is a sign of status, versus the lack of communal sports centres for the poorest. She pays little attention to the in-between – the more affordable gyms and sports centres that host similar quasi-religious exercise classes.

Pandya's research also brought to the fore the gender disparities, indicating that women are not only more likely to take part in yoga retreats but are also more receptive to their psychological benefits. Similarly, Raphael's research examines the American wellness industry from the perspective of women, noting that 'the majority of the book focuses on the groups most adoptive of commodified wellness – namely women' (Raphael, 2023, p. 13). Those observations resonated with my own experience as a fitness instructor: the majority of the people attending my classes are women. Furthermore, only one of my research participants identified as male – specifically, a gay man. I will later explain why I believe that his sexual orientation may carry significance.

Raphael suggests that the 'self-love talk' present in the fitness studios, the encouragement to make space for oneself, to find what feels good, to cultivate emotional health and the body–mind connection is like catnip to women (Raphael, 2023, p. 30). In reflecting on the potential causes behind gender disparities in gym-class participation, I wondered if these very things might also act as 'men repellent' in our culture. Emma Hogan explores why, despite live classes being the most popular 'gym-type' activity according to the 2021 Global Fitness Report, men are seriously under-represented on the studio floor. Hogan concluded that this under-representation stems from the prevailing perception that classes are feminine activities, ultimately depriving men of opportunity for fun and connection (Hogan, 2022, online).

Exercise as spiritual engagement

Raphael also looks at the gym as a site for communal spiritual engagement. The book highlights that the gym can offer a sense of community and meaning that is often associated with organized religion. 'I can never live anywhere where there's not a SoulCycle', one follower noted in a report on non-religious communities by Harvard Divinity School (Ter Kuile and Thurston, 2016, online). Raphael observes that group exercise can be deeply immersive, characterized by its own rituals, language and symbolism. She also draws parallels between the language of fitness and the language of religion, noting the use of terms like 'connection', 'devotion' or 'sacrifice' in both contexts where such attitudes 'induced religious fervour' (Raphael, 2023, p. 98). Kevin Lixey, approaching the subject from the Church's perspective, also observes similar trends, however this is in relation to team sports in general rather than just gym classes. Lixey argues for renewed appreciation for 'ascetical dimensions' of sports, like responsibility, discipline and sacrifice, and respect, from which churches may learn (Lixey, 2013, pp. 257–66). It appears that both authors, albeit approaching the topic from different angles, reach the conclusion that exercise can indeed enrich one's spirituality. Constructing his argument, Lixey cites Christian religious leaders, such as Pope John Paul II and Pope Benedict XVI. The latter wrote, still as Cardinal Ratzinger at the time, that sport 'compels a man to take himself in hand so that through training, he may gain control over himself; through control, mastery; and through mastery, freedom' (Ratzinger, cited in Lixey, 2013, p. 260). While Pope John Paul II, drawing on 1 Corinthians 6.19–20, offered the perspective that:

> Sport is making good use of the body, which brings marked consequences of psychological well-being ... From our Christian faith we know that, through baptism, the human person in his or her totality and integrity of soul and body becomes a temple of the Holy Spirit. (John Paul II, cited in Lixey, 2013, p. 262)

Connection and euphoria

In a study conducted by researchers at Brown University in Providence in Rhode Island, it was found that class participants frequently spoke about their relation to one another and their instructors, speaking of 'the expression of feelings and the installation of hope' (Brown University, 2021, online). For people who go to exercise classes, this intrinsic motivation often outweighs the potential of bodily transformation. Raphael (2023, p. 101) observes that the altered state experienced in group exercise is achieved by the combination of movement and music, similar to the way Electronic Dance Music concerts evoke euphoric emotions in ravers. In an essay exploring the ritualistic dimension of the underground rave culture and the DJ's techniques of liminality, Morgan Gerard cites the author Tara McCall, who vividly described her own euphoric experiences of the dancefloor music, which are strikingly similar to those encountered in a fitness class:

> ... wandering from warehouse to warehouse to have my soul awakened. The music thunders through my flesh, the notes swim through my veins. DJs spin their scriptures with eloquence, zest and assurance. The bass rattles my lungs and beats in unison with my heart. If I close

my eyes, I can watch my flesh melt away and my soul rise between the spaces of sound. (Gerard, 2004, p. 168)

Similarly, Graham St John, in exploring 'Liberation and the Rave Imaginary' brings our focus to the so-called 'Raver's Manifesto'. The manifesto articulates the idea of 'sharing the uncontrollable joy we feel from creating this magical bubble that can, for one evening, protect us from the horrors, atrocities, and pollution of the outside world. It is in that very instant, with these initial realizations that each of us was truly born' (St John, 2004, p. 22).

Many people form close bonds not only with their fellow gym buddies but also with their trainers who are there to foster the sense of belonging. Raphael cites an instructor who said that for some people classes can feel like the church they were never quite welcome at. 'When instructors mouth Lady Gaga's lyrics such as "I'm beautiful in my way, 'cause God makes no mistake", [the LGBT people] can feel seen in a way that feels nearly therapeutic, a radical acceptance in a society that doesn't always extend it' (Raphael, 2023, p. 110). This brings me back to my observation regarding the fact that the only men who were willing to talk to me about exercise as a spiritual practice were gay.

I wonder whether faith groups overlook, albeit inadvertently, the extent to which gyms are like places of worship for those who do not feel welcome elsewhere. I remember one particular aerobics class I attended at the end of a long day of theology lectures. An openly gay instructor had us jumping plyometric lunges to the beat of a remixed version of Hozier's song 'Take Me To Church', proclaiming as we hit the cardio peak the slightly changed lyrics: 'Good God, let me give you my lunge!' To be frank, the spiritual high and the sense of connection with others that I had experienced in that moment stopped me in my tracks. It forced me to ask whether studying for ordination was the best way to minister to people and help them cultivate their inner life.

The essence of this highly emotional connection was beautifully captured by Julie Rice, one of the founders of SoulCycle (SoulCycle's renowned classes combine HIIT, resistance and strength training while riding a stationary bike, and are known for their ambience, energizing music and motivating instructors):

> Your foot was on the same beat as their foot was on, and all of a sudden it became connected, and it became tribal ... The music was amazing, and an instructor is telling you that you could be more than you thought you could be ... There's something about a moving meditation with other people that are rooting for you, that are holding space for you,

that aren't there to compete with you, that are there to elevate you so that they can be elevated as well. (Rice, cited in Raphael, 2023, p. 101)

However, alongside the economic, class and gender dimensions when it comes to the ability to exercise, *The Gospel of Wellness* also acknowledges the ways in which the gym experience can be exclusionary, with certain body types and fitness levels being privileged over others. Even the most caring fitness instructor cannot pretend that their classes are for all. A wheelchair user, a person sensitive to loud music or someone who cannot afford a gym membership would know that well. But Raphael also offers a glimpse of hope as she points to the rising number of influential body-positive fitness gurus, such as Jessamyn Stanley, co-founder of the Underbelly Yoga (Stanley, 2021, online) and the author of *Every Body Yoga* (Stanley, 2017). Similarly, Les Mills, the company with which I trained, prides itself on inclusivity. As instructors, we are taught to create an environment that is inclusive of all levels of fitness. We are reminded to use inclusive language in the studio, and to look out for our participants to provide them with appropriate work-out modifications if needed. Those who attend my classes are probably tired of hearing my mantra that 'We exercise because we love our bodies, not because we hate them.'

Researching the connection between exercise and spirituality

'As the spiritual landscape continues to expand beyond organised religion, we start to see that faith isn't disappearing, it's evolving' (Raphael, 2023, p. 116). According to Raphael, fitness classes have become unapologetically spiritual and can feel like a safe refuge for those who feel alienated by traditional religious communities. The presence of other people, repetitive behaviour and language used in fitness studios are what add the spiritual dimension to what otherwise could be a mere act of physical exercise. This human need for spiritual connection and meaning is alive and well outside of organized religion, in the popular culture and in places such as fitness studios. The sentiments shared by many fitness instructors and coaches echo the comments made by Oprah Winfrey, who told Stanford University students in 2015: 'I am not telling you what to believe and who to believe, or what to call it. But there is no full life, no fulfilled or meaningful, sustainably joyful life without a connection to the spirit. You must have a spiritual practice' (Winfrey, cited in Raphael, 2023, p. 221).

I came to this research project with a number of assumptions. My personal experience of attending exercise classes, my experience as an instructor, and the literature I reviewed in preparation for this research indicate that some people already perceive exercise to music as a broadly understood spiritual practice. I was not trying to find out how common this phenomenon is, but rather to ask in what ways exercise classes *can* serve as a spiritual practice. Therefore, I decided to target the people who self-identified as those who already perceive group fitness as a somewhat spiritual tool. In other words, this research was interested in what can potentially happen to a person (emotionally, mentally, spiritually, holistically) in the midst of an exercise class that bear marks of spiritual experience. My approach to research was qualitative. I found participants mainly through the gym where I teach, both class participants and other instructors. Initial questionnaires were followed up by individual interviews.

Despite the differences in their faith traditions, all of my participants seemed to be, by and large, in agreement when it comes to the meaning of 'spirituality'. For every person this meant realizing the importance of relationships and reaching beyond oneself. The word that came up often was 'values'. People commented that spirituality is what connects us to our highest values or helps us in living those out. Chloe spoke about 'disconnecting from her feelings but connecting with others', while others preferred to emphasize awareness of oneself. Only one person, who identified as a non-practising Roman Catholic, explicitly linked 'prayer to God' with 'spirituality'. Ultimately, all of the participants agreed that spirituality has something to do with bettering oneself, letting go of ego, being attuned to emotions (or releasing them), and creating a state of peace.

Although our 'liturgy' requires us to say certain 'compulsory cues' (those are the basics that let our class know what to do and how to do it safely), we are also encouraged to bring our authentic self into the studio. Therefore, to say that the workout routine is scripted would be only partially true. Kylie Gates, one of the top fitness leaders of Les Mills and the creative director for several of their programmes, always reminds her trainee instructors that authenticity is key, teaching them her mantra: 'If you don't feel it, don't say it.'

Instructors are trained to deliver classes, thinking about moving with their participants through a 'layered coaching model'. During each 'track' (a distinct piece of music with its own choreography and goals), instructors progress with their class through three coaching layers. The 'Layer 1' coaching cues are the basics that tell the participants what to do and how to do it safely. Instructors set up the position, execution and timing. They provide the class with some options and modifications to accommodate different levels of fitness, pregnancies and injuries. Breathing patterns are being established. Once the class participants have learnt the basics, instructors can move their coaching to the 'Layer 2'. This means driving the intensity of exercise, improving execution and educating the participants on the benefits of the workout. This is also where silence begins to take over, allowing the class to feel and experience for themselves. Finally, instructors move to the 'Layer 3'. Here is where they turn to positive intrinsic motivators, share the feel of the workout with the class and celebrate with them. This is much more about how the workout makes us feel, rather than what it does to our bodies. I suspect that this is what Raphael called 'quasi-liturgical platitudes'. How instructors achieve this varies from track to track, depending on the genre of the music and the kind of exercise. For example, coaching a class through stretches to soft and delicate melodies will sound vastly different from performing heavy chest presses on a bench to the beats of a hard rock song.

I will examine track number 4 from BODYPUMP™ release number 124 (Spring 2023) as an example of utilizing the layered coaching model in order to take class participants on a journey through their emotions, making it more than mere exercise. I chose this track as it struck me as being particularly powerful in impacting emotions, and I had recognized some participants in class drying their eyes at the end of the track.

The track trains muscles of the posterior chain (the back of the body), thus the participants are encouraged to work with heavy weights. It comes roughly 18 minutes into the class, meaning that the participants are not only fully warmed up but also begin to feel the first signs of fatigue. It is performed to the song called 'Won't Make a Sound' by ARMNHMR & Nurko, featuring Micah Martin. It lasts six minutes and 27 seconds and is constructed out of three blocks of workout that follow the pattern of three verses and three choruses in the song. The choreography notes provide the timing and succession of exercises through the song and number of repetitions. The 'track focus' at the top of the choreography page encourages the instructor to 'team-teach with the music to create a musical experience'. I have recorded myself teaching this track to a class, to analyse how I 'team-taught' with the music, and note my 'Layer 3' cues, which some may call 'platitudes'. I did so to examine how I, as an instructor, contribute to the sensations of emotional release that my research participants spoke about. The table below analyses what I have said during the third and final block of work, contrasting it with the kind of exercise performed, the feel of the music, and the lyrics of the song.

Exercise/Intensity	Musical feel/ emotions in the song	What I said
Low intensity. Lightweight plate work. Single dead rows.	Music softens following the previous peak. The singer sings softly.	*(conversational voice)* Bravery is not absence of fear. It is being scared but doing something anyway *or* Bravery is facing our doubt.
No change	No change	Sometimes all you have to do is wait for the right moment. And dare to hope, that the sun will rise.
Intensity rises. Triple dead rows. Class stays low.	The singer shouts with frustration.	*(I raise my voice)* Get DOWN!
If a person wasn't ready for the sudden drive of intensity, they may feel unsteady on their feet.	Music steadies again.	*(conversational voice)* If the weights knock you around, brace stronger. Unmovable, like a rock *or* How does it feel? Shaky? Wobbly? You are still in control.
Exercise continues and settles in the rhythm.	The singer sings quietly again. There is emotional pain in his voice.	*(whispering)* Hush. In your quiet centre there is strength. Timid, but stronger than you could ever imagine.
No change.	No change.	Waiting for the right moment. Waiting until you are ready to emerge *or* Load all your frustrations on to the weights.
Class switches from lighter weight plates to much heavier barbell.	Music builds up, feels brighter and expectant.	*(I remain silent)*
Slow deadlift with the barbell, the weight is slowly lowered to the knees.	Music accelerates.	The time is now. *or* We are ready.
Class slowly raises from the deadlift.	Pre-drop	*(I sing along to the music)*
Brief pause.	A split second of silence.	*(I shout)* With all your FURY! *or* Throw it like there's no tomorrow!

Exercise/Intensity	Musical feel/ emotions in the song	What I said
Clean and press on repeat – the most powerful move of the class. Participants stand tall and push heavy barbells overhead. Cardio peak.	Bass drop. Music and vocals become messy and explode. Music peaks.	*(I remain silent, mouthing* 'How does it feel?' *with music and maintaining eye contact with my class)*
Weights down. Exercise ends.	Music softens and concludes.	*(I smile, congratulate my class, and allow them time to come down and breathe)*

The exhortations I offer pick up on the themes and messages of the song lyrics (see Martin et al., 2022). It doesn't take a genius to figure out how such a combination of the music, lyrics and motivational statements turn mere exercise into a powerful emotional experience. This might be especially true for those who have experienced any kind of marginalization, either recently or at some point in their lives. The song lyrics and words said by the instructor have the potential to be poignant and liberative for someone who feels that they have been silenced, discriminated against or bullied – for example, women who are suffering from a controlling partner; harassment in the workplace; or gay men experiencing homophobia. As already explored, women and gay men are over-represented on the studio floor.

The part of the workout analysed above was its third and final block. That means that at this point the participants are already seriously fatigued and probably tempted to abandon the workout. When the class reaches the cardiovascular peak, which lasts roughly 25 seconds, they are expected to follow the instructor in performing eight repetitions to the beat of the music, lifting overhead one of the heaviest weights of the class. This means that the heavy barbell 'hits the sky' roughly every three seconds, putting their entire body through immense strain: from legs and core muscles, and the entire posterior chain, to shoulders and arms. Class participants point to such a physical peak as one of the two occasions when a spiritual experience is likely to happen during an exercise class. Considering the parallels between what I have described above and Rave culture and spirituality, the comments made by my research participants and those that Raphael spoke to led me to believe that this physical intensity, which releases adrenaline and endorphins, is what drives the heightened emotional or spiritual experience. In other words, listening to the same song and the same 'platitudes' while sitting on a sofa (or in a church pew) would not have a remotely similar effect on an individual. This leads me to conclude that it is the very act of physical exercise that sets the foundations for any potential emotional or spiritual experiences that follow in the class. These take root in what happens in our physical selves when the body is driven to the edge of its comfort zone, and the racing mind is numbed by loud music and meditative repetition. The music, coaching cues and being together are also necessary to create this powerful experience, but I am being led to believe that the physical strain is its fundamental ingredient.

In 2022, TikTok user FionnTimes uploaded a short workout video to the sound of a narrator saying:

> Going to the gym is more than just exercise. It's about turning all your emotional pain into something quantifiable, so you can handle them (*sic*) in an adequate manner. Most people will never understand how good it feels to lift a weight and have a weight lifted from your shoulders. Some people go to the gym to look better, but most of us go to feel better. You start to wonder how something so simple can change your life and mindset so much. I used to think I was the one lifting the weights, but it turned out the weights were lifting me. (TikTok, n.d.)

The sound has now been used by over 10,000 users, attracting hundreds of millions of 'likes' across tens of thousands of videos. This is probably a modest underestimation. It is hard to know exactly how many people found that this statement resonated with them, as FionnTimes's sound has since been posted by multiple accounts separately, severing the link to the original creator. It also appeared independently across other social media platforms, including Instagram, and it was available to the users of the video editing app CapCut, making it virtually impossible to keep track of its actual usage.

How my research participants viewed the relationship between their faith tradition and their perception of group exercise as a form of spiritual practice was fascinating, mostly because of what has *not* been said. Ed, who grew up in the Church of Scotland but currently identifies with Quakers, recalled a story from his childhood to describe the relation between exercise and his broader spirituality: 'I remember when being a child at Kirk, that when doing the Lord's Prayer, we would incorporate movements to focus our hearts and minds. I think this is the role that exercise plays in my spirituality.' He also reflected that it is important to him that, like Quaker Meetings, gym classes are very much LGBT-friendly. I was reminded of the comments in Raphael's book that gyms become like places of worship for those who do not feel welcome at churches – namely, LGBT people (Raphael, 2023, p. 110).

Laura, who grew up in the Hindu tradition, said that both group exercise classes and her Hindu background help her 'connect with the good values of kindness and tolerance'. She also said that both teach her to be empathetic with others and provide her with a sense of stability and belonging.

The combination of music, choreography, coaching cues and physical exertion creates an environment conducive to cathartic emotional release and guides the participants through a journey that goes beyond mere physical exercise. The scripted choreography, along with carefully selected music and instructors' authentic expressions, contribute to the creation of a quasi-liturgical experience. Furthermore, the sense of unity and communal experience within group exercise classes fosters a feeling of interconnectedness, both with fellow participants in the studio and with individuals following the same programmes worldwide.

It is worth noting the significance of these classes for individuals who may have experienced marginalization or discrimination. Women and gay men, who are over-represented in group exercise settings, can find respite from the challenges they face in other aspects of their lives, empowerment and a sense of belonging in the gyms. My research appears to suggest that despite shrinking affiliation with religious groups in the UK, individual human spirituality is alive and well, withdrawing to spaces that are typically understood to be secular – like fitness studios. Such spiritual expressions are often hidden in plain sight, and those experiencing them may be reluctant to talk openly about it out of fear of being ridiculed.

Conclusions

The findings of my research demonstrate that for some people physical and sensory engagement is an effective way of getting in touch with their deepest selves. I am not suggesting that worship spaces should be turned into fitness clubs, but I do want to encourage those involved in chaplaincy ministries and beyond to consider whether they cater for those who need to fully employ their bodies to effectively practise their spirituality and engage with their deepest selves.

I also want to question the roles and responsibilities that fitness centres have for caring for their members. Those who turn to group exercise often start during times of distress, seeking solace. And yet the underlying assumption is that people go to gyms to train their physique. I wonder what role fitness instructors and sports centres play in caring for the members in difficult life circumstances. The combination of hard physical work, music and emotional engagement can trigger all sorts of responses. This leads me to conclude that gyms should seriously consider the provision of chaplains or, at the very least, mental health first-aiders, and that faith organizations such as the Unitarians could embrace the need and possibility in gyms for inclusive, body and life-affirming, spiritually attuned ministries of service.

Bibliography

Brown University (2021), 'For Mindfulness Programs, "With Whom" may be More Important than "How"', *Health and Medicine*, 16 February, available at https://www.brown.edu/news/2021-02-16/mindfulness (accessed 7.07.2024).

Faith RXD (2023), available at https://faithrxd.org/ (accessed 7.07.2024).

Gerard, M., 'Selecting Ritual: DJs, Dancers and Liminality in Underground Dance Music', in G. St John (ed.), *Rave Culture and Religion*, Abingdon: Routledge, pp. 167–83 (quoting from T. McCall (2001), *This is Not a Rave: In the Shadow of a Subculture*, Toronto: Insomniac Press, unpaginated).

Guthold, R. et al. (2018), 'Worldwide Trends in Insufficient Physical Activity from 2001 to 2016: A Pooled Analysis of 358 Population-Based Surveys with 1.9 Million Participants', *The Lancet, Global Health* 6(10), 4 September, doi: 10.1016/S2214-109X(18)30454-6.

Hogan, E. (2022), 'Why Are Men Missing Out?', *Les Mills Insider*, 29 September, available at https://www.lesmills.com/uk/fit-planet/fitness/men-are-missing-out/ (accessed 7.07.2024).

Lixey, K. (2013), 'The Vatican's Game Plan for Maximising Sport's Educational Potential', in N. J. Watson and A. Parker (eds), *Sports and Christianity: Historical and Contemporary Perspectives*, Abingdon: Routledge.

Martin, M. et al. (2022), 'Won't Make a Sound', available at https://www.musixmatch.com/lyrics/ARMNHMR-Nurko-Micah-Martin/Won-t-Make-A-Sound (accessed 7.07.2024).

Pandya, S. (2018), 'The Culture of Yoga Retreats, Active Followers and Peripheral Associates of New Religious Movements: Wellness Enterprises Promoting Well-being', *Mental Health, Religion & Culture* 21(5), pp. 443–57.

Raphael, R. (2023), *The Gospel of Wellness: Gyms, Gurus, Goop and the False Promise of Self-Care*, London: Souvenir Press.

Sports Chaplaincy UK (2023), available at https://sportschaplaincy.org.uk/gymchaplaincy/ (accessed 7.07.2024).

St John, G., (2004), 'The Difference Engine: Liberation and the Rave Imaginary', in G. St John (ed.), *Rave Culture and Religion*, Abingdon: Routledge, pp. 19–45 (quoting from 'Raver's Manifesto', http://www.ecstasy.org/experiences/trip98.html).

Stanley, J. (2017), *Every Body Yoga: Let Go of Fear, Get on the Mat, Love Your Body*, New York: Workman Publishing.

Stanley, J. (2021), 'Jessamyn Stanley: Underbelly Yoga', available at https://jessamynstanley.com (accessed 7.07.2024).

Ter Kuile, C. and A. Thurston (2016), 'How We Gather: Part 2. SoulCycle as Soul Sanctuary', *On Being*, 9 July, available at https://onbeing.org/blog/how-we-gather-part-2-soulcycle-as-soul-sanctuary/ (accessed 7.07.2024).

The Unitarians (2023), available at https://www.unitarian.org.uk/who-we-are/ (accessed 7.07.2024).

TikTok (n.d.), 'FionnTimes: fionnwharton2006', available at https://www.tiktok.com/@fionnwharton2006 (accessed 7.07.2024).

PART FOUR

Chaplaincy and Christian Mission

14

Cross-cultures: Hospital Chaplaincy as a YWAM Missionary

CAROL HATTON

Making sense of Christian chaplaincy as a part of the Church's mission has come to the fore in recent times as declining numbers in church attendance continue to demonstrate wider society's move away from organized or institutionalized religion. The Church itself has responded by moving outside its walls into the community, to engage with people where they are through grassroots projects, rather than trying to entice them into the church building. In an endeavour to have a more contextual approach to faith and belief, the Methodist Church (2020) adopted *God for All: The Connexional Strategy for Evangelism and Growth,* and in 2019 the CofE launched 'The Pioneer Build' with the remit, 'Pioneers are people called by God who are the first to see and creatively respond to the Holy Spirit's initiatives with those outside the church', and also stating, 'Pioneering is a big part of the Church's mission to be a growing church for all people in all places' (Church of England, 2019, online). These modern developments in traditional churches' ecclesiology and missiology are attempts, as Slater suggests, 'to adapt to its context in dialogue with the prevailing culture in order to remain faithful to its mission to discern where God is at work in the world and join in with that work' (Slater, 2015, p. 10).

Similarly, there is a recognition that chaplaincy needs to re-establish its theological grounding as proposed by Walters, who (2018, p. 45) suggests 'Every chaplain is an attempt to integrate sacred and secular, eternal and temporal, Church and world.' Ryan (2018, p. 79) agrees that 'there ought to be some unifying theology that can group together the nature of this public-facing religious work – even if the contexts in which it is employed remain remarkably disparate.'

The diverse nature of chaplaincy means it does not neatly fit into one field or another, instead borrowing from several in order to form its own identity. Andrew Todd (2018, p. 40) locates chaplaincy within the realms of incarnational theology in which chaplaincy points 'towards the discernment of the incarnate Christ within the diversity of humanity ...

realised through dialogue and pastoral care'. In a discussion of a case study of chaplaincy within the discipline of pastoral theology, Don Browning (2000, p. 91) takes chaplaincy towards a 'practical theology of care'. Whipp explores the idea of chaplaincy being an 'apologetic presence' while promoting a practical theology for chaplaincy (Whipp, 2018, p. 105). In contrast, Slater's mentioned argument above focuses on theologies of mission and *Missio Dei*: God's mission in the world, in which the followers of Christ discern and join in with his work. She quotes David Heywood: 'Rather than following a universally applicable blueprint, the community is called to discern the shape of God's mission for each place and time and allow its own life consistently to be renewed by the Holy Spirit so as to fulfil that mission' (Heywood, cited in Slater, 2015, p. 72). The whole theological approach to chaplaincy for Slater is then summed up as 'co-creative collaboration with God's work in the world; it seeks to collaborate both with God and with the communities and people it serves' (Slater, 2015, p. 74).

It is into this discussion that I step; from a lifetime calling to an international missionary movement where practical and missional theology is embedded in the day-to-day realities of lived experience, to chaplaincy in the NHS. My identity, for want of a better expression, is that of 'missionary'. It is who I am. Wherever I go, even in the hospital, while I wear my name tag with the title 'Chaplain' on it, I am a missionary.

The missionary model encompasses the notion that God is active and present in the world and that, following Jesus' example, the chaplain's role is to partner with God in being the living breath of the gospel to the people to whom they are sent. Baker (2021, pp. 13–21) argues for the missiology of chaplaincy from a scriptural perspective: chaplains imitate various actions that Jesus and other biblical characters demonstrated, including cross-cultural engagement, human connection, intentional initiation, inclusivity, compassion, presence and meaning-making. These examples of Jesus in ministry unequivocally characterize and form the basis for the missionary model of chaplaincy. The mandate for chaplains is to be like Jesus and a Christian presence outside the walls of the Church, called by God and sent into the world as a witness to the gospel and the coming kingdom of God, empowered by the Holy Spirit.

It is worth noting, before going further, that there are many blurred lines between the various models of chaplaincy that have been proposed by Threlfall-Holmes (2011, pp. 116–26). The missionary model shares similarities with the incarnational model, the former being more the motivation of the chaplain and the latter having more to do with the chaplain's method of engagement with the care seeker. The motivation of the chaplain will form later discussion.

The chaplaincy provision that I am in serves a local population of around

400,000 people, offering 'Spiritual, Pastoral and Religious care and support to all'. The core employed chaplaincy team of around ten chaplains are currently Christian and Muslim. They are supported by volunteers from faith traditions including Hindu, Sikh and Jehovah's Witnesses. There are generally two to three chaplains working 8 a.m.–4 p.m. daily, with one then remaining 'on call' out-of-hours. The team is bolstered by trainee chaplains and local volunteers whose numbers vary. The demography of the surrounding area is growing in its ethnic, cultural, social and religious diversity, with more than 30 languages spoken. The most common languages after English include Hindi, Polish, Urdu, Lithuanian, Romanian Punjabi, Bengali, Gujarati, Arabic and Tamil.

Chaplains do not fit comfortably within the recognized professions of the NHS but they are none the less 'professional staff qualified and contracted to supply spiritual, religious, or pastoral care to patients, service users, carers and staff ... one of the smallest professional groups working in the NHS' (NHS England, 2015, p. 7). It has been the responsibility of the NHS to employ chaplains since 1948 and, I would suggest, they are the only group of professionals in the hospital who have the remit of a service provision to the whole hospital population, which in 2018 was around 5,000 people in any 24-hour period on our site, not including the family and friends of patients (Care Quality Commission, 2018, p. 2).

These numbers demonstrate that the chaplain, as a professional giving spiritual and religious care to those from all faiths and none, has an enormous task – especially when each encounter with a care seeker can be as individual as the care seekers themselves. One of the key strengths of the missionary model is that the chaplain is aware of the need to adapt to the circumstance in front of them. It is their motivation that takes them into the situation but, as will be discussed later, their method of ministry is adaptable, diverse and inclusive.

The mandate to take the gospel into the world is easily fulfilled in the vastly diversity-hospital population where I work. When the missionary call is practised appropriately, the host culture (in this case the hospitals and their beneficiaries) will be approached and treated with respect. This is the underlying principle of any cross-cultural ministry and is also dictated by the guidelines set out in the NHS's *Promoting Excellence* in pastoral, spiritual and religious care. In this context, cross-cultural can be understood as 'any ministry in which one interacts with people who have grown up learning values and lifestyle patterns that are different from one's own' (Lingenfelter and Mayers, 1986, p. 11).

Threlfall-Holmes cautions that the missionary model might be 'feared' by institutions outside of the Church as it conjures up images of forceful proselytization, prejudice and narrow-mindedness. She goes on to suggest that 'Those who become chaplains to share the love of God with people in hard-to-reach places need to be particularly skilled at the task of discerning the best means and tools of mission in a particular context' (Threlfall-Holmes, 2011, p. 119). There is in my experience still a misperception within the population of the hospital, both staff and patients, that the role of the chaplain is that of either proselytization or uniquely for end-of-life care. This lack of understanding has led to conversations that include equating my visit with past experiences of conversion attempts by doorstep evangelists from groups such as the Jehovah's Witnesses or Mormons. Conversely, I have been greeted by comments such as 'I'm not dying, so why are you here?' or 'Are you here to tell me I'm dying?' Once the context of the visit and specifically the role of the chaplain have been explained and clarified, patients and staff are mostly happy to engage with me as a Christian chaplain.

Herein lies one of the dilemmas of the missionary model. When explaining my role and why I'm visiting a patient, if I identified most strongly with the missionary model I could not describe that I'm there 'sent by the church to do my part in the mission of God in the world' since this would be entirely inappropriate and confusing, especially to those of a no-faith or a non-Christian background, even if it was for the most part accurate. In addition, to do so would be to expound upon my motivation for being a chaplain as this is what the missionary model of chaplaincy denotes. It is a motivational model explaining the 'why' behind my purpose for being in chaplaincy, but not the 'how' of my chaplaincy practice and what it might signify for the care seeker. Unlike the other models that Threlfall-Holmes proposes, which are more descriptive of what a chaplain does practically, the starting point of the missionary model is the chaplain herself as the one sent, her motivation and calling to be a chaplain; it is not the method of her ministry to those to whom she is sent, and how she will interact with this care seeker. Over the course of her day, a chaplain may use many different methodologies, as described by the other models, in how she will interact. She may offer pastoral care, spiritual care, civic service, officiate at a religious service or offer sacramental services, or she may simply be a presence, embodying her faith. All of these are actions, not motivations. This could, however, be seen as a strength of the missionary model: 'Because the needs of people and means of communicating the gospel vary widely between different contexts, there is no one typical pattern of ministry for those who see their ministry primarily in this way' (Threlfall-Holmes, 2011, p. 119). The chaplain therefore has the ability to contextualize or vary her methods according to the needs of the care seeker. The missionary model is also further supported by the fact that by investing and being embedded in the life of the hospital, chaplains fulfil their calling in the same way a missionary does: being sent by the Church to a foreign culture. In the context of the NHS, they learn the host culture's medical language, observe their rhythms and protocols (protected mealtimes, doctors' rounds, PPE observance, occupational health and safety training etc.) and take part in their rituals (report-writing for the trustees, ethics committees, annual reviews etc.), just as a missionary on the field embeds in the host culture.

It is important to recognize that different meanings are attributed to the terms 'mission' and 'missionary'. Coming from an evangelical background, Moreau, Corwin and McGee argue: 'Mission that does not include evangelism is missing the core' and 'Mission that does not include incorporating those led to Christ into a local body of believers or teaching them to obey all that Christ commanded ... is, at best, truncated mission' (Moreau, Corwin and McGee, 2004, p. 89). It could be argued that 'missionary' is not the right terminology to use for a model of a person who is sent by the Church or who feels called by God into chaplaincy in the context of the NHS, since the NHS Chaplaincy Guidelines (NHS England, 2015) clearly affirm: 'Patients and service users have a right to expect that chaplaincy care will be experienced as neither insensitive nor proselytising.' Discussions of language and meaning are important within the missionary model of Christian chaplaincy since the chaplain is being sent from one sphere and culture – that is, the Church with its distinct religious language and customs – to another, in this case healthcare and the hospital. Both settings have distinct and very different languages, customs and world views.

Although there is a growing recognition of new and alternative therapies and treatments, some rooted in ancient philosophies such as meditation practices and yoga, by and large the medical professionals practising in the NHS have traditions that are rooted in science, medicine and evidence-based research. The language used is obviously that of medicine and science, where the patient is often spoken to using vocabulary unfamiliar to them (unless medically trained). The dominant theme and culture in the medical profession values knowledge, empirical evidence and meta-science. Patients, in my observation, are spoken to in a language that they are far from familiar with. They are told of various tests or scans they need, which will inform the next round of medication or treatments they require, using technical language, which is often incomprehensible to them and leaves them confused and sometimes frightened as well.

Operating from the missionary model the chaplain can be cross-culturally relevant in the NHS setting. Missionaries who go out to the people, working cross-culturally, learn the language of the people they are sent to and embedded with. The hospital chaplain is therefore bilingual, having an understanding of the language of the employing institution, the NHS, and speaking the language of the care seeker's lived experience. In the hospital context it is often the language of uncertainty, fear, longing, mortality, pain and suffering, loss, searching and meaning-making, and sometimes of their faith background. Conversely, chaplains can translate and interpret the language of the care seeker for the medical professional attending to them, as evidenced in the Theos report on chaplaincy in the UK:

> The authority and expertise in their [the chaplain's] own faith is especially important in areas like mental health, where chaplains are involved in working with doctors to identify patient beliefs that are the norm for their particular faith, beliefs that are a bit extreme, but still not necessarily dangerous, and patients who exhibit beliefs that are not to do with their faith but may be a part of a wider mental health problem. (Ryan, 2015, p. 53)

When writing about the different aspects of the chaplain's role, Carr (2001) agrees that chaplains are uniquely placed as interpreters. As care seekers from any background attempt to process and make sense of their lived experiences in the hospital, as part of their journey in life, Carr (2001, p. 30) suggests that 'Because of the ambiguous position (between centre and margin, between religion and spirituality, between institutional role and person) that he or she occupies, the chaplain can be used to interpret what may be happening to people.' Swift (2009, p. 143) also proposes that, despite the pluralistic and increasingly secular nature of society, in the hospital, although the language of religion might be changing, the concepts concerning spirituality remain, especially in matters of meaning, suffering and death. He writes: 'In a world where religious belief prevails over atheism and where such beliefs are fragmentary, the need for skilful interpreters must surely be in the ascendant.'

Despite the chaplain often being called on for their 'authority and expertise' in areas of their faith as evidenced above, a contrasting position can also be presented in which chaplains come to care seekers with empty hands to discern and then join in with what God is doing.

The outcomes of the chaplain's influence on a care seeker's health and well-being are difficult to evidence using the more acceptable scientific empirical evidence methods of the medical world; however, the language the chaplain uses is more often the language of the patient: relatable, real, comforting and familiar. In addition, the chaplain has more time to spend with each individual care seeker in order to 'read' and respond to their spiritual or pastoral needs. Chaplains identifying with the missionary model therefore on occasion attend to the care seeker not as a religious specialist or expert but, as Whipp proposes, 'the chaplain's purpose is to make room for the spirit' (Whipp, 2018, p. 115). This is the essence of *Missio Dei*, joining in with what God is already doing in the world and the lived experience of the care seeker. Slater (2015, p. 95) describes this characteristic of the chaplain as 'the capacity to be culturally "multi-lingual" in order to offer and witness to the insights and values of the faith tradition in a culturally plural context in ways which contribute to human flourishing and the common good and so to the flourishing of the kingdom of God'.

In the future, patients will probably no longer relate in as great a number to the traditional churches but may still consider themselves Christian. Increasingly, statistical analysis of data on church attendance is revealing a trend that shows the decline of the traditional established Church and an increase in attendance at Pentecostal and Free Churches (Brierley, n.d., online). The aged demographic mainly being admitted to the hospital today are of the generation who grew up with institutional church attendance being very much part of their lives and many are nominal Christians. As the youngest so-called 'baby boomers' become the aged population of the future, the chaplain who is more attuned to their style of contemporary Christianity will be well suited to attend to their religious needs and to 'the reality of the patient's experience' (Swift, 2009, p. 169).

Those from Evangelical/Pentecostal denominations may most readily identify the missionary model as being their predominant motivational calling to chaplaincy and to the practical outworking of their ministry. Their approach to faith has a contemporary edge often more flexible and accommodating of others than that of their more traditional colleagues. They operate generically and inclusively as they provide spiritual and pastoral care but are also available to offer specific religious care. However, one of the key issues facing the chaplain who favours the missionary model is the challenge to serve the multi-faith and secular community of the hospital with integrity and respect and without compromising their own convictions. As already discussed, they need to possess many skills in their practice, both bilingually and cross-culturally, and have a comprehensive understanding of the people whom they are employed to serve. When an approach is adopted where a chaplain sees the care seeker as their own key resource, the chaplain's faith background or world view should not be a hindering factor. When done well in this context, a pastoral and spiritual carer will listen to the narrative of the care seeker with sacred and cultural humility and support them as they explore meaning. This meaning-making endeavour and the skill of interpathy, as Grefe, McCarroll and Ansari (2022, p. 80) suggest, is the key for chaplains and 'often includes code-switching, whereby chaplains use care seekers' spiritual/religious language to move inside their meaning-making systems with them'. This meaning-making approach reinforces the missionary model of chaplaincy and its scope to minister in the world, as it promotes the notion that chaplains can provide a therapeutic presence to anyone so long as they are able to 'bracket out their own worldview ... and move inside that of another, viewing life and circumstances from within' (Grefe, McCarroll and Ansari, 2022, p. 80). However, it could be argued that in 'bracketing out their own worldview', the motivation of the Christian chaplain has not changed and that although they are providing a listening ear to the care seeker, they are still pursuing their Christian mission. This will forever remain a tension for the chaplains who must exercise self-awareness in their generic inclusive practice.

At first glance, the missionary model, as explained by Threlfall-Holmes (2011, pp. 118–19), is presented as a way of placing and locating chaplaincy within the mission of the Church. Slater proposes that 'chaplaincy needs to be understood as being at the cutting edge of mission, a prime locus of the Church's participation in God's mission in the world for the building up of God's kingdom and the flourishing of all God's people' (Slater, 2015, p. 19). There seems to be an effort here to legitimize chaplaincy as a profession within the [Anglican] Church where this acknowledgement might previously have been lacking. In addition, far from explaining the model in which the chaplain practises, the missionary model appears to be an explanation for the chaplain's motivations for being in this particular type of ministry and a way to justify their place outside the walls of the Church among the people. However, upon closer examination, as the model is unpacked through a more practical lens, it can be demonstrated that, if equated with missionary practice, the chaplain as missionary has valuable contributions to make to her context, especially in the secular institution of the NHS hospital. The challenges faced by the Christian chaplain in a multifaith, pluralistic context can be met with the proficiencies of a missionary who equally feels 'called and sent by God'. These skills include cross-cultural awareness, learning and participation, translation, interpretation, respect for values and world views, and what I would call practical evangelism. Here the chaplain both explicitly and implicitly demonstrates God's love for the care seeker through who they are and what they say and do, thus living out the *Missio Dei*.

Bibliography

Baker, A. T. (2021), *Foundations of Chaplaincy: A Practical Guide*, Grand Rapids, MI: Eerdmans.

Brierley, P. (n.d.), *Christianity in the UK*, available at https://faithsurvey.co.uk/uk-christianity.html (accessed 7.07.2024).

Browning, D. (2000), 'Pastoral Theology in a Pluralistic Age', in J. Woodward and S. Pattison (eds), *The Blackwell Reader in Pastoral and Practical Theology*, Oxford: Blackwell Publishing.

Care Quality Commission (CQC) (2018), *Luton and Dunstable Hospital NHS Foundations Trust Inspection Report*, available at https://api.cqc.org.uk/public/v1/reports/08fff295-f512-4a2c-b230-115c7aec4d13?20210115060533 (accessed 7.07.2024).

Carr, W. (2001), 'Spirituality and Religion: Chaplaincy in Context', in H. Orchard (ed.), *Spirituality in Healthcare Contexts*, London: Jessica Kingsley Publishers, pp. 21–32.

Church of England (2019), *Pioneer Ministry*, available at https://www.churchofengland.org/faith-life/vocations/pioneer-ministry (accessed 7.07.2024).

Grefe, D., P. McCarroll and B. Ansari (2022), 'Meaning Making in Chaplaincy: Presence, Assessment, and Interventions', in W. Cadge and S. Rambo (eds), *Chaplaincy and Spiritual Care in the Twenty-first Century: An Introduction*, Chapel Hill, NC: University of North Carolina Press, pp. 66–89.

Lingenfelter, S. and M. Mayers (1986), *Ministering Cross-culturally: An Incarnational Model for Personal Relationships*, Ada, MI: Baker Book House.

Methodist Church (2020), *God for All: The Connexional Strategy for Evangelism and Growth*, available at https://www.methodist.org.uk/media/16362/counc_mc20-38-evangelism-and-growth_mar_2020.pdf (accessed 7.07.2024).

Moreau, A., G. Corwin and G. McGee (2004), *Introducing World Missions*, Ada, MI: Baker Academic.

NHS England (2015), *NHS Chaplaincy Guidelines 2015: Promoting Excellence in Pastoral, Spiritual & Religious Care*, available at https://www.england.nhs.uk/wp-content/uploads/2015/03/nhs-chaplaincy-guidelines-2015.pdf (accessed 7.07.2024).

Ryan, B. (2018), 'Theology and Models of Chaplaincy', in J. Caperon, A. Todd and J. Walters (eds), *A Christian Theology of Chaplaincy*, London: Jessica Kingsley Publishers.

Ryan, B. (2015), *A Very Modern Ministry: Chaplaincy in the UK*, available at https://www.theosthinktank.co.uk/cmsfiles/archive/files/Modern%20Ministry%20combined.pdf (accessed 7.07.2024).

Slater, V. (2015), *Chaplaincy Ministry and the Mission of the Church*, London: SCM Press.

Swift, C. (2009), *Hospital Chaplaincy in the Twenty-first Century*, Farnham: Ashgate.

Threlfall-Holmes, M. (2011), 'Exploring Models of Chaplaincy', in M. Threlfall-Holmes and M. Newitt (eds), *Being a Chaplain*, London: SPCK, pp. 116–26.

Todd, A. (2018), 'A History of the World', in J. Caperon, A. Todd and J. Walters (eds), *A Christian Theology of Chaplaincy*, London: Jessica Kingsley Publishers, pp. 21–42.

Walters, J. (2018), 'Twenty-First Century Chaplaincy: Finding the Church in the Post-Secular', in J. Caperon, A. Todd and J. Walters (eds), *A Christian Theology of Chaplaincy*, London: Jessica Kingsley Publishers, pp. 43–58.

Whipp, M. (2018), 'Embedding Chaplaincy', in J. Caperon, A. Todd and J. Walters (eds), *A Christian Theology of Chaplaincy*, London: Jessica Kingsley Publishers, pp. 101–17.

15

The UK Oil and Gas Chaplaincy

LEE HIGSON

As of 2018, there were 184 offshore rigs in the North Sea (Statista, 2023), making it the busiest area in the world in terms of oil and gas exploration and production. In 2021, 28,400 people were employed directly in the UK offshore energy industry, with a further 172,400 connected with the industry in the supply and service sectors as well as those in the wider economy supported by the industry (Offshore Energies UK, 2022, p. 8). For almost 40 years, the industry has been served by one chaplain: this is a huge parish!

The UK Oil and Gas Chaplaincy exists to provide 'pastoral and spiritual care to those who work or have worked in the industry, past and present, and their dependants' (Oil and Gas Chaplaincy, 2014). Although the commercial extraction of gas on the UK continental shelf began in 1966 (oil in 1975), it wasn't until 1986 that the need for a permanent chaplaincy for the industry was identified. In the early days, the industry was largely reactive in its approach to change, and it was the tragic ditching of a Chinook helicopter, used for crew transfers, with the loss of 45 offshore workers and flight crew, that provided the catalyst for establishing a permanent chaplaincy role. Just as the appointment process was being finalized, in July 1988, there was another tragedy: the Piper Alpha platform located in the North Sea was ripped apart by a series of explosions and a catastrophic fire resulted in the loss of 167 lives. This was, to date, the UK's worst offshore disaster.

The need for a permanent chaplain was recognized throughout the industry and it is funded completely by Offshore Energies UK. A full-time administrator is also employed by the chaplaincy. Contributions to this work, as well as to the chaplaincy welfare fund, are made by various oil companies and service providers. Similarly, office space for the work of the chaplaincy is provided by various oil companies. Because the chaplaincy is 'owned' by everyone, and no single company 'runs' it, the chaplaincy remains completely impartial and independent, which is a healthy foundation to build this ministry on.

Offshore chaplaincy today

The chaplaincy role is both a reactive and a proactive one. Even in recent years, and with a paradigm shift in the offshore safety culture since Piper Alpha, there have been several fatal offshore helicopter accidents. Between 2009 and 2018, there were six crashes resulting in the deaths of 33 people and the rescue of 65 others (Husseini, 2018). It is standard procedure for all oil companies operating on the UK continental shelf to call and mobilize the chaplain in the event of a serious incident offshore. Police Scotland will also notify the chaplaincy if any death offshore has been reported to them.

Even without accidents, the offshore workforce is an ageing community and deaths from natural causes can and do occur offshore. Following such a death, the chaplaincy will be informed and it is often the case that the chaplain will be mobilized offshore, perhaps at the time of the funeral to allow an act of remembrance to take place among the deceased's colleagues. Occasionally, the family may request that ashes are scattered offshore and this role too may involve the chaplain mobilizing offshore, or at least providing direction for the offshore crew and management.

Throughout 2022–3, I supported the chaplaincy as an assistant chaplain and conducted offshore visits to assets both in Morecambe Bay and in the North Sea. This followed a 22-year career working in the energy industry. It is vital that the chaplain understands the pressures of living and working away from home, and so prior experience in the industry, or a similar field, is helpful. Many of the past and present chaplains come from a forces background and all are ordained clergy, often from the Church of Scotland as a result of the main base being in Aberdeen.

Anyone mobilizing to a UK offshore installation must have a valid offshore medical certificate as well as certification to prove they have received training in how to respond to various offshore emergencies and helicopter ditching. Chaplains must also hold public liability insurance. Prior to mobilization, there will almost certainly be a company-specific induction that is completed online. The chaplain will normally email the Offshore Installation Manager outlining the reasons for his or her visit and what the crew should expect. Offshore visits are normally requested by the oil companies, who liaise directly with the chaplaincy administrator.

On the day of mobilization, the chaplain travels to the heliport where they, along with the mobilizing crew, complete security checks. A pre-flight safety briefing is given and, following this, the outbound passengers don survival suits and hearing protection before being escorted to the helicopter. The mobilization is a great way to get conversations started with the offshore crew over a cup of coffee in the departure lounge. As the heliport staff and aircrew are just as much part of the oil industry as the offshore workforce, I will always speak with those on duty and tell them about the work of the chaplaincy and how it can support them.

Helicopter transit times can vary from as little as ten minutes to just under two hours. Most passengers are asleep within minutes of the lift – the vibration and noise of the helicopter along with the warm snugness of the survival suits make it easy to doze off. Just prior to arrival, the flight crew will wake everyone up via the tannoy to prepare for landing.

If it is a chaplain's first visit, or if he or she has not visited the platform in the previous 12 months, a full safety induction and tour of the installation will take place. This will highlight the muster stations, designated lifeboats, how to escape to sea, where different emergency escape equipment is located, and a tour of the accommodation will also be given. This can often take several hours. A platform will typically have between 60 and 180 offshore workers onboard, all overseen by the Offshore Installation Manager (OIM). Facilities onboard a modern oil rig are comparable to hotels. Internet access is standard and the food is restaurant quality and is looked forward to by all the crew. There are TV lounges, recreation rooms, modern gyms, saunas, cinema, library, quiet rooms, a fully equipped hospital and often rooms to pursue hobbies and interests. Cabins are normally twin berths with day and night shifts sharing the living space.

The chaplain will normally meet with the Offshore Installation Manager on the day of arrival. Offshore installations are producing oil and gas 24 hours a day, seven days per week, except when planned maintenance is taking place, and a plan will be agreed to get to see as many workers as possible across the various departments and shifts. The locker room is a good place to catch the workforce, especially at the start of tea breaks. There is a natural curiosity about the work of the chaplaincy and most crew, after a bit of banter, are happy to engage with the chaplain. Most of the conversations are secular in nature – the chaplain being there for all faiths and none. Mental health often comes up, along with talk around the pressures of family separation, especially when children or family are ill or having a hard time. If the platform is approaching the end of its field life, there will invariably be some anxiety onboard about finding new jobs and paying the mortgage once the rig is decommissioned. The chaplain can encourage the workforce in this time and feed back any specific concerns to the management.

If possible, the chaplain will arrange what is known as a 'town hall' meeting. This will be attended by as many people as possible who can leave their work for 30 minutes or so. During this meeting, the chaplain will outline the role of the chaplaincy, stressing the pastoral and spiritual support that is available for the workforce and their families, regardless of faith or no faith. Many offshore workers are surprised to discover that the chaplaincy administers a charitable trust that can act as a bit of a safety net when workers face financial hardship or go on long-term sick leave and find that the statutory sick pay is not enough to cover bills. We will also run campaigns, for example around mental health wellbeing, or encouraging all offshore crew to ensure they have an up-to-date will by highlighting real-life situations that have occurred when offshore workers have died without a will in place.

The chaplain normally has freedom to go in any non-restricted areas onboard so will walk around the accommodation visiting the control room, galley, talking to the catering crew, visiting the various offices and section leaders, perhaps visiting the hospital or sickbay, and talking with the medic. Following this, the chaplain may don his or her boiler suit and safety equipment and go for 'a walk on the park' – walking around the production decks and drilling module, talking with the various teams on the platform. We find people are often more open outside, where they are not generally seen to be talking with the chaplain, and it is in these conversations that we pick up the things that are bothering individuals.

I've found that there are often practising Christians on board the rigs and they will invariably seek me out for a chat, coming to sit with me at mealtimes or finding me after a shift in the recreation room, where the chaplain will spend some of his or her time to be accessible to everyone. It is a good opportunity for the chaplain to encourage such workers, perhaps offering to pray for them, leaving them some resources or just talking with and encouraging them in the work that they do and the light that they shine to others.

I've found offshore workers to be very open to discussions around faith, and often just sharing my story about how I became a chaplain will stir their interest, leading to some quite profound questions. I'm frequently asked if I can pray for a situation at home – a teenage daughter struggling with anxiety or an elderly mother with deteriorating health. I was once asked how to answer questions a six-year-old daughter was asking her dad about God and what happens when people die – though I did wonder if this was Dad's way of asking the questions for himself.

An offshore visit typically lasts 24–48 hours, which is normally long enough to get around at least half of the crew. Prior to departure, I will often spend 20 minutes or so with the Offshore Installation Manager sharing my perception of morale onboard, what they are doing well, and maybe a couple of areas where there might be some room for improvement. I'll remind them that I'm completely impartial and that I'm there for them whenever they may need me or the chaplaincy. Onshore managers will also sometimes ask us for feedback on specific concerns and we are happy to provide this without breaking confidentiality. During our visits to installations, we cannot come across as either 'management spies' or 'ex-officio Trade Union members' as we must always remain neutral. Our role is simply to support everyone and sometimes that might involve challenging a misconception doing the rounds and sometimes it might involve sharing a concern with the appropriate person in the management chain. Whatever we do, our golden rule is to stick to hard facts and not to act on rumours.

Other roles and responsibilities

In addition to the offshore role, there is also an onshore civic role in providing memorial services, particularly on the anniversaries of tragic events such as the Piper Alpha disaster or helicopter crashes. The chaplaincy maintains a book of remembrance to commemorate all those who have died offshore on the UK continental shelf. The remembrance book is held at the oil chapel in the Kirk of St Nicholas in Aberdeen. An annual service is held on the first Saturday of November to remember those who have died. The chaplain is routinely called upon to conduct the offices of baptism, weddings and funerals as well as various memorial services, and needs to be confident in talking with all levels of the workforce, from the roustabouts on the drill floors right up to senior onshore management leaders at an upmarket hotel presentation evening or similar. He or she may sometimes act as an advocate standing up for those who feel they're not being heard – living out the words of Micah 6.8.

Reflecting theologically from a Christian perspective

Arguably, the first reference to mission at sea was through the work of St Paul who, in Acts 27, fulfilled many of the roles of an offshore chaplain – providing guidance (v. 10), encouragement (v. 22), proclamation (v. 23), prayer (v. 35) and fellowship/communion (v. 36). Very little has been written specifically on oil and gas chaplaincy, but there are some remarkable similarities to seafarer chaplaincy, and I now draw on some of this research.

The maritime missiologist Roald Kverndal makes an interesting observation, arguing that Christ, preferring the poor and disadvantaged as agents for mission, selected seafarers (fishermen) for the task as they were 'social outsiders' and people 'constantly on the move' (Kverndal, 2008, p. 7). Critics may question whether it is correct to define Galilean fishermen as offshore workers in the true sense of the word. Galilee was an inshore freshwater lake of limited reach – very different from the North Sea, for example. However, there are strong similarities in that they both faced unique dangers associated with working on the sea and were at the mercy of the wind and weather.

Peer ministry has long been a feature of the Mission to Seafarers. One of the more famous converts is John Newton, Anglican minister and writer of the hymn 'Amazing Grace'. Formerly a slave-ship captain, he came to faith after being influenced by a fellow Christian captain. The Oil and Gas Chaplain has an important part to play in encouraging Christians in the offshore workforce to maintain their faith and share it with others.

Kverndal (1994) proposed a dual strategy based on both shipboard peer ministry (witnessing to colleagues) and shipboard fellowship groups (as expressions of Christian community at sea). Some Christians do this on their own initiative, with ad hoc informal shore-based support from the various ministry teams during the brief port stays, perhaps in much the same way that the offshore chaplaincy and support groups interact with a platform. In Aberdeen, the main shore-base for UK oil exploration and production, there is one such support group called the Light Offshore Christian Fellowship, whose objectives are: 'The spreading of the Word of God and the Gospel of Salvation within the Oil Industry by distribution and placing of Bibles and all forms of Christian literature in Oil Industry premises and installations' and 'The promotion of Christian Fellowship amongst Christians working in the Oil Industry' (Total Giving, 2023).

The Revd Dr Paul Mooney of the Mission to Seafarers wrote with a view to refocusing mission away from seafarer centres and ship visitors/chaplains and back to the seafarers themselves:

> No matter how empathetic; meetings with seafarers in the course of ship visiting and duties in the seafarers' centre cannot be but occasional and almost random elements in an overall strategy of pastoral care. Sustained and empowering pastoral care can only be primarily exercised by ministering seafarers working among their peers. (Mooney, 2004, p. 5)

This essentially is calling for a paradigm shift in the entire approach and raises questions about what this may look like on an offshore installation.

As editor of *Watermarks*, Kverndal remarked, 'If we are to be serious about Christian ministry in a pluralistic world, we will have to intentionally focus ... on how to promote witnessing and worshipping fellowship at sea' (Kverndal, 1988, p. 1). This, I feel, is a much-undervalued part of the chaplain's role and one that is critical to the flourishing of Christian fellowship offshore. Having had seven years' experience myself running a 'cell-church' on an offshore installation, this is a mission that is close to my own heart.

The Apostleship of the Seas, a Roman Catholic seafarer mission, have stated that 'Seafarers who make up a Christian community on-board embody a new way of being Church' (Kverndal, 2008, p. 4). This is truly a fresh expression of church. Christians offshore will invariably find fellowship at a separate church during their home leave periods, but for the two or three weeks they are offshore, a Christian fellowship can be a real bonus for them. Kverndal argues that 'It is as indigenous peer ministry among fellow seafarers that such witness "from below" gains grassroots relevance as contextualized' (Kverndal, 2008, p. 177), and the missiologist David Bosch supports this view, stating: 'Nothing can compare with the very being of a Christian community to impact sceptical onlookers' (Bosch, 1996, p. 414).

Conclusion

UK Oil and Gas production peaked in 1999, and there has been a steady decline since this time. There have been no 'major' finds for many years now and as platforms age and the water cut (the percentage of water in the output) increases, many operators are choosing to decommission their assets, which is now a boom industry in itself. The Oil and Gas Chaplaincy is in the process of rebranding to become Offshore Energy Chaplaincy – this in turn, although still focusing on offshore Oil and Gas production, will also embrace offshore wind and other forms of green offshore energy. It is an exciting time for the energy industry as pressure ramps up to reduce carbon emissions and our dependence on fossil fuels. There will, I believe, always remain the need for dedicated chaplains to serve this enormous parish.

Bibliography

Bosch, D. (1996), *Transforming Mission: Paradigm Shifts in Theology of Mission*, New York: Orbis Books.

Husseini, T. (2018), 'Offshore Helicopter Crashes: Improving Safety and Saving Lives', available at https://www.offshore-technology.com/features/offshore-helicopter-crashes/?cf-view (accessed 7.07.2024).

Kverndal, R. (1988), 'Seafarers fellowship – No Goodbye but New Beginning! Towards a Maritime Theology of Mission: Effective Witness has to be Fellowship Focused', *Watermarks*, available at https://iasmm.org/2020/07/14/watermarks-1973-1990/ (accessed 7.07.2024).

Kverndal, R. (1994), 'A New Maritime Mission Paradigm?', *International Association for the Study of Maritime Mission Newsletter*, Spring Issue 1, available at https://iasmm.org/wp-content/uploads/2018/10/IASMMNewsletter_Spring1994.pdf (accessed 7.07.2024).

Kverndal, R. (2008), *The Way of the Sea: The Changing Shape of Mission in the Seafaring World*, Pasadena, CA: William Carey Library.

Mooney, P. (2004), 'Maritime Missions', *The International Association for the Study of Maritime Mission Newsletter*, Spring Issue 23.

Offshore Energies UK (2022), *Workforce Insight 2022*, available at https://oeuk.org.uk/wp-content/uploads/2022/11/OEUK-Workforce-Insight-2022.pdf (accessed 7.07.2024).

Oil and Gas Chaplaincy (2014), 'Welcome to the UK Oil & Gas Chaplaincy's Website', available at https://www.ukoilandgaschaplaincy.com/ (accessed 7.07.2024).

Statista (2023), 'Number of Offshore Rigs Worldwide as of January 2018 by Region', available at https://www.statista.com/statistics/279100/number-of-offshore-rigs-worldwide-by-region/ (accessed 7.07.2024).

Total Giving (2023), 'Light Offshore Christian Fellowship', available at https://www.totalgiving.co.uk/charity/light-offshore-christian-fellowship (accessed 7.07.2024).

16

Chaplain as Fire-tender: Envisioning a Model of Chaplaincy for Clinical Pastoral Education in the USA and Beyond

ANJEANETTE ROBERTS

I've always loved the literal warmth and light that a campfire brings to a cool evening. The smell of burning wood mingles with the scents of surrounding wood or field. A distinct sense of satisfaction comes from building a good fire: finding enough kindling, a few other small pieces of wood placed in criss-cross fashion with plenty of room for air, and then the larger pieces that go on last, sustaining the fire's warmth and character. Successful, one reposes beside the burning invitation for gathering.

Campfires indiscriminately draw friend and stranger by their warming and mesmerizing nature. Would-be warmers circle round, attentions fixed on dancing flames, with intermittent glances to others' fire-lit faces. As congregants gather side-by-side, they relax and find a listening ear, or two, from others who are not directly focused on them. These shared fires provide a sense of intimacy and anonymity. When one faces another, it is through the buffer of the fire, or she turns to face the other to draw them deeper into conversation. Fires hold space for reflection, for shared and common human desires and for experiences of the sacred.

Encountering the sacred

In life's recent seasons, I recognize an impoverishment of soul born of the absence of campfires. Not just the campfires per se, but the social, contemplative and transitional space they imbue. I wonder, 'Has this absence sparked my vocational shift to chaplaincy?' I wonder too whether this recognition has been feeding my consideration of chaplaincy as a vocation best modelled as one who tends, fuels or preserves a fire – a fire-tender.

My chaplaincy training contexts have primarily been in healthcare settings: Yale New Haven Hospital (YNHH) in the USA, and the Christie

NHS Foundation Trust, one of the UK's top cancer hospitals and the largest single-site cancer centre in Europe.

The seed for the model emerged as I was completing my first unit of Clinical Pastoral Education (CPE) training at YNHH. The Association for Clinical Pastoral Education (ACPE) is the premier, US Department of Education-recognized organization that provides rigorous accreditation and certification processes for CPE centres and educators (ACPE, 2020). For US Board Certification in Chaplaincy, one must have completed at least four units of CPE in addition to meeting other educational and professional requirements. ACPE is one of three recognized, accredited organizations overseeing CPE training: the National Association of Catholic Chaplains (NACC) or the Canadian Association for Spiritual Care (CASC) are the other two (BCCI, 2023).

In my final evaluation of Level I CPE I was asked: 'What theological image best describes your experience in patient encounters?' I responded: 'Moses, as he removes his sandals, aware that he is standing on holy ground in the presence of God in the burning bush' (Exodus 3.5, my wording). I chose this image because I often experience a sense of the sacred when I am with a patient. As I think of each person being made in the image of God (Genesis 1.27), I see each encounter with another person as an encounter with the sacred. For me, the fire in the burning bush symbolizes the holy or sacredness of the presence of God found in the person made in God's image. I hope I never lose this sense of awe and humble privilege, this sense of sacredness, when entering a patient's room.

Clinical training in CPE contextualizes and expands theological and professional education for spiritual care professionals of any faith. Many CPE cohorts are, thus, multifaith cohorts. I realize now that a model of chaplain as fire-tender might provide helpful language that could have bridged some of the gaps or removed some of the obstacles experienced by my CPE cohort peers with regard to the multifaith context of CPE training. My cohort was comprised of Christian, humanist and Jewish, cis-gendered and non-binary students of various sexual orientations. Two of my peers often expressed tension in our group sessions and in verbatims, where we shared patient encounters as part of the act-reflect-act again clinical model in CPE. When Christians used overly Christian-embedded models to describe their theological reflections and patient encounters, these non-Christian peers felt marginalized by a dominant Christian sub-culture. A model of fire-tender could provide alternative metaphors for the expression of theological reflections and might remove some of the tension unintentionally created in multifaith cohort training.

Spiritual care and models of chaplaincy

Hospital chaplains engage in a wide range of institutional activities. These include promoting and ensuring diversity and inclusiveness in the workplace and in patient care, recognizing and marking religious holidays or institutionally significant events, promoting mental health and well-being among the staff, offering prayer or religious services and serving in medical ethics consultations. These activities contribute to the well-being of the institutional whole, and in this respect could be seen as a type of spiritual care. However, Jacobs identifies the practice of 'spiritual care' as addressing transcendent issues in a patient's life, such as identity, meaning and purpose, which may or may not be expressed in religious or cultural (or spiritual) terms and explains that the chaplain ensures this care in a variety of ways 'by focusing on the emotional and spiritual needs of the patient' (Jacobs, 2008, p. 15).

It is this patient-centred spiritual care that is the focal point of the fire-tender model. Although narrowed from the broader activities of a chaplain to patient-centred spiritual care, it is critical to recognize the underlying breadth of patient-centred, individualized spiritual care. Transcendent issues of identity, meaning and purpose are highly individualized for each patient and, for any given patient, their emotional and spiritual needs may change over time and in different contexts. Therefore, spiritual care is broadly divergent from patient to patient and must be tailored to a patient and their current context.

Lartey (2003, p. 140) states that spirituality 'means different things to different people and is notoriously difficult to encapsulate in a neat and comprehensive definition'. He provides a definition of spirituality that allows for personalization in the sense that it relies on the individual's characteristic style of relating, and that refers to the human capacity for relationship with self, others, the world, God and that which transcends sensory experience (Lartey, 2003, pp. 140–1). I find Lartey's definition helpful because it allows an understanding of 'the spiritual' as that which refers to a relationship with transcendence (Lartey, 2003, pp. 143–5), but also allows individuals to prioritize which relationships are central to them in determining what brings their lives meaning and purpose.

Thus, in order to provide spiritual care, a chaplain needs to discover a patient's needs as well as their desires and self-identified sources of resilience, strength and/or support through spiritual assessment during the chaplain's earliest patient engagements (Erşahin, 2021, pp. 74–6). For some patients these needs may be expressed as religious needs, but spiritual needs may also encompass those without religious contexts or references, as made evident by Jacobs's and Lartey's descriptions (see also Gordon, Ewan and Mitchell, 2011, pp. 57–62, and Todd, 2011, pp. 96–8, for how spiritual and religious care differ and overlap).

Chaplain as fire-tender

I gravitate to the model of fire-tender for the chaplain/spiritual care provider because fire-tender is an image that transcends various cultural milieux without importing specific religious language, while simultaneously holding touch points for various religious images and ideas of the spiritual, sacred, divine or holy. This model and imagery thus uniquely holds space for encounters involving individuals from diverse populations and ideologies within a wide range of situational contexts, not just hospitals but hospices, local or cross-cultural crisis sites, social-public gathering spaces, universities, prisons and so on. Each of these populations will reflect a plurality of ages, faiths, ethnicities, sexual- and gender-identities, personality types, spiritualities and socioeconomical and educational backgrounds found in their underlying population contexts. Just as a shared fire may indiscriminately draw a variety of people to warm themselves, a chaplain/fire-tender should expect to engage and care for individuals from different faiths or no faith, as well as individuals from the chaplain's own faith background, especially in these varied contexts. A fire-tender/chaplain is best situated to offer spiritual care in any individual encounter by laying aside preconceived notions of whom she will be serving, and by leaning in with curiosity and, hopefully, a sense of anticipation of the sacred.

Campfires

Although some literature suggests that fireside chats were for those of one's own group, history and literature are also filled with examples where fires draw strangers together. Peter warmed himself at a fire where he was mostly unfamiliar to those who shared the same fire (John 18.18, 25–26). Storytelling bards would often engage in the fireside gatherings of others to share tales and songs of imagined and distant places. Druids and pagans were drawn to fires of religious significance set by Patrick in the early days of Christianity in Ireland. From personal experience, during three weeks of camping in Czechoslovakia when it was a single country, my teammates and I made many friends around campfires. Even when a common language was not easily shared, bonds of friendship formed. And when common language is shared, stories exploring adventure, culture, history, meaning and beliefs flow easily from one person to another.

A characteristic of campfires is that they have for all of human history, and likely pre-history, served as gathering places for relaxed companionship, social bonding and storytelling (Boyd, 2018, pp. 4, 10; Dunbar and Gowlett, 2014, p. 277; Dunbar, 2014, p. 14013; Lauer, 2021, p. 5; Dana Lynn, 2014, pp. 983–4; Turnbull, 2015, p. 43; Wiessner, 2014, p. 14029), and as transitional spaces that facilitate and allow expanding self-reflection, deepening comprehension of others' thoughts and emotions, and igniting one's imagination (Wiessner, 2014, pp. 14027, 14032–3). Through shared stories and social interactions, fireside chats expanded and helped deepen individuals' senses of self, others, meaning and identity and imaginations of new stories. Additionally, Wiessner (2014, p. 14029) describes how on evenings gathered around the fire: 'Efforts by everybody present contributed to healing the sick, closing social rifts, and restoring spiritual cohesion.'

Keeping and tending

A good, a really good, or even great campfire doesn't just happen or spring into existence. Someone gathers the wood, creates the environment and structure for the fire, and brings the spark that sets the fire burning. The very possession of fire entails responsibilities as to care and preservation; one needs a predetermined, well-considered plan to keep (or tend) the fire (Hough, 1926, p. 8). These activities implicitly signify the importance of a fire-keeper or a fire-tender. The fire-tender knows when a fire is ready for more wood; they know too much wood, provided too early or too late, or improperly placed (context), may extinguish the fire. They know fires need space and air to breathe and burn. Hough describes many aspects of tending a fire, including the importance of air, draught, burning coals and fuel. In creating or inducing draught (air-flow) necessary for a fire's continued burning, Hough (1926, pp. 22–3) describes the attention to design provided by a fire-tender, including piling stones or raising a fire above a base level or, in fires where draught was less important, the need for blowing or fanning a flame. A well-seasoned fire-tender knows that a variety of fuels may sustain a fire, including wood, coal, peat, dung, bones, fish, birds and fat (Hough, 1926, pp. 53–8).

In this model, the fireside represents a space for gathering that is the chaplain–patient spiritual care encounter. The characteristics of fireside gatherings noted above parallel activities identified as critical for spiritual (pastoral) supportive care where the chaplain/spiritual care provider comes alongside a patient whose narratives of meaning and purpose have been interrupted by illness or health-related crisis. The fireside symbolizes the place where the chaplain attends to the patient, and through well-timed actions, such as empathic listening, paced-offering of questions, or comments and non-verbal signalling, helps the patient identify relationships of meaning that are central to their spiritual well-being. The chaplain offers a safe presence and holds space where patients can relax and share their stories, engage in self-reflection, grow in understanding of their thoughts and others' thoughts and emotions in light of the current challenge, and perhaps even engage imaginatively with new ways of being in relationship.

The fire represents the sacred, holy or transcendent, which encompasses the sacredness of the patient (as one made in the image of God) and the patient's self-identified spirituality. These skills of tending a fire are metaphorical representatives of the skills the chaplain possesses and utilizes in spiritual care, identifying and supporting the patient in their self-identified spiritual and emotional needs. The chaplain tends the fire by understanding what is most important to the patient in bringing meaning, purpose and transcendent significance to their life. The chaplain determines this through spiritual assessment, direct inquiry, empathetic listening, verbal and non-verbal communication skills, theological reflection and professional discernment, and offers the patient what is most likely to help them (re)connect with what is of greatest spiritual significance to them in their specific context. The questions, comments and communications are like the wood or fuel for the fire, and the attentive listening and space held for the other's story to emerge is like the air the fire needs to breathe.

Some patient encounters reveal stories that have major plot disruptions. Illnesses or prognoses have changed patients' abilities to function in particular roles or capacities central to their identities and/or relationships with themselves or others; or diseases challenge the narrative and meaning or purpose of their lives. Patients find the stories they have told up to this point no longer make sense or the roles they have played are no longer possible to play without major changes to the plot or script. Providing a place where they can begin to tell stories and imagine new scenarios can help relieve felt tension and can even create new imagined roles and narratives of meaning. Telling such stories and listening to the stories being told can help the teller incorporate plot twists into new stories that bring a renewed sense of meaning or purpose or resolve identities and roles within the narrative arch.

The role of the chaplain as fire-tender may also encompass religious rituals such as prayer or offering a blessing when such rituals are significant to a patient in making sense of, or restoring meaning to, her life's narrative when challenged or disrupted by illness, injury or a health crisis. The role may involve inviting another fire-tender to tend the fire for the patient, especially in such instances where the patient desires a specific religious or spiritual ritual that is from a different religion or faith practice than that of the chaplain.

Fire-tending and theological reflection

In instances where the patient's spiritual need is presented within the Christian tradition, or in instances where the patient identifies a desire for a Christian response, I have found that sharing from my own experiences of God's love and grace, or from my own theological reflections, often offers the patient a new way of considering or contextualizing their current challenge into a narrative of hope or meaning. In other words, in order to tend the fire, one may be called upon as a storyteller who can contextualize life's trials into the sacred story of God's love. As the fire-tender listens, she must also draw from a contemplative quality formed by personal experience, theological reflection and holy encounter. The experience of the sacred and theological formation is what sets the chaplain apart as a spiritual care provider from other professions of attentive listeners, such as counsellors or social workers (Newitt, 2011, pp. 106–7). In any faith context, and especially in a Christian one, the chaplain benefits from life-long contemplation of the Scripture-story and how it bears on spiritual formation or how the sacred stories of one's faith can help a patient make sense of meaning in his/her own life narrative.

This process is a type of narrative theology, rendering a Scripture-based response fostered by theological reflective practice of maintaining internal narratives in one's own faith tradition. This approach is not so much a canonical narrative theology, fitting the patient's story to scriptural accounts of the life of Jesus (Walton, 2014, p. 164), nor is it a strictly constructive narrative theology, where the patient is constructing their own story as an agent of narrative (Walton, 2014, pp. 165–6). What I have found personally helpful, and am suggesting, is a third type of narrative theology that looks to the scriptures to discover ways that others' lives and stories may parallel our own struggles and trials. As we see God in the scriptures, active in the lives of others, as their stories and struggles mirror our own lives, we can begin to imagine that God is active in our lives as God was in theirs. In this imagining, we may find renewed hope and renewed understanding of transcendence, meaning and purpose. The stories of others may help us find renewed relationship within our own stories. This third type of narrative theology helps us find meaning in our stories and tell our stories in the light of the Christian narrative, by bringing all biblical stories, and even biographical stories of historical Christians and the whole story of creation and salvation history, together as resources for asking, considering, and growing in understandings of how God may be present and active, even in our lives' most challenging crises. In finding meaning and purpose, Christians have the lives of Paul, Job and Thomas – and many others besides Jesus – to draw on for asking and discovering how God may be present in our own trials.

Munson (2022, p. 9) discusses the relationship of the sacredness of the stories of people and the stories of Scripture and similarly recognizes that the stories of Scripture inform us of God in relationship with us. He makes an important observation, stating: 'In theological reflection, one does not challenge the story (as in the events that occur). Rather one is challenging the story as interpreted through the lenses of culture and commentary, and challenging the storyteller' (Munson, 2022, pp. 9–10). He goes on to say: 'The sacred stories of our experiences should have their interpretations challenged by the sacred stories of scripture. The sacred stories of scripture should likewise have their interpretations challenged by the sacred stories of our experiences' (Munson, 2022, p. 11). Through attentive listening and theological reflection, the chaplain helps tend the sacred fires within patients by helping them discover new ways of considering current trials in light of God's story and character and by re-storying their life narratives. Through this fire-tending, patients receive critical spiritual support that contributes to their health and well-being, thus fulfilling the institutional expectation for patient-centred spiritual care.

Sacred fires

Others have done considerable work in describing how various cultures or religious sects, such as the Vedic, Parsees (Zoroastrians), Yezidis, Magi, Hopi Indians and even Pagans have found fire symbolic and integral to sacred belief and religious practice (Hough, 1926, pp. 130–1; Jayaram V, n.d., online; Fox, 2009; Beyer, 2018). In this next section, I offer a few reflections on Hough's findings, and provide additional source material, as I expand the idea of the link between fire and the sacred and the role of a fire-tender.

Hough (1926, p. 128) explains that although commonly called fire-worshippers, the Parsee specifically disclaim the worship of fire and affirm that, 'Fire is only the symbol of God, whom alone they worship' (Avery, cited in Hough, 1926, pp. 128–9). In the Pentateuch, God manifested God's self in a pillar of fire (Exodus 13.21) in addition to the burning bush cited earlier. In early Christian texts, Jesus' baptism of his followers is described as a baptism of the Holy Spirit and fire (Matthew 3.11; Luke 3.16) and the outpouring of the Holy Spirit at Pentecost, referred to as the birth of the Church, came with power and tongues of flame manifested on those receiving the Spirit of God (Acts 2.1–4). In many meditative and religious traditions, lighting of candles signifies the presence of God and/or the holy, thus indicating the enduring character of fire as a strong symbol of sacred space and holy presence.

Hough (1926, p. 142) also points to how the continuity of fire was also associated with the continuity of life, suggesting this was the result of an association of life and fire with warmth. Others have made this association through the concepts of a divine spark or light within each person (Parr, 2012, p. 4). In addition to an association with life itself, fire has been associated with healing properties (Hough, 1926, pp. ix, 81, 127, 136, 174; Dana Lynn, 2014, p. 984), and in the Christian tradition, directly associated with the Holy Spirit (Matthew 3.11; Luke 3.16; Acts 2.3; Joseph, 2023, online).

As I enter patients' rooms, I am curious as to what condition and kind of fire I will find. Will the sacred fire be a divine spark aflame? Or a smouldering wick? Perhaps glowing embers? Will the patient be aware of the fire within? How will they understand the fire, the source, the spark within? Will I find the fire, as the presence of God, the sacred and the holy, burning steadily? Will it be recognized or unrecognized by the patient? How might I tend the fire I find? Or will I merely draw near to its warmth and listen to the stories about to unfold into the transitional space of encounter? Will I need to stoke the fire, fan an ember or move a few logs to allow a draught to form? Will I, like Moses, know a desire to remove my shoes in the presence of the holy?

Reflections on tending

I've noticed in my years of building and tending many actual fires that sometimes others create a significant effect when they stoke or poke a fire without much knowledge of how a fire breathes or burns. Sometimes others know the fire needs air. They will try to increase the fire's burn rate by breathing on it, often eliciting a flame, but also often giving up after a flicker of flame dies back down. They don't realize that persistence will often set up the draught required to sustain a stronger burn rate. Sometimes they may intervene, closing gaps that were needed to allow air to find its way through, quenching aspects of the fire. The fire, in other words, may suffer from mismanagement; it may be inadvertently disrupted and need tending a little more carefully to recover. Similarly, I have seen other chaplains do just these sorts of things in patient visits. Impossible to tell what their motivations may be, they have intervened with a question or comment of little previous relevance, filling the quietness of a gap that could have provided the patient space and time to continue down a thoughtful process of story formation. Or they bring premature closure of a topic or a visit. These activities can be addressed in debriefs among the chaplain team. I have seen how just such attention to how we tend to a patient can lead to changes being implemented in subsequent visits. A patient is given more time for responses; interactions or the pace of liturgy and patient engagement is slowed; and, in lingering, smouldering fires have been tended back to healthy flames.

Other patient encounters, such as those with non-verbal or unconscious patients, perhaps near the end of life, may leave the chaplain doing the bulk of the reflection, internally, within their own theological context and narrative arc. Like sitting alone at the edge of the fire, ruminating on the stories we've known for ages, ones we've just heard or ones we've told ourselves, the fire and embers provide a rich focal point for quiet reflection. In the quiet, a chaplain can often hear the voice of God, or her own heart, speak into the evolving narrative of her own life's story.

A fire-tender model invites not just the chaplain but each of us to a new way of thinking about the presence of the God or the holy in the lives of others. Each person is aflame by the presence of God's Spirit within them. The Spirit is breath and life, and it is in God that each of God's image-bearers live and move and have their being. All of us are created in the image of God, yet it seems that not all of us are yet aware of God's presence or acts; because, as Jesus described to Nicodemus, some have yet to be born again of the Spirit. They have yet to come to an awareness of, let alone a surrender to, the Spirit of God that gives them life. If we understand that God alone enlightens each life and God alone brings spiritual rebirth, then we can focus on tending the fire and on not quenching a smouldering wick. At the end of life, we do not bear the burden to light the fire or to keep it going when the embers are dying because there is no more wood to sustain its burning; only God lights the fire and ultimately sustains it. Each human encounter holds an invitation to consider and acknowledge the presence of the holy, and to approach with humility and curiosity. We come as to a bush aflame with the fire of God and we acknowledge the sacred space as we wait, watch and listen. We look for the presence of God or the sacred in all things and encourage others to do the same.

Ryan (2018, p. 80) argues that good chaplaincy models feature personalism: an attitude that speaks to humanity's innate need for relationships, both between individuals and between individuals and God. In keeping with Ryan's assessment, I suggest that the fire-tender model features Ryan's personalism. It speaks to the need for relationships with one another in the relaxed companionship, social bonding and storytelling around the fire. With regard to the individual's relationship with the transcendent, a model of fire-tender allows greater adaptability to patient-directed identification of the source of the spiritually significant in their own lives, whether identified as God, or the sacred, or relational sources of transcendent meaning. In this sense, as the religious and social landscapes continue to evolve in the UK and the USA and as public awareness tends towards acknowledging the increasing numbers of those from minority faiths and no faith (Ryan, 2018, p. 81), the fire-tender model allows a theologically robust sense of the presence of the spiritual and tending of the sacred in relationships between the fire-tender and patient and between the patient and the sacred. Thus, the fire-tender model is a bilingual model (Ryan, 2018, p. 93), speaking the language of both secular (or not overtly religious) and faith needs of those involved.

Furthermore, a fire-tending model carries no overtly religious language or negative connotations for those of faiths (or no-faith) that differ from the predominantly Christian historical roots of chaplaincy in the UK and the USA. Yet a Christian will recognize the association of fire with the holy or sacred (God and the Holy Spirit), and the imagery will provide new ways of expanding thought and engagement from within a Christian tradition to those of the same or different faiths. In this sense, a fire-tending model for chaplaincy is not just particularly suited to a change in context from traditional settings, such as prisons and in the armed forces, into ever broader spaces (Ryan, 2018, pp. 81–2), but to changes within the evolving religious and social landscapes and the wide array of individual, personal spiritual identifiers. This adaptive model provides the chaplain with theologically rich metaphors for grounding her vocation even in a rapidly evolving environment. It also provides a malleable framework for accommodating other's experiences and perspectives. As ACPE (2020) implements the revised CPE outcomes and indicators from 2023, a model of fire-tender could provide a bridging framework for accommodating and communicating differences in a chaplain's and patients' narrative histories, spiritual-based orientating systems or other Category A–E revisions. The fire-tender model allows recognition of the essentially relational nature of humanity, the need for intercultural and interreligious humility and the role of chaplains in creating, tending and sustaining transitional or transformational space (ACPE, 2020; Ryan, 2018, p. 98; Gerkin, 1984, p. 137).

As I approach a new CPE residency cohort, educator and one-on-one supervision sessions, perhaps this adaptive, multifaith model can invite me to note the fire that burns in my own soul. Perhaps this model can help me sustain an image of a warming, fire-lit space where my sense of the sacred can be fanned into flame and kept burning as I look to the spiritual care of my own soul in the midst of caring for others. Perhaps I can foster and experience transformational spaces internally and externally and pray with St Catherine of Siena (Catherine of Siena, 1983, p. 104):

In your nature,
eternal Godhead.
I shall come to know my nature.
And what is my nature, boundless love?
It is fire,
because you are nothing but a fire of love.
And you have given humankind
a share in this nature,
for by the fire of love
you created us.
And so with all other people
and every created thing:
you made them out of love.

Bibliography

ACPE (2020), '2020 Accreditation Manual', available at https://www.manula.com/manuals/acpe/acpe-manuals/2016/en/topic/acpe-outcomes-and-indicators (accessed 7.07.2024).
BCCI (2023), 'Qualifications for Board Certified & Associate Certified Chaplains', Board of Chaplaincy Certification, Incorporated, available at https://www.apchaplains.org/bcci-site/becoming-certified/common-qualifications-and-competencies/ (accessed 7.07.2024).
Beyer, C. (2018), 'Purity and Fire in Zoroastrianism', available at https://www.learnreligions.com/purity-and-fire-in-zoroastrianism-95754 (accessed 7.07.2024).
Boyd, B. (2018), 'The Evolution of Stories: From Mimesis to Language, from Fact to Fiction', *Wiley Interdisciplinary Reviews: Cognitive Science* 9(1), e1444 (16 pages).
Catherine of Siena, St (1983), *The Prayers of Catherine of Siena*, Suzanne Nottke, OP (ed), New York: Paulist Press, available at https://archive.org/details/prayersofcatherioooocath/page/231/mode/1up?q=suzanne (accessed 7.07.2024).
Dana Lynn, C. (2014), 'Hearth and Campfire Influences on Arterial Blood Pressure: Defraying the Costs of the Social Brain through Fireside Relaxation', *Evolutionary Psychology* 12(5), pp. 983–1003.
Dunbar, R. I. (2014), 'How Conversations around Campfires Came to Be', *Proceedings of the National Academy of Sciences* 111(39), pp. 14013–14.
Dunbar, R. I. and J. A. Gowlett (2014), 'Fireside Chat: The Impact of Fire on Hominin Socioecology', in R. I. Dunbar, C. Gamble and J. A. Gowlett (eds), *Lucy to Language: The Benchmark Papers*, Oxford: Oxford University Press, pp. 277–96.
Erşahin, Z. (2021), 'Care, Spiritual Care, and Modern Health Care: Developments, Concepts, and Debates', in H. Weiss et al. (eds), *Care, Healing, and, Human Well-being within Interreligious Discourses*, South Africa: African Sun Media, pp. 66–84.
Fox, S. (2009), 'Solstice Fires of the Pagan Spirit Gathering', available at https://www.circlesanctuary.org/Solstice-Fires-of-the-Pagan-Spirit-Gathering (accessed 7.07.2024).

Gerkin, C. V. (1984), *The Living Human Document: Re-visioning Pastoral Counseling in a Hermeneutical Mode*, Nashville, TN: Abingdon Press.
Gordon T., K. Ewan and D. Mitchell (2011), *Spiritual Care for Healthcare Professionals: Reflecting on Clinical Practice*, Boca Raton, FL: CRC Press, pp. 57–69.
Hough, W. (1926), *Fire as an Agent in Human Culture*, Smithsonian Institution Bulletin 139, US Government Printing Office.
Jacobs, M. R. (2008), 'What Are We Doing Here? Chaplains in Contemporary Health Care', *The Hastings Center Report* 38(6), pp. 15–18.
Jayaram V. (2000–2019), 'Hinduism and Zoroastrianism: A Comparison', available at https://www.hinduwebsite.com/hinduism/h_zoroa.asp (accessed 7.07.2024).
Joseph, D. I. (2023), 'The Methodist Symbol: 5 Interesting Facts', available at https://christianityfaq.com/methodist-symbol/ (accessed 7.07.2024).
Lartey, E. Y. (2003), *In Living Color: An Intercultural Approach to Pastoral Care and Counseling*, London: Jessica Kingsley Publishers, pp. 140–52.
Lauer, G. (2021), 'Language, Childhood, and Fire: How we Learned to Love Sharing Stories', *Frontiers in Psychology* 12, pp. 1–8.
Munson, C. (2019), 'Models of Chaplaincy. Bukal Life Care' [slide deck], available at https://www.slideshare.net/CeliaMunson/models-of-chaplaincy (accessed 7.07.2024).
Munson, R. H. (2022), 'Theological Reflection through Storying in the Orality and Clinical Pastoral Training Movements', *Bukal Life Journal*, pp. 27–42, available at https://bukallifecare.org/resource-materials/ (accessed 7.07.2024).
Newitt, M. (2011), 'The Role and Skills of a Chaplain', in M. Threlfall-Holmes and M. Newitt (eds), *Being a Chaplain*, London: SPCK, pp. 103–15.
Parr, P. (2012), *Answering That of God: Discovering Spirit Within*, London: The Kindlers.
Ryan, B. (2018), 'Theology and Models of Chaplaincy', in J. Caperon, A. Todd and J. Walters (eds), *A Christian Theology of Chaplaincy*, London: Jessica Kingsley Publishers, pp. 79–100.
SCImago Institutions Rankings, 2023, available at https://www.scimagoir.com/rankings.php?sector=Health&country=GBR&area=2730 (accessed 7.07.2024).
The Christie NHS Foundation Trust, 'A Profile of The Christie' (n.d.), available at https://www.christie.nhs.uk/about-us/about-the-christie/a-profile-of-the-christie (accessed 7.07.2024).
Thompson, J. N. (2023), 'Jesus in the Room', *Fuller Magazine* 19, available at https://fullerstudio.fuller.edu/story/jesus-in-the-room/, originally published 3 February 2021 (accessed 7.07.2024).
Threlfall-Holmes, M. (2011), 'Exploring Models of Chaplaincy', in M Threlfall-Holmes and M. Newitt (eds), *Being a Chaplain*, London: SPCK, pp. 116–26.
Todd, A. (2011), 'Responding to Diversity: Chaplaincy in a Multi-faith Context', in M. Threlfall-Holmes and M. Newitt (eds), *Being a Chaplain*, London: SPCK, pp. 89–102.
Turnbull, D. (2015), 'Connections, Collaborations, Knowledges and Kin', *Arena Magazine (Fitzroy, Vic)* 139, pp. 42–4.
Walton, H. (2014), *Writing Methods in Theological Reflection*, London: SCM Press.
Wiessner, P. W. (2014), 'Embers of Society: Firelight Talk among the Ju/'hoansi Bushmen', *Proceedings of the National Academy of Sciences* 111(39), pp. 14027–35.

17

A Personal Reflection on Chaplaincy for Older People in Botswana and Scotland

OARABILE MOLAODI

One thing that makes me value pastoral and spiritual care support from a chaplain is my own experience of having to offer care to my father, who had dementia. This experience left me with a desire to always be present for those who are caring for their loved ones and empathetically listen to them, supporting them accordingly and offering prayer when needed.

In my own work, I have observed how family members really valued a chaplain's presence, and the confidence that they had to share freely what was bothering them, knowing that they would be listened to and supported. My chaplaincy experience has been with Methodist Homes (MHA), a large charity that provides care, including in residential homes, for older people, working in one of their care homes in Scotland. I am also the lead for care-home ministry in my local church and I get to visit several care homes with the team. This has caused me to reflect on how care is offered back in my home country of Botswana.

The context in Botswana

In Botswana older people are respected and recognized by society as a whole because of their age, knowledge and experience, and they are looked upon as father or mother figures. Hence at times you would find that someone would address an older person as Mum or Dad, not because they are their biological parent or related to them, but as a way of showing respect. Deferring to the older person and consulting them for advice is taken as a great sign of showing respect. To an older person, it is important for the cultural beliefs and practices to be respected, adhered to, protected and passed on to the next generation. Hence it is the role of the older people in the family or community to make sure that this happens. Therefore, you would find that even when an older person is restricted in their ability to do things, or is less mobile, if they are cognitively doing well they would still be consulted in matters that concern family or the community they live in, regardless of their age. Examples of this include resolving conflicts and planning and conducting funerals and weddings to make sure that cultural procedures are followed and traditions are kept. Not consulting an older person or taking their advice could result in breaking relationships that are considered crucial for the family and community to maintain. Older people are given special treatment in various ways as a sign of respect. They are given priority in seating, for example, and it is customary to wait for them to be seated before younger ones can take a seat. It is a must to greet the older person and say it in a certain way and action – for example, good morning/evening, Sir/Madam, while bending your body or kneeling down. Although the younger ones are expected to give respect to the older people, it is expected that the older ones should set an example for them. There is a saying in Setswana (Botswana's language) – *Susu ilela suswane gore suswane a go ilele*, which means that the older one must respect the younger one so that the younger ones can learn and give back to them the respect.

In general, in Botswana older people are cared for by their relatives either in their own home or in the home of their caregiver. The traditional belief is that parents have children so that the children can take care of their parents when old, hence caregiving is normally provided by their children. In situations where an older person has no children, one of the extended family members would help to provide caregiving for the older person. They get visits from extended family members and lack of visits can be offensive to the older person. In cases where the caregiver has to go for work during the day or is not able to be with their parent, they would look for a paid helper to assist the older person when they are away. There are particular customs regarding who should do certain caregiving activities; for example, intimate care – such as bathing the older person – can only be provided by a family member. The paid helper can only assist with general help such as cleaning and cooking. For those people who are very unwell, they get home visits from the community health nurses or community-based care teams.

Spiritual care of the older people in Botswana and in the UK

Botswana's population is predominantly Christian. The census of 2011 stated that 1,171,537 people (79 per cent of the population) were reported to be Christians, and 225,416 people (15 per cent of the population) had no religion (Statistics Botswana, 2015). Hence people are generally open to religious activities like prayer when offered, even when they not practising Christians. For most older people their faith is an important part of their lives that they highly value, and when they can no longer manage to go to church, in most cases the church minister visits to offer prayer, encouragement and administer communion in their homes. Other church members also tend to visit, and some families hold family prayers before bedtime and at times singing and reading of scriptures will be included, hence the older person can benefit from this.

In the UK census of 2011, 54 per cent of people in Scotland reported to be Christian compared to 65 per cent in 2001, and 37 per cent had no religion (The Scottish Public Health Observatory, 2023, online), so it seems that the UK population in general is moving away from religion to being more secular (Voas and Bruce, 2019, p. 30). When I started doing singing and worship services in the local care homes with my church, one thing that surprised me was that the residents who used to go to church had very limited or no access to religious activities. In most cases, those of the Catholic faith will get a visit from the priest to offer prayer and sacraments, but for people of other denominations this is very rare. Some residents say they would value visits from their own church friends and church minister, and one told me how she is struggling to get her own church minister to visit her.

Talking with activity coordinators in various care homes, they expressed how hard it is for them to get local churches to come in and provide worship services for the residents or visit those of their faith tradition. This surprised me because I thought it is an opportunity that church would easily take up, based on my Botswana experience. On the other hand, speaking with some churches, there is an assumption that because of the way Christianity is viewed in society, the care homes would not allow churches to come in. Also, the lack of response from the church may be due to the fear and lack of knowledge on how to support people with dementia, which I can sense at times when I try to encourage people to take part in the care-home ministry. This calls for education and training of the local churches on how to provide spiritual support for those with dementia. In the UK there are several organizations promoting spiritual and pastoral support of older people and offering training courses to the churches to support those in their churches and those in the care homes (Faith in Later Life, n.d., online). For example, MHA offers a training course to the churches on how to do worship in church and care homes for those living with dementia, and Anna Chaplaincy works with churches to train chaplains to offer spiritual support to older people. Furthermore, there are other organizations focusing on equipping the churches to be 'Dementia-friendly churches'. Although there seems to be a lot of information on the support and training offered to the church by several organizations, many churches do not seem to be engaging in this kind of training.

Most care homes are privately owned and do not employ chaplains, and this makes me wonder why, if they are providing spiritual care as required, they are neglecting the religious area, which forms part of spiritual care for those who need it. I think the care homes are failing the older people by not respecting them in matters like this. Also, I observed that loneliness is a big thing for most older people in care homes, because although the staff are around, they are mainly providing care duties and do not have time to sit and chat with residents. Their families come in to visit but for some I have observed that their families live far from them, maybe abroad, and they do not get those family visits often. Where there is a chaplain providing one-on-one pastoral care the residents appreciate it. It is always touching when, after having a conversation with the residents, they ask me when I will come back.

A chaplain can be a prophetic voice and speak about the need to value older people more than we do in the UK generally. One of MHA's charitable activities is in advocating and lobbying for older people by influencing policy, having, for example, an Older People's Commissioner who will act as an advocate for older people (MHA, 2022, online).

Providing opportunities for residents in care homes in the UK to worship can strengthen their faith and help them remember 'the sustaining presence of God' (Norris, 2013, p. 208). For example, one resident told me how grateful she was that she is now in a care home where she has the opportunity to have a worship service and express her faith. She said that after her husband passed away she was unable to attend the parish church because of her ill-health, and she felt all alone. This is supported and confirmed by Albans, who states that for some older people:

> the experience of entering in a care home or a retirement living facility can enable them to reconnect with a worshipping community … That alone can be enough to reawaken an important aspect of their personality and provide something that has been missing while frailty and isolation at home have prevented them attending the local church and cut them off from a vital part of the way of making sense of who they are. (Albans, 2013, p. 23)

Conclusion

Older people in Botswana are afforded much respect by the family and in society as a whole, and as a result it is a priority for their families to provide caregiving for them in the home. Hence they get to live in familiar environments, they are not cut off from family life and community and can still participate and influence decision-making by giving advice and imparting wisdom to the younger generation. They receive spiritual support from their local church by getting regular visits from their church minister, and church members' visits also play a role in helping them maintain their faith. In some families, older people benefit from prayers held by families in their homes before bedtime. Living with family and getting support from family and church helps lessen isolation and loneliness and the impact these have on health.

Care for older people is very different in the UK in the area of spiritual care, and this may be because of the way the prevailing culture views both older people and religion in general, but the situation needs to be addressed and improved. As in the NHS, it would be of great benefit for all care homes to have a chaplain, employed and/or voluntary, to provide spiritual care for older people. Another source of spiritual care for older people is the church, but in most churches the focus is on the children, youth and families while overlooking older people's needs and not giving them respect in matters related to their faith. Churches should have strategies for ministering to older people, as argued by Pinson, Register and Roberts-Lewis (2010, p. 191): 'Ensuring the dignity and worth of older people … must be a theological mandate of the ministries of local congregations.' A regular visit to care homes (and those housebound) by the local church and church members to offer worship service, prayer and one-to-one chats can help older people remain connected to the fellowship and strengthen their faith, give hope and lessen the feelings of loneliness and isolation. To try to address lack of confidence by the church on ministering to those with dementia, organizations that offer spiritual and pastoral care training may have to take a more targeted approach – for example, by speaking directly with the churches and sending them information on training courses and educational materials. This could increase awareness of the needs of older people, and of the training that is available which could empower the church to provide spiritual care to older people and help them to live their later life well.

Bibliography

Albans, K. (2013), 'Supporting and Learning from the Oldest Old: The Spiritual Journey of Ageing', in K. Albans and M. Johnson (eds), *God, Me and Being Very Old: Stories and Spirituality in Later Life*, London: SCM Press, pp. 20–36.
Faith in Later Life (n.d.), 'Reaching Out to Care Homes', available at https://faithinlaterlife.org/reaching-out-to-care-homes/ (accessed 7.07.2024).
MHA (2022), 'Policy & Influencing', available at https://www.mha.org.uk/get-involved/policy-influencing/ (accessed 7.07.2024).
Norris, A. (2013), 'Chaplaincy among Older People: A Model for the Church's Ministry and Mission', in K. Albans and M. Johnson (eds), *God, Me and Being Very Old: Stories and Spirituality in Later Life*, London: SCM Press, pp. 200–13.

Pinson, M. S., K. Register and A. Roberts-Lewis (2010), 'Aging, Memory Loss, Dementia, and Alzheimer's Disease: The Role of Christian Social Workers and the Church', *Journal of the North American Association of Christians in Social Work* 37(2), pp. 188–203.

Scottish Public Health Observatory (2023), 'Religion, Spirituality and Belief: Demographics', available at https://www.scotpho.org.uk/population-groups/religion-spirituality-and-belief/data/demographics/ (accessed 7.07.2024).

Statistics Botswana (2015), 'Population & Housing Census 2011: National Statistical Tables 2015', Gaborone: Statistics Botswana, available at https://www.statsbots.org.bw/sites/default/files/publications/national_statisticsreport.pdf (accessed 7.07.2024).

Voas, D. and S. Bruce (2019), 'Religion: Identity, Behaviour and Belief Over Two Decades', in J. Curtice et al. (eds), *British Social Attitudes: The 36th Report*, London: National Centre for Social Research, pp. 17–38.

18

Retail Chaplaincy and a 'Ministry of Encounter'

DEBORAH DALBY

As part of my curacy (ministerial training), I experienced the joy and tension of being part of the formational team for a new expression of town centre chaplaincy. We charted a path through myriad practical and theological issues to arrive at a model best described as 'Ministry of Encounter'. It could have saved time in the short term to have adopted an 'off the shelf' model of chaplaincy but I believe this would have inevitably caused a loss of unique contextual identity and value.

The Sanctuary chaplaincy began in an indoor shopping centre in Runcorn, Greater Merseyside, in the north-west of England, during the first national lockdown of the Covid-19 pandemic. This started with my colleague Tim, a borough-wide pioneer Methodist minister, who initiated a 'walking ministry' to become acquainted with local retailers and hospitality spaces. He was intentionally open to conversation and prayer requests as a visible, 'collared' ordained minister. When all but essential shops closed, he started to make weekly pastoral enquiries of all staff in the centre – retail, cleaning, security and centre management.

The centre management team saw the value of his visits for those working in difficult circumstances and proposed a partnership, using a vacant retail unit as a base. Donated furniture and equipment were sourced and a small amount of city region funding was secured to assist with the set-up.

The shopping centre is in an area of high economic and social disadvantage. An innovative space at inception in the early 1970s, this concrete structure very quickly became tired and a little uninviting, and many retail units were left vacant. The relatively new centre management and statutory development teams were committed to making the space more appealing and recognized the need for a focal point or sense of identity. As part of their partnership to reinvigorate the centre and bring 'new life' to the space, the idea of a physical chaplaincy was embraced. The basis of Christian faith for this approach was implicitly accepted and, on reflection, it would seem that lack of challenge came from a twofold stance of understanding the local context. First, the community was overwhelmingly Christian in heritage if not in practice and, second, the centre was designed to mimic a traditional town centre and there had been an omission of any kind of spiritual presence that a traditional church or chapel may have provided to a townscape. We may have been fulfilling that need for a 'Church in the Town Square' as a familiar and comforting presence even if most passers-by never actually crossed the threshold!

At the time I was based in a local Anglican parish and joined Tim as co-lead chaplain to offer two in-person drop-in sessions each week. We also undertook 'walkabouts' to ask how people felt and if they were coping with the restrictions. Hospitality was offered, with refreshments provided by the centre team to retail workers and facilities staff. We spent time in the mostly deserted centre, handing out drinks and talking to those we found in the remaining shops.

We genuinely did not have a sense at this time of who we were and what we wanted to do other than 'be a Christian presence'. The expansion of chaplaincies into almost all aspects of contemporary life has provided a tremendously rich field for analysis and advancement but it has also created manifold complexities and tensions in practice. The great diversity in the outworking of chaplaincy has created multiple stakeholders and participants in most contexts – not only in the UK but worldwide (Ryan, 2015). This rich but complicated field caused us as much confusion as it created focus for our fledgeling chaplaincy while trying to find role models or examples to learn from or to emulate.

Tim was aware of the Chaplaincy Everywhere course (Methodist Church, n.d., online), which he felt would acquaint us with scriptural, traditional, historic and contextual models of chaplaincy of place and sector. At this time a small number of prospective non-ordained volunteers were recruited from a local ecumenical partnership, including Free Charismatic Church members, Methodist, United Reformed Church and Roman Catholic colleagues. All 12 participants agreed to attend the course online, which took place over 12 weeks of heightened Covid restrictions. Sessions were taken at a very gentle pace to enable discussion and discernment.

This garnering of ideas gave shape to the eventual establishment of the Sanctuary. Straight away we took an ecumenical approach with no 'lead' theological stance or organizational influence. It was quite challenging at this stage as a few among our number had come forward with the hope of overt evangelism and proselytizing. The local ecumenical partnership had historically been dominated by conservative evangelical leaders, a tradition not shared by wider congregations or the community. There was an existing tension in this dynamic as 'Catholic' (Anglican and Roman Catholic) colleagues had withdrawn from the partnership as a result of feeling ignored or overpowered. It was, therefore, valuable to spend extra time undertaking initial discussion with the team, guided by training, to find common ground.

It was also important to build equitable relationships with our partners – the centre team and local council colleagues. Through our initial conversations, when exploring funding and support, they had explicitly requested we avoid an evangelical stance. We all recognized that our chaplaincy had unapologetically arisen from Christian foundations, but the offering was to people of all faiths and none, through hospitality of space, listening, pastoral care and through conversations – answering questions of faith and spirituality.

I now realize how fundamental this issue was and is to the ongoing development of the chaplaincy. There was a quiet tension between ecumenical partners pulling in one direction, requiring explicit evangelism of proclamation, and statutory and private-sector partners pulling in the opposite direction – wanting our 'Christianness' to be as gentle and unspoken as possible. Tim and I were very clear that our foundation was our faith, which could not be watered down, but our primary role in this context was focus upon those we encountered – their needs came first. We were as much to be shaped by them as they by us. This pivotal issue of 'managing' evangelism has subsequently moulded the unique and embodied expression of the Sanctuary's ministry of encounter.

Initial discussion established an outward-facing ethos rather than feeding into any specific congregation or connecting with a town-wide imperative for church growth, an intentionality captured by Scadron as being 'not a platform for recruitment to fill empty pews ... [but] as a ministry of presence, Christ is demonstrated in our actions more so than public evangelism' (Scadron, 2021, p. 32).

One strength of the Sanctuary utilizing the Chaplaincy Everywhere approach was to make scriptural reference and discussion a mainstay of discernment that was acceptable to all, regardless of tradition. A concentration on Genesis in Session One enabled consideration of the essential mission of God for creation to be in relationship, in mutual care and people of faith called to be transformed by connection and reconnection (Genesis 1.1–5, 26–31; 12.1–4). We did not dwell excessively upon contentious theological and traditional disparities. Other specific texts spoke of meeting people where they are and tuning into their needs, listening to their deeper questions and being responsive (John 4.1–42), and helping visitors to recognize and understand what is happening in their lives through accompaniment – no matter how brief (Luke 24.13–35).

The emergent need was not an imposed approach lifted from another context but a basic understanding of place and people. This process helpfully took the team through seven stages of identification:

1 God's mission in our space;
2 Our offer of a Christ-like presence;
3 Pre-existing Spirit-led movements to join;
4 Articulation of our understanding of chaplaincy;
5 Chaplaincy examples to inspire and guide us;
6 Key contextual issues;
7 Essential, practical tools and resources to establish, develop or adopt.

The concept of offering 'the shared cloak' of Martin of Tours (Session Four) proved most critical and fruitful. From this basic idea of Martin of Tours (on seeing a beggar, cold and in need, giving what he had to offer), all other aspects fell into place. The principal idea of sharing time and an open space grew, as did the aspiration to provide care through rest, hospitality and a listening service.

The contextual needs identified through consultation with statutory partners were loneliness and isolation, mental health issues and chronic illness leading to depression and economic disadvantage. These issues were recognized in our practice through the evaluation of weekly chaplaincy conversations. We identified certain features as essential to our approach – to be without prejudice or expectation and to demonstrate readiness to pray with or for visitors.

The values-driven concept of Care, Prayer, Share grew, with associated branding and badged clothing and a formalized recruitment and training process. This 'values statement' acted as the axis and screen through which all actions and decisions were to be cultivated.

Prayer was central to the approach created, but we agreed this would only be shared if requested or if gentle offers for prayer were accepted – never assumed or imposed. Each session started and ended with prayer for the team and the centre, its visitors and staff. The Sanctuary has now developed into both a drop-in space and a walking ministry. It is open daily on a three-hour sessional basis with a team of three present at the base and mobile around the centre. In delivery it is a simple model of people sitting, standing, talking and listening, with an ethos that is 'being ready' for encounter.

We explored our traditions and history to give solid and meaningful foundations to this emergent ministry. Crick and Miller (2011) trace ancient Israelite roots of caring for the sick, feeding the poor, speaking for justice and carrying out fair and accountable administration for those inside and outside the community. This interpretation delineates how chaplaincy is shaped by Jesus going outside the familiar and safe confines of the city, through the temple gates, to minister to all comers, inside and outside the Israelite community. We saw our 'encounter' approach having a deep scriptural underpinning, as with Jesus in the midst of people flowing around him and to him – in their familiar places. We were keen to communicate his principles of justice and reaching out with evangelism of word and deed.

Crick and Miller go on to trace chaplaincy roots through early church life, with Christian communities seen to be distinctive through 'good living' and compassionate to the vulnerable and excluded, yet being seen as outsiders themselves. This, we felt, was also distinctive in the Sanctuary approach, based in a retail space yet outside of the commercial – visibly demonstrating love (Crick and Miller, 2011, pp. 67–70).

Reconciliation was again a central theme between those persecuted or pressured to renounce faith and those who remained faithful yet potentially resentful. This spoke deeply to Sanctuary encounters with those who had been part of church life but felt they could not– or should not – re-engage. It also resonated with those who felt 'angry with God' because of what had happened during the pandemic or other personal losses and challenges (Crick and Miller, 2011, pp. 70–1).

Despite the overwhelmingly positive nature of the Sanctuary model there are significant limitations evident in this form of retail chaplaincy. Availability of chaplaincy in a retail context is scarce compared to many other public settings. Traditional models are often engaged directly by the managing agent for consistent attendance either through employment or commission. Essentially, there is a governing body or establishment that pays for the chaplaincy to exist and be maintained. The Sanctuary, despite having a nominal base, is voluntary and part-time, a limited ministry to a mainly transitory community. The nature of shopping means that the time for engagement is limited, incidental and fleeting. Traditional forms of chaplaincy offer a greater degree of stable connection with people. The initial ministry we offered regularly amounted to a brief interaction, especially because of social distancing restrictions, which was affectionately called the 'Ministry of Waving' – coincidentally coined by a contributor to the Chaplaincy Everywhere course.

The idea of sharing time and interest has also been central, with each person being valued as gifts to chaplaincy and not a problem to be solved or a situation to be endured. Empathic listening has been at the heart of the offering – as is a desire to demonstrate care for the individual and their situation – to ascribe worth and dignity. Although prayer is not imposed, it is at the core of the Sanctuary approach and is not concealed nor its importance diminished.

The Chaplaincy Everywhere process enabled the team to identify the 'why' – theological underpinning and motivation – and the 'how' – the distinctive characteristics of the ministry and its operational outworking. The strength of this tailored approach enabled the team to develop a unique identity in its unique context.

The simple and everyday nature of this form of chaplaincy comes with a potential risk in external perception – for stakeholders and onlookers the appearance of 'being' rather than observably 'doing' can appear to be doing nothing at all! However, anyone who has engaged with this form of ministry will attest that action is at a hidden level. After a three-hour session, all volunteers concur that the physical, emotional and mental effort of engaging intentionally with all those we see, listen to and 'touch' is a powerful yet draining experience. This has great relevance for most of the Sanctuary chaplains and perhaps is best captured by relating to Luke 8.43–48; when Jesus was merely touched by someone seeking love and healing, he felt drained. For our chaplains the act of giving oneself through time, listening, presence and prayer is central to this ministry, yet those who we encounter may not even recognize that they are seekers who receive.

The current agenda and understanding of 'well-being' can provide both a source of support and encouragement to chaplaincies but can also generate challenges through divergent culture and language use. Chaplaincies such as the Sanctuary can contribute significantly to local well-being plans and policy frameworks, but a degree of interpretation and explanation is inevitable. Often both are speaking of the same need, activity and response but in starkly different terms.

Just as we had learned to respond to those we encountered in the shopping centre square, so we had to adapt and learn to meet the needs of those in the Town Hall and NHS office. The ability to 'respond to policy' (Ryan, 2015) became as important as responding to the perspective of those who drew up the policy. Talk of pastoral care translated into 'well-being' for those who hold an agenda for client and staff welfare, while spiritual care could be the reference point for those with responsibility for holistic care. We found in developing and communicating the work of the Sanctuary that we had to understand the emphasis of specific roles or organizations and use their language. We learned to adapt to alternative discourse – so rather than speaking of 'love and treasuring' we began to speak of 'respecting and upholding diversity' and 'demonstrating positive regard for all'. This did not diminish who we were but added to our care and understanding of those we worked among.

Engaging in the Sanctuary's intentional presence has related to the incarnational undertaking of 'attending' others that Kelly (2012) expresses as central to pastoral ministry. For those involved this has been the self-giving act of being wholly present, in the moment, just waiting for and listening to another. This attending genuinely unites people from across traditions and faiths: appealing to charismatic colleagues for whom attending took the form of waiting upon the Holy Spirit; for liberal Catholic colleagues it lay in being ready to offer loving service and being witness to inequalities and injustices; for those of an evangelical background it is in being unashamedly visible and present in the public realm – communicating God's love through presence. As a theological manifestation it is truly sacramental – an outward expression of inner grace. Patient yet persistent accompaniment, wholly focused upon the needs of another, has the potential to resonate with those of all faiths and none as a means of spiritual connection.

Attending has been a valuable concept in the development of the Sanctuary but our chaplains have somewhat embraced the step further to 'encounter', to grow a new cross-discipline, cross-sector model. With encounter all that is valuable and relevant in other chaplaincy models is drawn together to suit the particular context of transitory and incidental retail chaplaincy. 'Just being here seems important' is how one volunteer chaplain articulated this model and how this enhances the value in walking, talking and acknowledging the presence of others as an expression of Christ's incarnational commitment and love. For charismatic colleagues, this 'encounter' has been in being attuned to the work of the Holy Spirit by discerning when to sit and pray for the centre, when to go out and walk among others and when simply to present love through a window display, imbuing simple acts with intense significance.

Encounter has recognized the proactive stance of the prophet, the service of the deacon, the quest of the missionary, the grounded and embodied perspective of the parish pastor and the sacramental, incarnational presence of the priest (Threlfall-Holmes, 2011, p. 118). It has meant leaving behind inactivity, unwelcome evangelism, exclusive and safe environments while fostering the unashamed intention of bringing who we are and speaking of Who sends us, through compassion and engagement.

Encounter captures a desire to reach out with an evangelism that responds rather than repels. Paas defines these roles of evangelism for the Church as pilgrim and priest. Pilgrims, or even exile churches, are a people not a place, who 'journey' out into God's world to be immersed in and shaped by it. They maintain integrity and identity while sharing veracity and distinctiveness as their Christian mission. Priest church is 'for and in' the community. It is here that chaplaincy really can exemplify a new way of being and seeing church: 'In short, while passing through the world as pilgrims, Christians bless God on behalf of the world and bless the world on behalf of God' (Paas, 2019, p. 182).

The experience of working with chaplains through the establishment of the Sanctuary has given me a deeper and more connected sense of ministry in general. Chaplains can enable people who are outside faith communities to communicate and engage with questions about God and spirituality in a way that is meaningful and contextual, giving hope in their own 'safe' space. This can also be prophetic, and the chaplain may be able to see and articulate what is happening in the world, spotting trends and being attuned to change, which if valued and fed back into church experience could be transformational. This is real and holistic 'encounter', meaning chaplaincy should no longer be seen as the poor relation or the inferior partner in church life. Chaplaincy 'on the ground' is a central resource for gaining understanding and growing wisdom of what God wants ministers of every sort to hear, do and be in modern society. Despite my initial trepidation regarding overt evangelism, I have been able to work with others to discover an approach to evangelism that I am much more at ease with and which I now want to explore further – that is the spirit of encounter.

Bibliography

Crick, R. D. and B. Miller (2011), *Outside the Gates: Theology, History and Practice of Chaplaincy Ministry*, Oviedo, FL: HigherLife Development Services, Inc.

Kelly, E. (2012), *Personhood and Presence: Self as a Resource for Spiritual and Pastoral Care*, Kindle (e-book), Edinburgh: T&T Clark/Bloomsbury.

The Methodist Church (n.d.), Chaplaincy Everywhere, available at https://www.methodist.org.uk/for-churches/ministries/chaplaincy/chaplaincy-everywhere/ (accessed 7.07.2024).

Paas, S. (2019), *Pilgrims and Priest: Christian Mission in a Post-Christian Society*, London: SCM Press.

Ryan, B. (2015), *A Very Modern Ministry: Chaplaincy in the UK*, London: Theos.

Scadron, D. A. (2021), *The Chaplaincy, Chaplains Certification Program: A Basic Guide to the Practice of Chaplaincy and Biblical Counseling*, Canton, MA: Author Reputation Press.

Threlfall-Holmes, M. (2011), 'Exploring Models of Chaplaincy', in M. Threlfall-Holmes and M. Newitt (eds), *Being a Chaplain*, London: SPCK, pp. 116–26.

PART FIVE

Research and Reflective Practice: Chaplain Theologians

19

The Story Behind the Transformative Anti-racism and Faith Schools Project 'Shades': A Case Study and Personal Reflection

NI-COLA SCOTT

The CofE's current Vision and Strategy has six outcomes, the first of which is to double the number of children and young active disciples in the CofE by 2030 (Church of England, n.d., online). It was with this in mind that, in 2019, Manchester diocese received funding to develop a brand-new children's discipleship programme: Children Changing Places (CCP). This programme aimed to support children and young people at key transition points – from toddler to primary school, primary to secondary school, and then from secondary school onwards. A large recruitment process ensued to employ children's workers and school chaplaincy assistants to help bring the vision to fruition in Greater Manchester. This chapter tells the story of my involvement in the programme and how a project aimed at addressing racism and inclusion in schools, the 'Shades' project, came to play a significant role in the chaplaincy work that arose from CCP. This is a case study, in many ways, but it is also a personal story and a reflection on how chaplaincy in schools can have a profound effect, not only on the life of young people but also in how it can speak into and seek to transform wider issues that are within contemporary UK education.

How Shades began

When I saw the advertisements for the CCP project, I was intrigued. I recognized the potential and possibility, but I was also very hesitant. My mum was a child of the Windrush generation. She grew up with her grandparents in Jamaica, as her parents had travelled to the UK by boat to help rebuild Britain after the Second World War. At the age of just nine, my mum was 'sent for' by her parents, who she barely knew, and so she herself made the life-changing journey to England. Culturally, my mum was Jamaican, and she had to navigate the 1960s British education system. Her Jamaican roots never left her and were very influential into her adult life as she became a mother. As I grew up, my home-world felt like Jamaica, through the food we would eat, the music we listened to, the church we attended and our family gatherings. The outside was England. I recall the discussions my parents would have with me and my sister from a very young age, explaining how we were different from the rest of the world and that our heritage and skin colour were not celebrated. At the time I did not realize that the same conversations were happening in lots of other black and brown families; it was our parents' way of preparing us for life outside of our homes. It was in this context that I had to learn to coexist in both worlds in order to survive and it was with this background that, as I walked through the reception doors towards my interview for the CofE initiative that was CCP, I questioned whether I even remotely stood a chance. I was not concerned about my lack of experience or qualifications but rather whether my skin colour and heritage would be a barrier. This institution, it seemed to me as an outsider, was steeped in white history and I wondered about the presence of unconscious bias, or racism, within it. To my surprise, I got the job, and I quickly found my feet. Some 11 months later, a life-changing event prompted me to develop what is now known as the Shades project.

I was driving to a school where I had been working with a small discipleship ethos group when I collided with a large Range Rover that drove into my driver's side. My injuries were significant enough that I had to be on sick leave for an extended period of time. My mobility was restricted, I was in severe pain, and I began to reflect on my faith and role. In March 2020, I had a meeting with my manager about when I might return to work, yet the very next day the Covid-19 pandemic sent us into lockdown. Several weeks into this first lockdown, a live video recording of the murder of George Floyd, the footage captured by a teenager who was walking by at the time, was watched by over 1.5 billion people worldwide. Here I was, off work sick during the height of a global pandemic, navigating questions around identity, and now experiencing and witnessing the outpouring of internalized pain for black and brown people worldwide. I began to have several conversations with friends and family members about the personal experiences of racism and unconscious bias that we had on a day-to-day basis. I discovered how so many of us shared similar experiences and how racism still played a significant part in the lives of many black and brown people here in the UK.

My job role within the CCP project was directed towards helping children develop their Christian discipleship pathway within our diocesan church schools. I looked at our social media accounts to see how our organization had responded to the George Floyd incident and its aftermath, but there was nothing. Silence. More questions about identity, institution and my place within it all began to flood my mind. Had this terrible event not affected anyone where I worked, the way it had affected me? Were people I worked with not outraged at this huge injustice? Were they not traumatized by years of racism the way that I had been?

On returning to work after the pandemic and after the outcry of the Black Lives Matter movement since the awful murder of George Floyd, I had a heavy heart and felt a level of re-traumatization about my own personal experiences of racism, including my apprehension about starting this job in the CofE. I had a one-to-one meeting with my line manager and ended up sharing about one of my first personal experiences of racism where, at the age of five, I had gone to the local shops and some kids walked up to me and pulled my neat braids out, laughed, and then walked off. This was decades ago, but I had never forgotten it. These micro aggressions continued throughout primary and secondary education and, sadly, I just got used to it. However, now, having had an extended time off work with injury, which had led to deeper reflections about who I was and what I may be called to do against a backdrop of a global Black Lives Matter movement, these micro aggressions were increasingly at the forefront of my mind.

As I reflected on these stories, I had begun to think about the children and young people in our schools and churches, and wondered if they too had these same painful experiences. I thought about the children who one day might feel a call to ministry but, having never seen reflections of themselves in their local church leadership, would question whether there was a place for them. I wondered if they too had been humiliated as a result of their Afro or curly textured hair or had experienced exclusion from their church or school communities. The Archbishop of Canterbury at the time, Justin Welby, had stated in several interviews that the CofE was institutionally racist and that one of his key priorities was to change this. I wondered about our schools and where the change would come from for the children we served. Underpinning all of this questioning was one thought – if you do not feel accepted because of the colour of your skin, then how could you possibly feel loved and accepted by God? I shared all of this with my manager and, with her support, I instigated a process to discern how the CCP project could address some of the issues I was raising.

The consultation and development process

Initially, I harboured a fear about how a project seeking to address some of the issues around racism in churches and schools would be received. Was the CofE, and the CofE schools that I worked in, ready for this real dialogue and work? To ensure any project or work had buy-in and sustainability, a detailed research, consultation and development process was initiated and I began to look at the wider context of racism and inclusion within education. In 2020 the YMCA undertook some research to investigate the experiences of young black people growing up in the UK, in terms of crime, education, employment, health, finance and accommodation (YMCA, 2020, online). The study revealed that many young black people in the UK grow up expecting to experience racism and perceive that racial stereotypes within UK education have the potential to negatively affect their development and opportunities. Furthermore, 95 per cent of young black people stated that they had heard and witnessed racist language at school and 70 per cent of the students felt under pressure to conform regarding their Afro hair. Half the young people questioned said that the biggest barrier in education came from being perceived as 'too aggressive' by teaching staff. Black and brown children saw 'identity and belonging' as a key barrier faced within the education system and a problematic statement repeated by teaching staff was 'I don't see colour'. This, however well-intentioned, had the effect of cultivating a sense of invisibility and inferiority among black and brown children, which could follow them throughout their time in education.

The first part of my consultation process involved raising the issue with headteachers to gauge their reaction. One headteacher I spoke to explained how the demographics of his school had significantly changed over the past two to three years to the point where 80 per cent of the student population identified as coming from an African background and being either Christian or Muslim. This swift change in demographic had left the staff feeling ill-equipped. They did not feel confident in responding to issues of racism, inclusion and wider movements such as Black Lives Matter, and were unsure how best to support the young people at their school. The headteacher explained that only the day before he'd had a meeting with a parent in his office who had told him that their child had tried to scrub off his black skin in the bath, so he wouldn't continue to be bullied any more at school. The headteacher looked at me and told me that, as a white male, he did not know how to adequately deal with such issues. Within the school, teachers were interacting with children every day without the necessary skills and knowledge about their diverse backgrounds, cultures and ethnicities, and therefore were finding it difficult to effectively teach and mentor their students. I had many conversations with leaders within the diocese, who had longed for a project like this but did not know how or where it would come from. One of the biggest surprises of the consultation process was the fact that people were open and seeking a project that could help them address issues of racism and inclusion. I remember meeting one headteacher who explained to me that they would not have been ready for a project of this kind a year ago, but felt that now was the right time to begin to broach this subject and work on racism and inclusion in their school.

Alongside the formal consultation work, I began to read books, watch films and access any learning I could in order to create a project that not only worked but also brought long-lasting change. I joined a diversity international leadership network, which helped me with peer support and sharing ideas and challenges. I found the consultation process personally costly. It was painful having conversations about my personal experiences with work colleagues who had no idea or appreciation of what it was like to be a black child or woman in contemporary UK. There were many questions and, sometimes, I was overwhelmed emotionally at the re-traumatization of revisiting these experiences. I had to lean on my support system, friends and family and peer support, who were empathetic, shared similar experiences, and who could therefore help me to process the journey.

As part of the consultation process, we explored biblical texts and the use of Christian imagery in schools. Traditional images of the European-styled blonde-haired Jesus were still present in school life, which contradicted Jesus' Middle Eastern heritage and further contributed to the exclusion of black and brown heritage and history. The language used in schools for inclusion was interesting too, as it belied a culture of tolerance rather than celebration. Tolerance can be defined as the ability to deal with something 'unpleasant or annoying', and to tolerate something can be to continue in the present existence despite 'bad or difficult conditions' (Cambridge University Press, 2023). The perception of toleration, therefore, can be based upon a negative sense of burden rather than an attitude of acceptance and celebration. It contributes to the lived historical and contemporary experiences of black and brown people in the UK who have felt as though they have been grudgingly endured by the majority population. We wanted to help schools create an environment where all students felt welcomed and accepted and where difference was seen as something to celebrate and learn about.

Next steps

After six months of consultation with teachers, headteachers, parents and key leaders within our diocese, we identified some key aims and objectives for the emerging project:

- Celebrate and Educate: Develop spaces where Black History role models could be celebrated and educate children about the contributions that black and brown people have made in the UK and worldwide.
- Develop Understanding and Empathy: Foster and develop an understanding around racial diversity and acceptance in school, church and communities.
- Encourage Belonging: Help to improve the sense of belonging for children and young people in school, church, the wider community and home.
- Foster Identity: Instil dignity and belonging; promote a strong sense of racial identity for black and brown children in school, church and wider community. In addition, help to prepare all children to be students who stand against racial injustice and celebrate who God has made them to be.
- Share God's Love: Embed a recognition that all children and young people are created in the image of God and create the building blocks for all children to grow spiritually and flourish wherever they are planted. Remove racial barriers to children experiencing faith in school/church and instil acceptance and belonging.
- Continuous Professional Development: Empower schools to lead in the area of racial justice, helping them to embed anti-racist practice within their curriculum. Support schools to create an inclusive environment of belonging and enable all children to flourish no matter their racial heritage, colour of their skin or background. Help schools to empower their students with the good news that all children are made equal in the image of God, and resource leaders and teachers with the ability to enable all students to flourish.

The Shades project

The Shades project was launched initially as a deanery-wide project, working across 33 CofE schools, both primary and secondary. An online resource bank was constructed for schools, churches, parents and teaching staff to use in their settings, to inspire, empower, equip and educate. Alongside this, a music video was created to accompany a new song written specifically for the project – 'A Million Colours'. Children from the schools involved took part in the design and filming of the video and this is now a resource used nationally (Manchester Diocese, 2022). An interactive musically led initiative was developed and implemented either as a one-off session in schools or a more detailed eight-week project that focused around this. The emphasis was on teaching the song to groups, using dance, movement and song to explore the difficult subject of racism and inclusion. The session would end with the participants being able to perform the song in their collective worship in their school or church setting.

As a chaplaincy team, we offered interactive and engaging assemblies and collective worship that would help the school communities start the conversation, build understanding, improve well-being of students, and embed Christian values and a strong sense of identity. We set up Shades Ethos Groups in schools, which sought to create a safe space for children and young people to share their experiences without judgement, find acceptance, find their voice, and empower them to be advocates for change. These were time-limited groups of eight weeks, with the hope being that those within the group would then continue developing their own activities in ways that were contextually appropriate for them. During Black History month, we ran a 'Live Lounge' in high schools, which involved having live Gospel music, celebrating the vast contributions black people have made to music and how Gospel music carried faith on a melody. We ran Shades cooking sessions, exploring faith and culture and the contributions black people have made to our food in the UK, and we held drop-in sessions with young people at youth clubs to talk about Shades and racial inclusion and justice.

A major part of the Shades project focuses on the children in schools, recognizing the research that demonstrated how black and brown children faced multiple barriers within the education system. With this in mind, we initiated a Shades ambassador programme, where small groups of children and young people were given the opportunity to take the lead in creatively delivering racial justice and anti-racism projects in their schools. They initiated work with children and staff to embed diversity and inclusion within the curriculum, school environment, culture and ethos, by raising awareness around school with creative approaches. This included leading collective worship, working with the senior leadership team to embed racial justice values underpinned by Christian values, and providing peer support to students experiencing racism that is trusted and has a safe reporting system.

The impact of Shades

Gathering feedback from the schools where our chaplaincy team implemented the Shades project was an essential part of the endeavour. We did this through informal conversation, observation and via a more formal questionnaire that was sent to school leaders and students. Feedback often related to the fact that, for those in multicultural schools (which were the vast majority), the children had benefited greatly from the focus on representation. Students felt as if they were able to use their voice more effectively in discussions and that they would be heard. Comments in the feedback from students included statements like 'I feel more confident in my identity and who I am' and 'I am proud of who I am and feel like I belong here'. One teacher reported that a pupil who had been subjected to racist comments at school was observed to develop a greater sense of self-confidence during the Shades project work and became more comfortable talking about her religious background and sharing religious experiences with others. The creative element of Shades enabled some students to find ways to express themselves for the first time. One 16-year-old student shared her experience of racism, and the emotions she felt, through poetry writing, which led to her ultimately performing for other students at Live Lounge in the library.

A 'no bystanders' pledge was created for each class to sign, which stated that no student or staff member would stand by if they heard upsetting comments or discriminatory language in or around school. The messaging that centred on empowering children to be proud of who they were and recognizing that they were all made in God's image was another highly valued aspect of the project. Including the children and young people in the ongoing work enabled the development of some creative responses that were student-led, such as displaying posters on inclusion, having a Shades book section in the school library, and conducting mini class assemblies. Children and young people reported gaining a greater understanding of equality and diversity and felt able to discuss this with their peers. At one Shades youth group, where all the members identified as white, the Shades project enabled the young people to open up, ask questions and explore issues around race. This led to one memorable moment when one young person stated that he was proud of his ADHD because it was a part of who he is!

Staff reported high value in the way in which the Shades project enabled them to confidently approach issues that were sensitive and out of their own realm of experience. Teachers described how they changed their practice to become more proactive in discussions, rather than their previous practice of being reactive to situations or avoiding difficult and challenging conversations altogether. Staff reported how the project had enabled them to work more closely with the children and be guided by their ideas. One teacher, responding to the feedback questionnaire, wrote about how the Shades ambassadors would come to senior staff and share what they had heard, or voice any worries that they had and, together, they would discuss the best way forward. The emphasis on staff professional development needs was appreciated. For example, learning from the staff training helped not just the teaching staff but also the wider chaplaincy team to intentionally highlight contemporary black voices within the Church, such as Guvna B, and to highlight the African heritage of St Augustine, thereby helping students to see that Christianity is not a white religion. As one teacher stated: 'It helped to reinforce all the work that we do as part of our church school and the wider curriculum.'

The positive impact of the Shades project extended beyond the walls of the school building and into the wider school community. Parents were very supportive of the project and another example of its effect upon the lived experience of those involved was illustrated when a parent came into school to tell me that her child now felt confident to wear her Afro hair how she wanted it and not how she felt she should have it. One school held a community event, attended by parents and people in the wider community, where food from all over the world was shared.

Looking to the future

The Shades project, conceived when I was experiencing a great deal of personal challenge compounded by witnessing the horrendous racist murder of George Floyd and the aftermath, has transformed chaplaincy practice in the schools where it has been piloted. The role of a school chaplain is multifaceted, from providing pastoral care and spiritual guidance to educating students and supporting staff. It was fundamental to the Shades project that the Christian understanding of all humans being made in the image of God was central, because that gave language and understanding with which we could demonstrate how this meant that every student had worth, value and was precious in the eyes of God. From this foundation, we were able to create spaces for exploration, safe discussion, creative outlets, education for staff and students, and wider community connections. It also enabled the chaplaincy team themselves to grow in understanding the issues faced by young black and brown people. Although this was, at times, costly for me, as I disclosed the racial traumas I had experienced, it was a real example of post-traumatic growth and healing. The nature of chaplaincy is that it is a vocation rather than a job, and therefore it impacts on our whole life, our faith and the way in which we understand ourselves, the world and God. Being a chaplain is about being open to challenge and being disturbed and, ultimately, being transformed by the God whom we seek to represent in the spaces we inhabit.

While the Shades project was delivered by the chaplaincy team, it has ultimately taken on a life of its own in many schools, with students and staff taking the lead and developing contextually appropriate responses. Again, I would argue that this is chaplaincy practice at its best: seeking to empower people in their own spaces, giving spiritual guidance and support that enables all to grow in their own understanding of what faith means in their context, and how faith values can be lived out. The success of the project has meant that more funding has been made available to roll it out much more widely, and there has been huge interest not just from within the diocese but across the CofE, indicating how much such a project is needed. This model of school chaplaincy practice is a model that contributes to the transformation not only of individuals but also of contexts and systems. My hope is that this will contribute to a positive change to the wider educational system so that the inequalities faced by black and brown people within it are systematically addressed.

Bibliography

Cambridge University Press (2023), 'Tolerance', *Cambridge Dictionary*, available at https://dictionary.cambridge.org/dictionary/english/tolerance (accessed 7.07.2024).

Church of England (n.d.), 'Vision and Strategy', available at https://www.churchofengland.org/about/vision-and-strategy (accessed 7.07.2024).

Manchester Diocese (2022), 'A Million Colours' [Video], 6 October, YouTube, available at https://www.youtube.com/watch?v=8VHoLsXJCsA (accessed 7.07.2024).

YMCA (2020), 'Young and Black', 29 October, available at https://www.ymca.org.uk/research/young-and-black (accessed 7.07.2024).

20

Toxic MasKulinity and Gender-sensitive End-of-life Care: A Research Proposal

ANDREW WEBSTER

This chapter sets out a proposal to research how contemporary British hegemonic masculinity impacts on the work of hospice chaplains and how they might use 'gendered access points' and theological resources to create gender-sensitive pastoral care at the end of life.

In recent years there has been an increase of interest in masculinity in both the formal academic spheres and at a more popular level. One area of interest is that of male mental health and wider well-being. There have been significant pieces of work from both theoretical and practical perspectives (Hemmings, 2017), including contributions from a theological viewpoint (Moore, 2022). The topic is ripe for further investigation since masculinity is operative at an individual, communal and societal level and, given the pervasive nature of masculinity, it is inevitable that it will impact on the work of hospice chaplaincy. As a discipline, chaplaincy is rooted in practical theology and, as such, is an ideal location to research masculinity as well as to utilize any subsequent findings. If masculinity, or indeed masKulinity, a term I coined some years ago and that I have found is beginning to be used in other research areas for when men 'mask and perform what they perceive to be the commonly accepted version of their masculinity' (IATL, 2022), impacts all areas of life then it is interesting to ask how it might shape experience at the end of life.

The research will contain a literature review that traces some of the trends in understandings of masculinity. Masculinity has received increasing amounts of scholarly attention in recent decades, emerging as a field of enquiry in its own right. To summarize, and inevitably oversimplify a nuanced debate, there is increasing consensus that masculinity is a socially constructed phenomenon alongside a rejection of essentialist arguments based on such things as biology or 'common sense'.

I am persuaded by the argument that draws on feminist scholarship and emphasizes the significance of power within gender construction and how the dominant form(s) of masculinity serve to preserve patriarchy (Connell, 1987; Butler, 1990). Connell is a significant voice within Men's

Studies whose concept of 'hegemonic masculinity' is helpful for this research:

> The concept of hegemony ... refers to the cultural dynamic by which a group claims and sustains a leading position in social life. At any given time, one form of masculinity rather than others is culturally exalted. Hegemonic masculinity can be defined as the configuration of gender practice which embodies the currently accepted answer to the problem of the legitimacy of patriarchy. (Connell, 2005, p. 77)

The current version of hegemonic masculinity operant in the UK places an emphasis on, among other attributes, ambition, independence, stoicism, control, competition and self-sufficiency. I identify these attributes as particularly relevant for end-of-life care. Consequently, it discourages vulnerability, emotional literacy and places low value on shared tenderness and asking for help. Colloquially this situation is often described as 'toxic masculinity'.

The notion of a hegemonic masculinity can be combined with ideas drawn from the work of Butler (1990), who emphasizes that masculinity involves performance in that it is a plethora of actions and discourses that men are expected to perform throughout their lives. Society posits certain 'codes' of behaviour that shape how men should conduct themselves. This school of thought draws heavily on the notion that gender is socially constructed, with the accompanying optimism that if it has been created by society then there is potential for deconstruction and reconstruction. The reason masculinity might benefit from deconstruction is that the current hegemonic expression can be seen to be extremely damaging not only to women but also to men: there is a cost to them in maintaining patriarchy, an idea explored in numerous cultural arenas such as novels (Szalay, 2016), biography (Webb, 2017) and cinema (Palahniuk and Fincher, 1999). A key argument is that many of the challenges facing men can be traced back to the gap between the idealized version of masculinity promoted by society and their lived reality.

This impact is increased when combined with the negative consequences of living according to the demands of this expression of masculinity. A growing body of opinion promotes the idea that the widely reported issues in male mental health are rooted in the perpetuation of a 'toxic' version of masculinity (Thornton, 2012). From a pastoral perspective, a significant amount of research and subsequent praxis has been conducted around male mental health. An example would be the high-profile examination of suicide statistics for young men in particular (Thornton, 2012, pp. 8–9). Examples of practical outworking are the numerous iterations of support groups established with the aim of supporting men in their mental well-being and reducing the likelihood of suicide, with Men's Sheds being a prime example (UK Men's Sheds Association, no date).

There have been some efforts to engage with masculinity from a theological and spiritual perspective (Eldredge, 2010; McCloughry, 1992). Some of these might be regarded as reactionary in that they are resistant to some of the influences of feminism within the Church and espouse an essentialist understanding of gender, offering a solution to the challenges men face through rediscovery/reconnection with the essence of what it is to be a man; an essence that is understood as God given. Such an approach could be seen as a Christian version of a mythopoetic method, exemplified by the likes of Bly (1991), so called because of the frequent use of mythology, fairy tales, archetypes and poetry. In an important paper, Kummer (2019) engages with various strands of Men's Studies, with the aim of developing a gender-sensitive pastoral practice. He points out that the mythopoetic approach, while undoubtedly influential in both the Church and society, lacks evidential rigour and the protagonists fail to 'provide detailed reflections on how they arrive at knowledge about their subject' (p. 31). Kummer is more sympathetic to the sociological approach of Connell and advocates that practical theologians engage with this material to create gender-sensitive pastoral care that takes spirituality seriously. The work of Rohr (2005; 2012) is offered as an example of such an approach, though this author is perhaps also susceptible to the criticism of lacking firm evidence in social science. In outlining a gender-specific approach, Kummer is at pains to avoid a reactionary attitude that accommodates patriarchy and instead advocates the role of pastoral care to men as involving 'un doing gendering' – that is, 'the deconstruction of ideological gender codes' (p. 34), which involves a liberation from the harmful effects of hegemonic masculinity. This requires building on Rohr's concept of 'gendered entrance points' (Rohr, 2012, p. 339), which are imaginative ways of engaging with men so that they are able to access pastoral care in a meaningful way.

In contrast to the work around mental health, I am not aware of any gender-sensitive material for the hospice context. Therefore, I am interested in engaging with hospice chaplains to discover if they believe that hegemonic masculinity impacts on their efforts to provide pastoral care at the end of life. One such example might be the aforementioned reluctance to show vulnerability or emotional openness, which might manifest as an inability to be open about fears of dying. Anxiety around loss of control could also be a significant challenge. If chaplains do perceive an impact, then I am interested in whether they have insights into how their work can be gender-sensitive with 'gendered entrance points', and if they are aware of theological resources that might help 'de-gendering' in the context of end-of-life care.

Methodology and method

It is important to have an understanding of the methodological foundations for research as well as providing clarity with regard to method. While clearly related, these are distinct. The former concerns the nature of knowledge and how it has meaning, with the latter focusing on the practical tools used to access and analyse information. Swinton and Mowat (2016) provide a comprehensive overview of the methodological basis for practical theology. From an epistemological perspective they make the case for practical theology generating idiographic knowledge. This emphasizes that a great deal of 'meaningful knowledge can be discovered in unique, non-replicable experiences' (p. 41). From a paradigmatic point of view this is constructionist and interpretative, based on the understanding that truth and knowledge are constructed by individuals and communities and are then subject to a process of interpretation with regards to their meaning(s), which can be many and varied.

This type of knowing and understanding is most relevant with regard to the subject of masculinity, especially if it is understood in the sociological terms outlined above. Slater (2015, p. 65) affirms idiographic knowledge and its place in chaplaincy research and challenges the societal privileging of the alternative, nomothetic, form. The latter, with its emphasis on quantitative research methods, is of limited value when exploring complex arenas of human experience such as masculinity. Slater goes on to advocate qualitative methodologies, in particular a praxis-based approach that draws on reflective practice. The qualitative nature of such an approach allows for some of the complexity and 'thickness' of the issue to emerge. Engaging with the findings of social sciences is another methodological feature of the research. Engagement with social science is a distinctive feature of practical theology and has opened up many fresh and fruitful insights, which have helped equip the Church's mission, including chaplaincy. This requires some theoretical grounding by which the work of social science could be integrated into the theological project. There have been various proposed models, with that offered by Pattison being especially helpful. Building on Tillich's concept of critical correlation, Pattison proposes the idea of a 'mutual critical conversation' (2000, p. 139) in which social science discoveries are brought into a respectful conversation with the Christian tradition.

A perennial challenge for practical theology and resulting practice is the need to counter social science having too much influence. Thus, I will be at pains to encourage chaplains to think about what resources they bring to the question of masculinity that are drawn from the Christian tradition. Hopefully, the results will provide a useful and distinctive contribution to the hospice context. A number of writers, who embrace a qualitative methodology in the field of chaplaincy, advocate the use of case studies (Kruizinga et al., 2020). While clearly of value, this approach would be more suited if my research was engaging with patients themselves and their experience of masculinity and pastoral care at the end of life. Rather, as the focus is on chaplains and their understanding of their work in relation to masculinity, I propose to use the method of unstructured, or focused, interviews. As described by May, this method lends itself to eliciting accessible data but does so in such a way as to enable the necessary freedom to interviewees, thus there is scope for flexibility and the opportunity for interviewees to bring their own interpretations forward (May, 2001, p. 125).

May (2001, p. 130) outlines how developing a rapport with interviewees is a foundation for focused interviews. I am hoping that an element of this already exists in that I propose focused interviews with between five to ten hospice chaplains I already know through our local branch of our professional association – Association of Hospice and Palliative Care Chaplains (AHPCC). In so doing, there is no pretence of detached objectivity but rather I am myself a factor in the dynamic of any interviews. This need not be an issue as long as the research foregrounds the importance of reflexivity and self-awareness, as outlined by Swinton and Mowat (2016, pp. 56–8).

For successful focused interviews, May (2001, pp. 128–9) draws attention to the importance of preparation, accessibility, cognition and motivation:

- Preparation: Through initial contact via email, participants will be provided with an information and consent form that outlines what the project is for and the substance of the research and method used, confidentiality issues, permission for zoom sessions to be recorded, who will see the completed dissertation and confirming that data will be kept according to General Data Protection Regulation (GDPR, 2018) good practice involving digitized, password-protection techniques.
- Accessibility: Once consent is in place, each participant will be provided with a summary of what I understand by hegemonic masculinity and a hypothesis as to how it might shape men in the UK receiving hospice care. A description of 'gender-sensitive pastoral care', based on Kummer (2019) and including the concept of 'gender access points', will also be given. A third document will be a working understanding of what chaplains try to do as pastoral carers in a hospice based on the AHPCC guidelines. Finally, the participants will be sent a copy of the questions we will be exploring during the interview. The documents will be sent out two weeks prior to the focused interview, along with

the opportunity via email, zoom or phone for clarification. This is to ensure interview participants have the necessary information.
- Cognition: Prior to the focused interview I will establish that participants have 'an understanding of what is required of them in the interview' (May, 2001, p. 128) so they feel confident to engage in the process. I want to ensure that while I will have provided a basic structure as a starting point for reflection, it is their reflections on their own practice that I want to hear about.
- Motivation: Throughout the process it is important that participants feel their contribution is valued; this will be achieved via active listening and, hopefully, a shared recognition as to the value of the subject matter.

In order to develop my method, I propose to conduct two pilot interviews, including the dissemination of the various preparatory documents, so I can be as sure as possible that the necessary levels of information have been provided. Once the preparatory stage is complete the main part of the research will be a focused interview via zoom, which will be recorded. Initial questions will be information gathering, in the sense that I will ask for a description of the person's role, how long they have been in the role, and the size of their hospice. This information will be anonymized. The more qualitative part of the interviews will be focused on the following questions:

1 Based on the description of hegemonic masculinity, can you see where it might manifest in your work in providing spiritual care to men in your hospice context?
2 Could you give anonymous examples of where you have seen hegemonic masculinity manifest in your role?
3 Are there ways in which you have introduced some gender sensitivity to your pastoral role? For example, do you create 'gender access points'?
4 In your work with men are there any resources from the Christian tradition that help with the 'de-gendering' process that enables your palliative pastoral care? The resulting transcripts will be analysed thematically around the four areas of enquiry.

The focused interview format allows for conversation to take place, which enables the interviewer to offer illustrations from work they are aware of as prompts, if necessary. For example, at question 2, examples of 'gendered access points' can be presented drawn from male mental health approaches; and at question 4, work from writers such as Moore (2022) and his 'unravelling' of biblical gender myths is a demonstration of Christian faith-based de-gendering resources.

Ethical considerations

In addition to the use of a full process of consent, data handling and eventual destruction of data, the main ethical consideration is the well-being of the participants, including the interviewer. It is possible that, during the exploration of what can be a sensitive topic, participants will become aware of their own lives being impacted negatively by hegemonic masculinity. It will be made clear that participants can withdraw and return at any stage of the interview or exit completely. There will also be a 'cooling off' period of two weeks after the interview during which participants may request the redaction of certain sections, or to withdraw from participating in the research. After this point, the analysis means withdrawing a single participant becomes impractical. Furthermore, the confidential and independent services of an experienced chaplain will be made available to participants for support.

Aims and outcomes

The hope is that this piece of research will produce some evidence for the value of gender-specific pastoral care that will inform the work of hospice chaplains and the wider field of end-of-life care. It might also contribute to the work of other chaplains in addition to the growing field of Male Studies and well-being. The nature of the data collected faces the issue outlined by Swinton and Mowat (2016) of generalization (pp. 44–8). They are clear that qualitative research findings cannot simply be transferred to other situations, nor can they be replicated in the same way as quantitative findings. Nevertheless, it is reasonable to talk in terms of resonance between situations that share similarities: 'Qualitative research can therefore claim a degree of transferability in so far as it offers insights that reach beyond the particularities of the situation' (Swinton and Mowat, 2016, p. 45). Based on this claim I hope that while my findings will be drawn from specific chaplains working in specific contexts, some of what we find will provide insights that will be of use in other hospice contexts and more widely.

Bibliography

Bly, R. (1991), *Iron John: A Book about Men*, 2nd edn, Shaftesbury: Element.
Butler, J. (1990), *Gender Trouble: Feminism and the Subversion of Identity*, New York: Routledge.
Connell, R. W. (1987), *Gender and Power: Society, the Person, and Sexual Politics*, Redwood City, CA: Stanford University Press.
Connell, R. W. (2005), *Masculinities*, 2nd edn, Cambridge: Polity Press.

Eldredge, J. (2010), *Wild at Heart: Discovering the Secrets of a Man's Soul*, rev. and expanded edn, Nashville, TN: Thomas Nelson.

GDPR, Data Protection Act 2018, c. 12, available at https://www.legislation.gov.uk/ukpga/2018/12/contents/enacted (accessed 7.07.2024).

Hemmings, C. (2017), *Be a Man: How Macho Culture Damages Us and How to Escape It*, London: Biteback Publishing.

IATL (Institute for Advanced Teaching and Learning) (2022), Community Values Education Programme (CVEP), 'CVEP at Warwick Inclusion Conference (Overview of Talks: 2. Maskulinities Project)', available https://warwick.ac.uk/services/dean-of-students-office/community-values-education/news/?newsItem=8a1784 1a80f5871d0180ffb198902e3c (accessed 26.08.2024).

Kruizinga, R. et al. (eds) (2020), *Learning from Case Studies in Chaplaincy: Towards Practice Based Evidence and Professionalism*, Utrecht: Eburon Academic Publishers.

Kummer, A. (2019), 'Reforming Pastoral Care: Masculinity, Pathologies and Gender-specific Pastoral Care', in A. Vähäkangas, S. Angel and K. Helboe Johansen (eds), *Reforming Practical Theology: The Politics of Body and Space*, Oslo: International Academy of Practical Theology, Conference series, pp. 29–36.

May, T. (2001), *Social Research: Issues, Methods and Process*, 3rd edn, Maidenhead: Open University Press.

McCloughry, R. (1992), *Men and Masculinity: From Power to Love*, London: Hodder & Stoughton.

Moore, W. (2022), *Boys Will be Boys and Other Myths: Unravelling Biblical Masculinities*, London: SCM Press.

Palahniuk, C. and D. Fincher (1999), *Fight Club*, 20th Century Studios.

Pattison, S. (2000), 'Some Straw for the Bricks: A Basic Introduction to Theological Reflection', in J. Woodward and S. Pattison (eds), *The Blackwell Reader in Pastoral and Practical Theology*, Oxford: Blackwell Publishing, pp. 135–48.

Rohr, R. with J. Martos (2005), *From Wild Man to Wise Man: Reflections on Male Spirituality*, Cincinnati, OH: Franciscan Media.

Rohr, R. (2012), 'Men and Spirituality', in P. Tyler and R. Woods (eds), *The Bloomsbury Guide to Christian Spirituality*, London: Bloomsbury, pp. 338–46.

Slater, V. (2015), 'Developing Practice-Based Evidence', in C. Swift, M. Cobb and A. Todd (eds), *A Handbook of Chaplaincy Studies: Understanding Spiritual Care in Public Spaces*, Farnham: Ashgate, pp. 63–78.

Swinton, J. and H. Mowat (2016), *Practical Theology and Qualitative Research*, London: SCM Press.

Szalay, D. (2016), *All That Man Is*, London: Vintage.

Thornton, J. (2012), *Men and Suicide: Why it is a Social Issue*, Surrey: Samaritans.

UK Men's Sheds Association, 'Happy Healthy Men', available at https://menssheds.org.uk/ (accessed 7.07.2024).

Webb, R. (2017), *How Not to Be a Boy*, Edinburgh: Canongate.

21

Organic Chaplaincy: Supporting the Spiritual Care of Persons with Learning Disabilities

ANDREW JYOTHI ISAAC SUSAN

This research arose from the emerging question of how chaplaincy might be supported and understood as something delivered not by a single individual or a separate resource but as an organic process where engagement is embedded within the holistic and integrated care of persons with learning disabilities. The outcomes of the research could lead to the shaping of a chaplaincy role that could provide the necessary frameworks of oversight, support and education for delivering chaplaincy provision as part of this holistic care offered by personal assistants, with or without their own faith and/or spiritual commitments.

Spirituality is identified as an important dimension in the lives of persons with learning disabilities (Hunter and Kivisto, 2019, p. 23; Swinton, 2004a, p. 1; Demmons, 2009, p. 14). John Swinton, through a study in 1999 involving persons with learning disabilities, carers and support workers, demonstrated that individuals with learning disabilities of all levels have a keen interest in spirituality (Swinton, 2001, p. 1). It was also understood that spirituality can serve, for a person with learning disabilities, as a language and a means of self-expression, impacting how they see themselves and their place in the world as well as how they deal with and react to significant life events (Research Excellence Framework, 2014, p. 1).

Spirituality is reported as a source of comfort and hope in times of difficulties (Lemos, 2017, p. 20). Sango and Forrester-Jones (2022, p. 199) explored the relationship between spirituality and quality of life and concluded that spiritual/religious belief can positively contribute to quality-of-life perception in persons with learning disabilities. They suggest (2022, pp. 197, 199) that persons with learning disabilities who got the opportunity to express and nurture their spirituality reported 'more general life satisfaction', more empowerment and independence. It has also been identified that spirituality is an often-overlooked dimension of lives of persons with learning disabilities (Swinton and Powrie, 2004, p. 13).

Research evidence suggests that there exist assumptions by faith communities and care staff that spirituality requires a higher level of abstract thinking and that persons with learning disabilities are not capable of that (Lemos, 2017, p. 14; Hunter and Kivisto, 2019, p. 23; Raji, 2009, p. 125; Demmons, 2009, p. 10). Swinton (1997, p. 21) counters this idea and argues that faith and spirituality are relational realities and not intellectual concepts. A person's spirituality cannot be evaluated based on intellectual prowess (Raji, 2009, pp. 124–5). Studies also show that persons with learning disabilities are interested to learn more about religious beliefs, visit religious places of worship and talk about faith (Lemos, 2017, p. 21). Spirituality of persons with learning disabilities represents diversity: it could mean practising a particular faith; it could also be hybrid in nature, drawing from elements that may not be overtly spiritual (Lemos, 2017, pp. 16, 17).

Both personal spirituality and the communal dimension of spirituality has been found to be of significance for persons with learning disabilities (Swinton, 2004a, pp. 3–4; Carter and Boehm, 2019, p. 24). At a personal level, prayer has been identified as an important element of spirituality. In a study by Liu, Carter, Boehm, Annandale and Taylor (2014, as cited in Carter and Boehm, 2019, p. 38) involving young people with 11 learning disabilities, prayer was reported to be of primary significance by 'almost all participants' as an avenue of spiritual expression. Persons with learning disabilities have also expressed the desire to have personal time on their own to reflect, think and pray (Swinton, 2004b, p. 9). At the communal level it has been observed that spirituality explored through faith communities opens avenues for social inclusion, interactions, activities, friendships and a sense of belonging, which improve mental and physical health (Lemos, 2017, pp. 7, 23; Sango and Forrester-Jones, 2022, p. 6). Walter Kerns, writing from a Roman Catholic perspective, suggests that both the life of the church and the sacraments are essential for the spiritual life of persons with learning disabilities (Demmons, 2009, p. 77). It has also been noted that exclusive practices of faith communities can make spirituality inaccessible and have damaging effects on persons with learning disabilities (Swinton, 2004b, p. 12; Lemos, 2017, p. 14).

Persons with learning disabilities have reported that they wanted their spirituality to be recognized and supported (Swinton, 2001, p. 1). The benefits of supporting persons with learning disabilities in nurturing spirituality have been evidenced through several studies (Sango and Forrester-Jones, 2017b, pp. 12–13). Swinton (2004a, pp. 82–4) proposed several recommendations for spiritual care for persons with learning disabilities, such as inclusion of spiritual care in person-centred planning, training for support assistants in spiritual care, and adding spiritual care as a dimension of the professional role.

On similar lines, Raji (2009, p. 128) suggests that exploring the spiritual needs of persons with learning disabilities involves sensitive handling, and person-centred planning that has the person with a learning disability at the centre of the exploration. Staff perceptions of spirituality of persons with learning disabilities are recorded in several studies and reveal a mixture of attitudes (Sango and Forrester-Jones, 2017a, p. 11). Some staff recognize the significance of spirituality in the lives of persons with learning disabilities (Swinton and Powrie, 2004, p. 79; Lemos, 2017, p. 20). At the same time there is also evidence of care workers being unaware of this (Swinton and Powrie, 2004, p. 15; Lemos, 2017, p. 14).

The Nursing and Midwifery Council (2010, p. 36) state that in learning disability nursing, the spiritual needs of persons with learning disabilities must be taken into account while assessing, planning and delivering care. Narayanaswamy, Gates and Swinton (2002, p. 955) explore the positive outcomes of spiritual care provided by learning disability nurses to clients and families. They describe (2002, p. 954) two approaches used by learning disability nurses to address spiritual and religious needs in spiritual care for persons with learning disabilities – namely, the procedural approach and the personal approach. The procedural approach entails attending to the client's religious needs, such as accompanying them to a church service, while the personal approach involves the nurse directly attending to the client's spiritual needs. On similar lines, Sango and Forrester-Jones (2017a, pp. 1, 7, 12) differentiate religious spiritual care from non-religious spiritual care. Religious spiritual care is defined as assisting a person with a learning disability with overtly religious activities, such as attending worship on Sundays. One-on-one care between a caregiver and a person with a learning disability is referred to as non-religious spiritual care and it does not have to be openly religious.

Methodology

Swinton (2001, p. 3) suggests that research on spirituality and spiritual care of persons with learning disabilities must be 'narrative based' in order 'to capture the subtle and often deeply personal nuances of spiritual experience'. Hence, I chose to use the methodology of hermeneutic phenomenology.

Phenomenology is not a singular method but instead is comprised of three diverse approaches with distinct philosophical postures (Eddles-Hirsch, 2015, p. 252) – namely, transcendental phenomenology, hermeneutic phenomenology, and existential phenomenology (Kafle, 2013, p. 185).

This study employed the hermeneutic phenomenological approach. In hermeneutics, knowledge is understood as being the outcome of an interpretative process wherein an individual engages with an experience from a specific standpoint or perspective. Hermeneutics endeavours to better understand the manner in which individuals interpret and perceive their experiences (Swinton and Mowat, 2016, p. 103; Alsaigh and Coyne, 2021, p. 2). According to Gadamer, hermeneutics is about what individuals are, rather than what they do to interpret an experience. Hermeneutics is ontological rather than merely epistemological (Swinton and Mowat, 2016, p. 103). Hermeneutic phenomenology integrates both approaches to give a rich description as well as an interpretative perspective of the experience (Swinton and Mowat, 2016, p. 105). The researcher gives equal attention to both the participant's description of the phenomenon and their interpretation of the experience of the phenomenon (Eddles-Hirsch, 2015, p. 253). The methodology of hermeneutic phenomenology attracted me because it acknowledges that the whole truth can never be fully understood (Lindseth and Norberg, 2004, p. 151) but recognizes the presence of valuable knowledge within intricate details and nuances. In order to generate meaning and achieve understanding, it emphasizes these aspects of an experience that could be overlooked or taken for granted (Alsaigh and Coyne, 2021, p. 2).

The selection of participants in this study was determined by the specific phenomenon under investigation, employing a purposive sampling approach (Hycner, 1985, p. 294). The recruitment process consisted of field investigations (Berg, 2001, p. 32), which in this study consisted of my witnessing the assistants providing spiritual care for core members, the term used for persons with learning disabilities who are supported by L'Arche. L'Arche is charitable organization where people with and without learning disabilities live together in community (https://www.larche.org.uk/). Personal relationships aided in sample recruitment and none of the assistants whom I approached declined the invitation.

A significant limitation of the study is that in the study none of the assistants who participated had experience supporting in spiritual care a core member of a different religious tradition. One further observation I gained from the discussions was that all the interviewees exhibited a form of flexible spirituality, characterized by a departure from strict adherence to any specific religious group or faith. Those assistants who had been expressly agnostic reported a movement towards Christian values, as observed through their experiences in L'Arche. Similarly, assistants who previously held a deeper commitment to a particular denomination indicated a shift towards developing an appreciation for diverse value systems. So I could not get an assistant who embodies the tension of firmly held personal beliefs, and the different beliefs of the core members.

Research findings

The spirituality of core members

One significant aspect of L'Arche that I observed was the sensitivity of assistants to the spirituality of core members. The responses of assistants reflected an awareness of the general attitude in the care sector that care workers and organizations are often unaware of (Swinton and Powrie, 2004, p. 15; Lemos, 2017, p. 14), or do not acknowledge, the significance of spirituality in the lives of persons with learning disabilities (Sango and Forrester-Jones, 2017b, p. 4). Hannah critically reflected on the 'functional approach' (Swinton and Powrie, 2004, p. 75) in care for persons with learning disabilities:

> People with learning disabilities I think are often presumed although it's not said, but there is an implicit kind of saying of having a different human experience, [than] the rest of us, or lesser human experience and like they won't see the value of this ... and therefore often the care that is created around them is very basic. It's about basic human needs. It can be very unimaginative, it can be very limited, it can be very much like if you have eaten and drunk and dressed and you've had your medication like ... job's done. (Hannah)

In a study by Sango and Forrester-Jones (2017a, p. 11), it was reported that care staff in a care home suggested that persons with learning disabilities might not understand spiritual matters as a result of their 'mental capacity' and that they might not have a 'spiritual need'. It is also suggested that spiritual care for persons with learning disabilities may not be seen as equally significant as physical care given by caregivers (Sango and Forester-Jones, 2017b, p. 5). What Hannah explained further profoundly countered these attitudes:

> And I think that's not what human experience is about. Human experience is about love and connection and bravery and disappointment and complexity and joy and all of those things, those kinds of other emotions, like the sense of otherness of the world. And that's what I think people with learning disabilities absolutely have a right to because that's for me where the richness of life has happened. And also, people that have disabilities have just taught me so much about that, that they are ... not passive in wanting that. They're exploring and asking these questions. (Hannah)

Prayer

Prayer has been reported as being a significant form of religious expression by persons with learning disabilities (Turner et al., 2004, p. 164; Lemos, 2017, pp. 16, 28, 36) and there exists literature on the impact of prayer in their well-being (Sango and Forrester-Jones, 2017c, p. 12; Turner et al., 2004, p. 161). John shared how his understanding of a core member was transformed through observing her personal prayer:

> It was really interesting because she very much doesn't talk about [sic] in daily life. You don't hear her opinions on things. You don't really hear what she cares about or what's going on ... And then in this moment, we had this very touchy moment where she would say, 'Oh, I pray for this person and this thing I'm going through'. And I was just like, Oh my gosh, she's carrying so much ... do you know what I mean? In her life ... And it just made me feel like that she's going through so much that she's not vocalizing to anybody ... I think that was quite transformative for me because I almost viewed her in a completely different light because before that I just didn't hear that level of thought sharing. Yeah, intimate sharing from her. (John)

The sensitivity of this assistant to the personal prayer of the core member is of particular significance, as prayer is reported as a way of expressing the 'person's inner pain' (Swinton and Powrie, 2004, p. 54) and spiritual needs (Lemos, 2017, p. 28). Assistants also shared about their experiences of supporting core members in prayer, including Lydia:

> At first I found it, like, difficult and confusing because I hadn't had experience with praying since I left school, because I went to a Church of England school. But then it came quite easily because you realize how much it means to the core member. And it's almost like praying doesn't strictly have to be something linked to religion. So, I found that I could work through it. (Lydia)

Hannah reflected on being invited to pray as a privilege: 'And, um, that's a privilege. I think that's what I think those things are ... when someone is inviting you ... when they are asking for help, saying a prayer or recognizing something as deeply authentic and ... and precious.'

Sango and Forrester-Jones (2017a, p. 12) report care workers having feelings of 'doubt' and 'fear' in relation to preparing prayer sessions. My interviews supported the view that prayer forms a significant part of spiritual care for persons with learning disabilities and that it requires special effort and intentional commitment from support assistants to support persons with learning disabilities in prayer.

The spiritual milieu of L'Arche

Through interviews I discerned an active engagement by L'Arche with the perceived tension of how spirituality can be incorporated in the context of spiritual diversity (L'Arche USA, 2016, p. 4; L'Arche USA, 2017, pp. 1–2). The term 'moveable feast' (L'Arche USA, 2017, pp. 4–5) reflects this dynamic expression of spirituality. Participants shared their valuing of the ecumenical and interfaith dimension of the organization and an inclusive outlook where every member contributed to the spiritual life of the community.

The emphasis of community in the spiritual milieu of L'Arche is a theme that is explored theologically (Greig, 2015, p. 201). The celebration of community is special in L'Arche as evidenced through the different weekly and monthly gatherings, celebrating birthdays and anniversaries, and also in the daily mealtimes when all the core members in the house and assistants on rota come to eat together (L'Arche USA, 2017, pp. 5–7, 12; L'Arche UK, 2015, pp. 6–7). These narratives reflect an organizational awareness and sensitivity to spirituality. 'Organizational awareness of spirituality' is a significant aspect of 'spiritually competent practice': this has an impact on staff because, in the absence of organizational awareness of spirituality, even care workers who are willing to support in spiritual care will find themselves 'constantly having to work around (or even against) the system, rather than with it' (Wattis, Curran and Rogers, 2017, p. 192). Such attitudes have a negative impact on service users as well (Sango and Forrester-Jones, 2017b, p. 15). Swinton and Powrie (2004, p. 79) report care workers not getting the opportunity to reflect on their own spirituality and its impact upon addressing the spiritual needs of persons with learning disabilities, hence the significance of these spaces offered in L'Arche to explore the spirituality of core members as well as support assistants.

The relationship between personal spirituality and provision of spiritual care

The way James described his experience of supporting the core members resonates with Montgomery's (1991, pp. 91, 93) suggestion that personal, intimate involvement has profound significance on the 'caregiver' and the 'client'. It is also suggested that the way care workers perform their duties at work in relation to spiritual and religious care may sometimes be influenced by their personal beliefs (Sango and Forrester-Jones, 2017a, p. 12).

James reflected on caring in general from a sacramental perspective (Greig, 2015, p. 208) and this reflects L'Arche's understanding of spirituality being present in the 'most routine and mundane details of the day, when they are shared with each other' (L'Arche Atlanta, n.d., online):

> There are times of like, not always, but sometimes ... great kind of joy for me, like we're, we are connected and we're connecting to something bigger as well ... to be honest, they, they more often come into the day to day [activities], like I can think of a time when I was supporting [a core member] recently, I was using a flannel to kind of wash him down and that scripture ... popped into my head ... Whatever you do for the least of one of these, you, you did for me. And I was able to clean him in a way that I, you know, if I was doing that for Jesus, like I would've done it in that way ... So, it felt really deeply kind of dignifying for [the core member]. Like, I felt like I was putting him in the highest place and I was really kind of cherishing him and prizing him as a person. (James)

In the research, I found reflections from the vantage point of spirituality not tied to organized religion, from a personal morality perspective, and from a spirituality that is based in Christian faith. The reflections of these assistants demonstrated spiritual self-awareness, an essential component of spiritual competence (Huiskes, 2016, p. 4) and spiritual sensitivity (Callahan, 2015, p. 46) in health and social care.

Approach to spiritual care: the needs of the core member takes priority

Persons with learning disabilities should not be excluded from exploring their spirituality because of institutional restrictions or because of their perceived limitations (Lemos, 2017, p. 28). But it is also reported in studies that spiritual needs of persons with learning disabilities are often ignored or even shunned (Turner et al., 2004, p. 169) in favour of what is convenient for the care staff (Swinton and Powrie, 2004, p. 79). On the contrary, in L'Arche, the narratives of assistants consistently portrayed an attitude of flexibility in prioritizing the needs of the core members:

> I think if I am supporting somebody in their faith, my faith has to take a back seat because I am not there as me. [I mean] I am there as me, [but] I am there as an extension of them in that situation ... my only reason for being there is supporting them through it, and if I can't do that fully then things need to change. (Laura)

What was shared by Laura is how she addressed 'religious and cultural barriers' in spiritual care (Swinton and Powrie, 2004, p. 79). It is similar to a response by a participant in an action research project: 'Sidelining my own personal beliefs and looking at the emotional needs/beliefs of others' (Hatton et al., 2004, p. 33). John shared a similar view:

> Because it's just their life ... I'm here to support them, so I'm not [here for] my own needs. If I wasn't comfortable ... if there was a challenge, I think I would ask if there's a way I can amend the challenge to make it less of a challenge, if that makes sense, but if there was no wiggle room, I'd go with what was expected. (John)

I perceive these ideas as radical because the staff approach to spirituality has been identified as a significant aspect in how well the spiritual needs are addressed (Sango and Forrester-Jones, 2017a, p. 11). The challenges this may bring to assistants led to them identifying the importance of 'having those spaces like supervision or accompaniment'.

Spiritual care as mutually co-created fellowship

Every participant spoke from a perspective of doing something with, not for, the core member.

Demmons (2009), drawing from Karl Barth, writes about spiritual care being mutual and not unilateral. She argues that in spiritual care the fellowship experienced together is more important than the care itself. The fellowship points to the shared human need to care and receive care in the face of vulnerability, because vulnerability is a shared human experience. What is portrayed in the fellowship is a 'human camaraderie or solidarity' (Demmons, 2009, p. 183).

It has been proposed that spiritual care can also take the shape of intimate friendships and quality time spent together, especially for those with profound learning disabilities (Swinton, 1997, p. 26; Watts, 2011, as cited in Sango and Forrester-Jones, 2017a, p. 12). Hannah had something interesting to share about her experience of supporting and celebrating spirituality of core members, even when she does not necessarily agree with them:

> Elsa and I talked about doing [a community activity] and her mum would be so proud looking down on her from heaven. And I don't know if I conceive of heaven ... and I probably don't conceive of it in a similar way to Elsa. But that's not important. What's important is that Elsa is describing something that is very important to her, that gives

her a sense of meaning and context ... And your understanding of the experience doesn't need to be the same as [theirs] for it to be something shared and significant. (Hannah)

This shows that spiritual care is something that could be experienced together and is of benefit to the support assistant as well. It further buttresses the view that it cannot be delivered as a tick-box activity (Swinton, 2004b, p. 14).

Curating spiritual care: 'How do I know this is what they want?'

It is important that something is not forced upon persons with learning disabilities and that spiritual care is 'in line with their personal desires' (Sango and Forrester-Jones, 2017a, p. 14), 'meeting the aspirations chosen by the person' (Hatton et al., 2004, p. 4). With verbal core members, knowing their preferences is much easier and, during my time living in L'Arche, I have witnessed core members choose not to go to a particular event that they usually participate in. When a core member makes that choice then the care is curated around that choice. John shared how he gained feedback on the bedtime ritual that he co-created with a core member: 'And I got feedback in terms of how they reacted and that was positive. If it was negative, I wouldn't have done it ever again. Do you know what I mean?' Writing about 'spiritual safety' in the context of health and social care, Keenan (2017, p. 2) speaks of special care needed for individuals who 'struggle with understanding, defining and expressing their spiritual/religious concerns/needs'.

Similarly, for non-verbal core members, there is always a need for caution when assuming whether a particular thing is what they want and then interpreting their responses as indications of whether or not they like it (Sango and Forrester-Jones, 2017a, p. 10). Reflections from participants portrayed the complexity involved here, and the sensitivity required from the assistants, particularly reflecting on bedtime prayer that was part of the routine for a few core members:

So there's something about interpreting for [the core member] around what would he want to pray for ... It's hit and miss, right? You're hoping that your knowledge of that person and your relationship with that person will help you curate that space for him because it's very important for him. But also [what you have is] that understanding that you are creating it. You are choosing who the people are that are named. So that's also an interesting balance, isn't it? (Hannah)

The significant point here is that there exists in L'Arche an active engagement with the spiritual needs of the core member while being fully aware that there can be failure in understanding what the core member wants. But this does not mean it should be seen as a barrier and spiritual care ignored as it was reported in a study by Swinton and Powrie (2004, p. 80). The way forward is to engage with the core member sensitively, taking the cues and curating care catering to their preferences (Raji, 2009, p. 135). Along these lines, James shared how a non-verbal core member reminded him to pray for his family as part of the bedtime prayer, which was similar to an event reported by Sango and Forrester-Jones (2017a, p. 6):

> I recently forgot to pray for his [family]. Yeah. So, as I was ending the prayer, Johnson said [name of family member]. And ... that was quite a surprise really, because he barely says things like that. Yeah. But it was so important to him that I'd missed it and he reminded me. (James)

There was also an active effort to curate spiritual care for a core member whose family does not follow any faith tradition, which demonstrated the exploration of spiritual care beyond explicitly religious or spiritual activities. To actualize these requires the sensitivity of both the support assistants and the organization to the spiritual needs of the core member and person-centred planning (Raji, 2009, p. 128). With or without the ability to communicate verbally, a person could express their spiritual aspirations and needs (Lemos, 2017, pp. 28–9) through provision of opportunities and accessible information (Swinton, 2001, p. 1) as evidenced by this research.

Imaging the spiritual care roles of support assistants: guide-facilitator; interpreter; advocate

An interesting idea that came up in the conversations about prioritizing the core member's needs was seeing the assistant as an extension of the core member: 'I think if I am supporting somebody ... I am there as an extension of them in that situation.' Assistants also shared a few images on how they conceptualize their role in spiritual care, and in analysis I merged these images with the concept of the support assistant as the extension of the core member.

Guide-facilitator

> I think my role in someone's spirituality isn't sort of a leader or telling someone what to do. I think it's just more a guide. Yeah. I think supporting them to do what they want to do or even collaborating on something together. [John]

This image of guide-facilitator was reflected in what Laura said: 'It's the subtle things of, like, helping the person go up when they are [in communion] ... helping them give money to the collection in church.' This support of guiding and facilitating the subtle things is of significance in actualizing the spiritual needs of persons with learning disabilities, as absence of this support has been reported to restrict participation of persons with learning disabilities in communal religious activities (Swinton and Powrie, 2004, pp. 79–80).

Interpreter

> You are almost sometimes their verbalizer or the explainer between. Sermons can often be very complicated and very wordy depending on what part of the Bible they are going from or using big words or are talking too fast. Or the songs going on, them just kind of using different words for the songs. 'We are going to sing now', 'We are going to do a song', 'It's time to stand up and let's praise God'. All of those phrases being, 'stand up to sing', but only one of them said stand up and sing. So even those sorts of things, having to support somebody with those things if they are not used to it, or it's a new church so you know ... It's kind of like an interpreter as well. (Laura)

This transcript extract relates to the idea of intellectual access in spirituality. Intellectual inaccessibility has been reported to cause exclusion of persons with learning disabilities and can be compounded by various forms of social exclusion (Swinton and Powrie, 2004, p. 44). Hence the significance of this idea of being an interpreter.

Advocate

This was conceptualized in terms of advocating for the core member:

> I've supported a core member to have communion and they did a blessing with the core member instead of communion and I was like, Oh no, can they have communion please, because the priest didn't realize. It was an easy mistake. They assumed because they are [a person with a

learning disability] they wouldn't want communion. They would just want a blessing because the person is non-verbal. So, my job in that situation was to advocate for them that they need communion. (Laura)

And also in terms of advocating to the core member:

If a core member needs a lot of encouragement to stay focused on something or needs you, you need to advocate for the situation [to the core member] as well. 'Huh this is really fun, this is really good, we are going to enjoy it.' (Laura)

These images reveal the complexity involved in spiritual care and the sensitivity required by the support assistants in responding to the needs of the core member.

Outcomes and recommendations

The analytical findings of this hermeneutic phenomenological study are useful to gain new insights about the identified phenomenon. The new understandings gained should impact behaviour. This application of hermeneutic phenomenological interpretations is called appropriation (Lindseth and Norberg, 2004, p. 151). In this step of seeking to enable the research to have real-world impact I identified the following outcomes and recommendations:

- Assistants' sensitivity to the spirituality of a person with learning disabilities was identified as a key factor that impacted the provision of spiritual care. Hence, enhancing the awareness and understanding among assistants regarding spirituality and its significance in the lives of individuals with learning disabilities has the potential to improve the delivery of spiritual care. There is a need for the development of training resources for this.
- All the assistants reported providing support with prayer as a form of spiritual care. The knowledge of how to do it came from either being brought up in a church school or being part of a church. Workshops on prayer and spirituality could be helpful for assistants in this regard.
- The organizational awareness and sensitivity to spirituality in L'Arche was reflected by all the participants in the study. While L'Arche portrays this through its roots in the Christian faith, there needs to be further exploration on how secular care settings can achieve this. It could be possible through partnerships with religious organizations.
- The community ethos of L'Arche was observed to enrich the spirituality of not only the core members but also assistants. The weekly and

monthly events of celebration and fellowship are a pattern that can be adopted in secular contexts as well.
- Assistants must be given opportunities to reflect on their own spirituality as well as how it impacts their work. This need not be religious. Based on the feedback provided by the assistants, it became apparent that the presence of a dynamic spiritual environment in L'Arche positively influenced both their personal spirituality and the care for the persons with learning disabilities.
- Active encouragement to make friendship and relationship was found to have an impact on care in general and spiritual care in particular. This challenges the existing ideas on professional boundaries in care settings. This is a significant wisdom L'Arche portrays, that provision of safe care need not always be associated with clearly defined professional boundaries.
- Mutuality in spiritual care is another aspect that could be learned from L'Arche. Assistants received as much as they gave in spiritual care, even in the mundane events of practical support such as supporting a person to church. Frameworks should allow assistants to have this space to experience spirituality with persons with learning disabilities and also to try new experiences.
- The fundamental L'Arche ethos of prioritizing the core member, in my view, needs to be a core philosophy in any care for persons with learning disabilities. This approach goes beyond what I have learned as person-centred care. To put this in simple words, it is about reframing the basic question from 'Is it possible to make this happen?' to 'How can we make this happen?' and looking at every barrier through this lens.
- The philosophy of prioritizing the core member is closely associated with curating spiritual care and involves a proactive sensitivity to persons with learning disabilities. The variety of communication tools available can be employed for this and this is an area I believe warrants further research.
- The reflections of assistants on images points to the further possibility of developing theoretical frameworks for the roles of a support assistant in spiritual care, drawing in ideas from support assistants as well as persons with learning disabilities.

Bibliography

Alsaigh, R. and I. Coyne (2021), 'Doing a Hermeneutic Phenomenology Research Underpinned by Gadamer's Philosophy: A Framework to Facilitate Data Analysis', *International Journal of Qualitative Methods* 20(1), pp. 1–10.

Berg, B. L. (2001), *Qualitative Research Methods for the Social Sciences*, Boston MA: Allyn & Bacon.

Callahan, A. (2015), 'Key Concepts in Spiritual Care for Hospice Social Workers: How an Interdisciplinary Perspective Can Inform Spiritual Competence', *Social Work & Christianity* 42(1), pp. 43–62.

Carter, E. W. and T. L. Boehm (2019), 'Religious and Spiritual Expressions of Young People with Intellectual and Developmental Disabilities', *Research and Practice for Persons with Severe Disabilities* 44(1), pp. 37–52.

Demmons, T. A. (2009), 'Toward a Post-Critical Theology of Knowledge of God for Persons with Intellectual Disabilities: with Special Reference to Karl Barth's Church Dogmatics III:2', unpublished doctoral thesis, Scotland: University of St Andrews.

Eddles-Hirsch, K. (2015), 'Phenomenology and Educational Research', *International Journal of Advanced Research* 3, pp. 251–60.

Forrester-Jones, R. et al. (2018), 'Including the "Spiritual" within Mental Health Care in the UK, from the Experiences of People with Mental Health Problems', *Journal of Religion and Health* 57(1), pp. 384–407.

Greig, J. R. (2015), *Reconsidering Intellectual Disability: L'Arche, Medical Ethics, and Christian Friendship*, Washington DC: Georgetown University Press.

Hatton, C. et al. (2004), 'Religious Expression, a Fundamental Human Right: The Report of an Action Research Project on Meeting the Religious Needs of People with Learning Disabilities', London: Foundation for People with Learning Disabilities.

Huiskes, S. (2016), 'Medical Social Worker's Understandings of Spirituality in Patient Care', master's thesis, St Catherine University and the University of St Thomas, Minnesota.

Hunter, C. and S. E. Kivisto (2019), 'Significance of Spirituality among Individuals with Intellectual and Developmental Disabilities', master's thesis, Bethel University, IN, available at https://spark.bethel.edu/etd/311/?utm_source=spark.bethel.edu%2Fetd%2F311&utm_medium=PDF&utm_campaign=PDFCoverPages (accessed 7.07.2024).

Hycner, R. H. (1985), 'Some Guidelines for the Phenomenological Analysis of Interview Data', *Human Studies* 8, pp. 279–303.

Kafle, N. P. (2013), 'Hermeneutic Phenomenological Research Method Simplified', *Bodhi: An Interdisciplinary Journal* 5(1), pp. 181–200.

Keenan, P. (2017), 'Spiritual Vulnerability, Spiritual Risk and Spiritual Safety – In Answer to a Question: "Why Is Spirituality Important within Health and Social Care?" at the Second International Spirituality in Healthcare Conference 2016 – Nurturing the Spirit', *Religions* 8(3), p. 38.

L'Arche Atlanta (n.d.), *L'Arche Spirituality*, available at http://www.larcheatlanta.org/larche-spirituality.html (accessed 7.07.2024).

L'Arche UK (2015), 'Survey of Community Faith Life Practice in 2015', unpublished.

L'Arche USA (2016), 'Guide to Practices that Provide Meaning', available at https://archive.larcheusa.org/wp-content/uploads/2019/01/LArche_Spiritual_Practices_Guide.pdf (accessed 7.07.2024).

L'Arche USA (2017), 'Enhancing and Nurturing L'Arche Spirituality in the Communities of L'Arche USA and Beyond', available at https://archive.larcheusa.org/wp-content/uploads/2018/01/White_Paper_Enhancing_and_Nurturing_L_Arche_Spirituality_in_US_and_Beyond.pdf (accessed 7.07.2024).

Lemos, G. (2017), *Looking Together: Spiritual Beliefs and Aspirations of People with Learning Disabilities*, London: Lemos and Crane.

Lindseth, A. and A. Norberg (2004), 'A Phenomenological Hermeneutical Method for Researching Lived Experience', *Scandinavian Journal of Caring Sciences* 18(2), pp. 145-53.

Montgomery, C. L. (1991), 'The Care-giving Relationship: Paradoxical and Transcendent Aspects', *Journal of Transpersonal Psychology* 23(2), pp. 91-104.

Narayanaswamy, A., B. Gates and J. Swinton (2002), 'Spirituality and Learning Disabilities: A Qualitative Study', *British Journal of Nursing* 11(14), pp. 948-57.

Nursing and Midwifery (2010), *Standards for Pre-registration Nursing Education*, London: NMC.

Raji, O. (2009), 'Intellectual Disability', in C. C. H. Cook, A. Powell and A. Sims (eds), *Spirituality and Psychiatry*, London: Royal College of Psychiatrists, pp. 122-38.

Research Excellence Framework (2014), 'Impact Case Study – Spirituality and Health and Social Care', available at https://ref2014impact.azurewebsites.net/casestudies2/refservice.svc/GetCaseStudyPDF/43376 (accessed 7.07.2024).

Sango, P. N. and R. Forrester-Jones (2017a), 'Spiritual Care for People with Intellectual and Developmental Disability: An Exploratory Study', *Journal of Intellectual and Developmental Disability* 44(11), pp. 1-11. (Note – open access author's accepted manuscript downloaded from Kent Academic Repository. Url: https://kar.kent.ac.uk/61810/.)

Sango, P. N. and R. Forrester-Jones (2017b), 'Intellectual and Developmental Disabilities, Spirituality and Religion: A Systematic Review 1990-2015', *Journal of Disability & Religion* 21(3), pp. 280-95. (Note – open access author's accepted manuscript downloaded from Kent Academic Repository. Url: https://kar.kent.ac.uk/61314/.)

Sango, P. N. and R. Forrester-Jones (2017c), 'Spirituality and Social Networks of People with Intellectual and Developmental Disability', *Journal of Intellectual & Developmental Disability* 43(3), pp. 1-11. (Note – open access author's accepted manuscript downloaded from Kent Academic Repository. Url: https://kar.kent.ac.uk/61315/.)

Sango, P. N. and R. Forrester-Jones (2022), 'Spirituality and the Quality of Life of Individuals with Intellectual Disability', *Journal of Long-term Care*, pp. 193-204.

Swinton, J. (1997), 'Restoring the Image: Spirituality, Faith, and Cognitive Disability', *Journal of Religion and Health* 36(1), pp. 21-7, available at http://www.jstor.org/stable/27511088 (accessed 7.07.2024).

Swinton, J. (2001), 'Spirituality and the Lives of People with Learning Disabilities', *Updates* 3(6), pp. 1-4.

Swinton, J. (2004a), 'Why Are We Here? Spirituality and the Lives of People with Learning Disabilities', *Updates* 5(11), pp. 1-4.

Swinton, J. (2004b), *No Box to Tick: A Booklet for Carers and Support Workers on Meeting the Spiritual Needs of People with Learning Disabilities*, London: The Mental Health Foundation.

Swinton, J. and E. Powrie (2004), 'Why Are We Here?: Understanding the Spiritual Lives of People with Learning Disabilities', unpublished report, London: Foundation for People with Learning Disabilities.

Swinton, J. and H. Mowat (2016), *Practical Theology and Qualitative Research*, London: SCM Press.

Turner, S. et al. (2004), 'Religious Expression amongst Adults with Intellectual Disabilities', *Journal of Applied Research in Intellectual Disabilities* 17(3), pp. 161-71.

Wattis, J., S. Curran and M. Rogers (2017), *Spiritually Competent Practice in Health Care*, London: CRC Press.

22

Re-writing the Play: Reflections on a Theodramatic Approach to Decolonizing my Teaching of Chaplaincy and Pastoral Care

GRACE THOMAS

Chaplaincy is a discipline that holds together a multitude of different models and approaches to practice. This book is a clear example of the many ways in which chaplaincy is lived out and the diversity of contexts it inhabits. While there are many facets to the work that chaplains do, one central theme is pastoral, or spiritual, care. And it is this theme that has interested me for over 15 years. How do we learn about pastoral care and where does our understanding come from?

In this chapter, I will tell the story of a journey I took during a year-long decolonizing project I embarked upon as tutor of pastoral care and chaplaincy. My initial intention was to develop a course that reflected a global, inclusive, decolonized perspective that would equip students for practice within our multicultural, diverse contexts and would enable them to critique some of the dominant Eurocentric approaches that remain within the field. What emerged from the project did, to an extent, serve to reach my initial aim, but it raised far more complex questions as it became apparent that reshaping and decolonizing the modules I teach could not be done in isolation from the institution within which they were taught and the wider social landscape. Here, I give a small glimpse into my story and how I experimented with a new framework of reflection: namely, theodrama. As with so many stories held within this book, the narrative is ongoing, extending beyond the realms of these pages and, hopefully, into the narratives of others who, like me, are exploring what it means to truly diversify, decolonize and, ultimately, deconstruct many long-held structures.

Using theodrama as a reflective tool

As a tutor in pastoral care and chaplaincy for five years, I was becoming increasingly aware of the ways in which the subjects were shaped mainly by white Western theologies and experiences. I decided, somewhat ambitiously, to embark upon a year-long reflective project. Tools of reflection inevitably shape the process and influence outcomes. The most common methods within a transformative praxis paradigm are versions of the pastoral cycle, such as Green's spiral (Green, 2009), Swinton and Mowat's cycle incorporating mutual critical correlation (Swinton and Mowat, 2016) and Lartey's intercultural cycle (Lartey, 1996). These all encourage a linear, 'progression' approach to reflection. Beaudoin and Turpin highlight that organizing procedurally is a trait linked with the practice of white Europeans and their cultural descendants, in order to increase efficiency and convenience (Beaudoin and Turpin, 2014, p. 261). They argue that 'procedural rationality' has become a distinctive marker of influential approaches in white practical theology. Such approaches have then been applied in diverse, indigenous communities with an underlying predisposition to 'setting the terms of the field' (Beaudoin and Turpin, 2014, p. 261) in a manner that parallels colonial power.

In a project designed to explore decolonizing practice, I was keen to avoid methods that had the potential to enforce colonial systems and normative Western approaches, and I became drawn to Nell's use of theodrama. Ian Nell is a South African theologian influenced by the Swiss theologian Hans Urs von Balthasar, whose extensive works proposed that the relations between God, the world and the Church could be best conceived as a play, which demonstrates the dramatic, complex and tense nature of the story of redemption (von Balthasar, 1988). Nell adopted a theodramatic approach to his teaching of practical theology and missiology, which enabled him to look at the issues through the themes of stage, script, plot and role (Nell, 2021). Rather than operating on a trajectory, theodrama creates a picture. There is no progression between steps, as each element of stage, script, plot and role is freestanding. Yet at the same time the elements frequently transgress their boundaries into one another. This non-linear nature took me away from the most frequently used models of transformative praxis and allowed me the opportunity to reflect more creatively. Therefore, I framed my project using theodrama as a reflective tool through which I could begin to explore the process of decolonizing in the way I taught pastoral care.

The stage

The stage is the 'local, national and international context (culture) in which we theologise' (Nell, 2021, p. 5). In my case, the drama unfolded in the theological college where I taught pastoral care and chaplaincy. Luther King Centre (LKC) is named after Martin Luther King and the foundational ethos of LKC is articulated on the college's website:

> We are inspired by Martin Luther King's vision of equality, justice and peace and seek to be a small part of making that dream, and the dreams of our students and faith communities, a reality in our world. (Luther King Centre, n.d.)

The college has a long history of exploring theologies and ideas on the 'edges' of mainstream theology and challenging perspectives that may not reflect diverse outlooks. Yet the staff team are honest in recognizing that they still have a long way to go to achieve the 'dream'. This includes me, of course, and despite the fact that I have a South Indian heritage, my learning and teaching in pastoral care and chaplaincy have been wholly formed by a Western perspective. The result of the Western foundation of theological education has been an academic framework shaped through a lens that many theological educators like myself are unaware of. This has led to the development of pedagogical practices that privilege one main way of learning. We teach within a globalized context, meaning that students come to colleges like Luther King Centre with diverse learning styles – such as the oral culture. Yet they are often 'colonized to a European-rooted model of paper writing', which does not allow those from global backgrounds 'to access the worlds from which they come and to which they will return and engage' (Day, 2021, p. 125). The default option, or even the 'gold standard' form of assessment, remains the written submission, which is the form of assessment I have required.

Decolonization initially referred to independence from colonial rule, but recently it has been used to refer to what Shahjahan et al. call a 'reconfiguration' of the world – a 'decentering' of Western, Eurocentric norms (Shahjahan et al., 2022, pp. 81–2). This highlights the breadth of the decolonizing landscape – one that is often not fully acknowledged. The stage has a backdrop – the local context is, inevitably, part of the wider national and international context, and a growing body of evidence points to wider issues within theological education that have made decolonizing both essential and challenging. Eve Parker states that theological education has 'validated hierarchies created through white male supremacy and colonialism' (Parker, 2022, pp. viii–ix) yet, in the UK in 2020, only 24 out of 128 universities stated that they had one or more faculties committed to decolonizing the curriculum, and only 11 were committed to decolonizing the whole university (Batty, 2020). As I reflected on my own practice with the aim of effecting change, I did so with strong local support, yet among a wider backdrop of what appeared to be apathy, or even a lack of recognition of need. The stage, as von Balthasar states, is not neutral – it is both influenced by the action that is due to take place there, and it itself influences the unfolding play (von Balthasar, 1990, p. 173). The local stage, LKC, had the willingness to create a more diverse, decolonized play, but was restricted by wider cultural norms and standards, where the will to progress was less defined. As I began to recognize this, I began to reflect on my position, my ability to effect change and my naivety, in a sense, that I could simply 'decolonize a module'. The picture being developed through this theodramatic process was far more complex than I had originally imagined.

The script

Having taken a look at the stage, I then began to look at the script – namely, what was shaping the narrative of pastoral care and chaplaincy in theological education. The limitations of the prevailing script have been highlighted for decades. Pattison, for example, in 2000, critiqued the influence of dominant Eurocentric culture in narrowing the focus of pastoral theology and care to an individualized approach to well-being (Pattison, 2000, p. 17). The field of chaplaincy is, similarly, dominated by research undertaken mainly by men and women from Western perspectives. The lack of global voices and perspectives is stark and stands in contrast with the hugely diverse contexts within which pastoral care and chaplaincy practice are often lived out.

There has been a growing recognition of the need for diversity and inclusion in ministerial training and practice, yet the painful reality is articulated by Paul Gorski, in his paper 'Good Intentions are Not Enough' (2008). Without due reflexivity and honest interrogation of whole practices, Gorski argues that much of what is considered to be 'intercultural education practice' actually accentuates, rather than reduces, 'existing social and political hierarchies' (Gorski, 2008, p. 516). The script, in many cases, is tweaked rather than overhauled. Structures are left intact, while minor changes are made that are then hailed as progress. This was, in all honesty, reflected in my original approach and proposal, and as the drama of this reflection continued to unfold I was becoming increasingly aware of this challenge and, at times, quite overwhelmed by it.

For Nell, the plot centres on the various acts that arise from the focus of the script (Nell, 2021, p. 5). I had, by this point, acknowledged that the script needed re-visioning and was set on a stage with a complex backdrop. The outcome, or the resultant plot, of the traditional script had led to the exclusion and limitation of global voices and practices within the field of pastoral care and chaplaincy. In keeping with an intersectional, non-linear way of approaching theological reflection, I began by discerning what plot I was seeking to achieve so that this could be used to shape a new script of a play that was set within a stage that, itself, needed work.

A decolonized plot centres around the liberation and empowerment of global voices and practices that can be added to the Eurocentric voices that have long dominated the subject. It also needs to empower students from diverse backgrounds to take part in the academic forum in ways that liberate and value their cultural pedagogical practices. As Parker points out, decolonizing a curriculum is not about the denial or removal of Eurocentric epistemologies (Parker, 2022, p. 155), but rather it is a reassessing of theological truths in the light of an understanding that such epistemologies are, by themselves, insufficient at best and oppressive at worst. The plot of the 'traditional' Eurocentric script in theological education elevates one perspective to the oppression, exclusion and, even, elimination of all others. Western knowledge, Tuhiwai Smith asserts, established 'positional superiority', and this is evident in some of the accounts emerging from within theological education (Tuhiwai Smith, 2021, p. 68). Beaudoin and Turpin powerfully illustrate how white theology has historically occupied an unquestioned space, the byproduct of colonial Christianity being that white theology presumes to speak for and about 'others' (Beaudoin and Turpin, 2014, p. 253).

The impact of this in the theological classroom has been multifaceted. It involves both the content of materials presented and also the way in which they are presented and the modes of assessment that are offered. In contemporary theological education, Parker argues that there has been disdain and distrust for black/queer/feminist theologies because they deviate from the deeply ingrained privileged white Western male norm (Parker, 2022, p. 9). 'Classical' theologians such as John Calvin and Karl Barth are deemed to have universal, foundational relevance whereas 'contextual' theologians such as James H. Cone are seen wholly through the lens of black theology and are deemed optional (Day, 2021, pp. 48–50). In my initial deliberations, I had highlighted the need for broader materials in the exploration of pastoral care practices that incorporate global perspectives, and within the LKC context I found that this aspect of decolonizing was already taken seriously – there was a breadth of material available in study spaces and on reading lists. This demonstrated good intention, but this intention needed to translate into embedded, transformative practice.

Day points out that students of colour are often told that they are not 'theoretical enough' or their work is not valid because they are working from different scholarly paradigms and frameworks – possibly the result of having encountered different dominant cultural traditions of knowledge assimilation, such as the oral tradition (Day, 2021, p. 58). She also articulates how students find themselves faced with Eurocentric rigid structures where they are told their experiences are 'cultural', not theological, and therefore irrelevant (Day, 2021, p. 62). So the desired plot, or outcome of a script that is on a journey of decolonizing, is that students in theological education settings have greater access to pedagogical practices and resources that support their diverse ways of assimilating knowledge, and are broadened to feature global voices, perspectives and practices.

Being open to creative pedagogical methodologies is central in a decolonizing approach, to ensure equal access for students of all backgrounds. Elina Hankela notes the importance of cultivating spaces where students are able to locate their life narratives within the curriculum, so that their experiences 'become auto-ethnographic archives' (Hankela, 2020, p. 88). The Black theologian Anthony Reddie concurs, arguing that approaches that push personal narratives to the sidelines are deductive and unhelpful for student development in Black theology (Reddie, 2008, p. 60). In my teaching practice, I noted that I tried to facilitate spaces that allowed for class and group discussion, sharing of ideas and enabling of peer-to-peer learning. However, the discussions centred around case studies I presented and images and models of pastoral care and chaplaincy arising from Eurocentric epistemologies. This perpetuated the individualistic nature of pastoral care practice and, while it generated some space for people to reflect on their own reactions to situations, I limited the potential for students to fully explore and locate their own narratives within the subject. Similar to my critique of methods of theological reflection, the danger here was that I was drawing students into a process of assimilation with preconstructed norms, by directing them to focus their personal reflections on case studies chosen by myself, instead of creating spaces where their personal narratives could emerge more organically and authentically.

My reflections enabled me to see that a decolonized script that seeks to develop a plot of inclusion and decentring of Eurocentric pedagogical norms incorporated far more than simply addressing sources used and content delivered. It centres the student voice and adopts pedagogical practices that actively acknowledge different learning cultures, reflecting this in the modes of delivery and assessment. To this end, I began to allow more space in my teaching for students to bring forward their own pastoral case studies and, instead of requiring a written formative submission, I asked students to do oral presentations that could facilitate discussion within the class. While these were small changes, I found that during the year the depth and breadth of conversations and whole-class learning grew richly.

Roles

To perform the play, everyone must have an idea of their roles within it (Nell, 2020, p. 34). It was evident that one role to consider was my own and what I needed to do to decolonize the teaching that I delivered and the materials and perspectives that were being shared. What was becoming more apparent in this process was that the complex, wide-reaching nature of decolonizing required the drama to go beyond the classroom walls to consider the roles of the faculty and, possibly, even wider socio-political institutions.

Gorski warns that often, in decolonizing discourse and action, we are socialized to expend energy addressing symptoms of oppressive conditions, instead of the conditions themselves (Gorski, 2008, p. 519). In this project, I was regularly reminded of how the different elements of the drama impacted upon one another. The stage, and not just the script, needed re-visioning and, as a main actor within this project, I needed to accept a level of responsibility in trying to effect change. In Shahjahan et al.'s comprehensive review of decolonizing practices within higher education, they identified four ways that enable decolonization to be actualized: regularly evaluating the sources of knowledge in educational spaces; constructing an inclusive curriculum that extends beyond dominant knowledge systems; development pedagogical practices that foster collaborative learning between tutor and students; engaging with the wider community, and socio-political movements (Shahjahan et al., 2022, p. 86). The first three roles listed have been addressed earlier but the fourth point highlights the work needed by tutors such as myself to critique, and potentially dismantle, the continued colonial practices of Eurocentrism, and inequalities being actively pursued within wider structures.

True decolonizing needs significant investment. As Parker points out, serious efforts to address power imbalances cannot be resolved by simply adjusting reading lists or adding new modules that leave the existing power institutional dynamics undisrupted (Parker, 2022, p. 4). This only further serves to validate normative practices and keep the status quo, whereas decolonization should be disruptive and disturbing enough to be noticed (Tuck and Yang, 2012, p. 8). Educators frequently go for pragmatic and immediate strategies (Gorski, 2008, p. 522) and this was my default. Yet these changes do not facilitate the type of social and cultural changes that are needed. Authentic intercultural practice requires a shift in consciousness, as otherwise changes can further colonize rather than liberate (Gorski, 2008, p. 522), and this requires a much higher level of commitment and work. It serves as a wider reminder of the messiness of theological reflection, which linear approaches sometimes do not accommodate.

It is within this year-long theodramatic reflection that this book itself began to unfold. Inspired by movements in co-creation, operating more and more from a decolonizing perspective and conscious of the importance of voices that are, all too often, sidelined, I became acutely aware of the wealth of wisdom and experience within the classroom. Kim and I discussed this at length – often sharing the stories of chaplaincy from different contexts that we were hearing. This was enhanced by the fact that some of our modules were taught via zoom, giving greater access for students living in different areas of the world. It was in these spaces that we heard Basil talk about his work in a prison in Nigeria, and Angus talk about the unique role healthcare chaplains often took on in Hong Kong. Agatha shared her journey towards ordination and healthcare chaplaincy, and some of the tensions she experienced in the place she now found herself, and Nik poignantly recalled how healthcare chaplaincy had given him a second chance at ministry. All of these stories had so much depth, and Kim and I found ourselves gaining a deeper understanding of contemporary chaplaincy, which in turn enhanced our own learning and teaching. These were stories we had not encountered before, told first-hand by practitioners in the field, most of whom had never published their accounts before. Our script was being changed through these narratives and we felt it was hugely important, as a way to change the broader academic pastoral care and chaplaincy script and start to reshape some of the structures of learning, that we used the roles and power we had to bring them to a wider audience. This was a lengthy and, at times, challenging process. Having done a lot of work in the year around decolonizing and the dangers of assimilation, we were conscious of the need for some form of flow throughout the book but, at the same time, we wanted to ensure that the writing was authentically in the voice of the authors. If the cultural codes, norms and standards that have historically shaped such spaces remain, the script will not change (Day, 2021, p. 60). If the script remains superficial, the resultant plot will not deliver the depth of response needed. This book, emerging at least in part through my journey of decolonization, tries to address the script in a way that may impact the plot.

Conclusion

I began this journey of reflection on practice, thinking about how I could change my teaching content and my practice to embrace a decolonized approach. The exploration, however, drew me into a drama that extended far beyond the four walls of the classroom. The theodrama approach enabled me to think creatively, and to build up a visual picture of the various elements. Its non-linear nature meant it was messier, yet this gave it a greater sense of authenticity – theological reflection is rarely tidy – and it correlated more with a project that sought to move away from rationalized, sequential methods, and embrace ways of undertaking research that reflected a more diverse, inclusive paradigm.

Decolonizing cannot be 'achieved' in a year-long project. This became acutely apparent very early on. However, what can happen is the development of a new mindset and culture that consciously seek to scrutinize practice and wider structures. During the year, I was profoundly challenged by the call not simply to skate over the surface but to dive deep into the heart of the issues at hand. As the scales began to fall from my eyes regarding the enormity of the task, my desire to share this challenge with others and to work out collectively how to address some of the embedded issues grew and grew. I am extremely grateful to the co-editor of this book, Kim, who shared my passion, and to the students, many of whom are featured in this book and whose voices are helping to shape my outlook. The drama is ongoing, with both the timing and the shape of the finale yet unknown. I imagine it may be a play that unfolds throughout my ministerial and academic career, with this being simply the first act.

Bibliography

Batty, D. (2020), 'Only a Fifth of UK Universities Say they are "Decolonising" Curriculum', *The Guardian*, 11 June, available at https://www.theguardian.com/us-news/2020/jun/11/only-fifth-of-uk-universities-have-said-they-will-decolonise-curriculum (accessed 7.07.2024).

Beaudoin, T. and K. Turpin (2014), 'White Practical Theology', in K. Cahalan and G. Mikoski, *Opening the Field of Practical Theology: An Introduction*, Washington DC: Rowman & Littlefield, pp. 251–70.

Day, K. (2021), *Notes of a Native Daughter: Testifying in Theological Education*, Grand Rapids, MI: Eerdmans.

Gorski, P. (2008), 'Good Intentions are Not Enough: A Decolonizing Intercultural Education', *Intercultural Education* 19(6), pp. 515–25.

Green, L. (2009), *Let's Do Theology*, Woonsocket, RI: Mowbray Publishing.

Hankela, E. (2020), 'Liberating the Classroom: Ethnographic Elements in Liberation Theologies Curricula', *Teaching Theology & Religion* 23(2), pp. 84–95.

Lartey, E. (1996), 'Practical Theology as Theological Form', *Contact* 119(1), pp. 21–5.
Lartey, E. (2002), 'Embracing the Collage: Pastoral Theology in an Era of "Postphenomena"', *Journal of Pastoral Theology* 12(2), pp. 1–10.
Luther King Centre (n.d.), 'Our Community: About LKC', available at https://www.lutherking.ac.uk/community/about (accessed 7.07.2024).
Nell, I. (2020), *Together in God's Theatre: Practical Theology in an African Context*, Wellington, South Africa: CLF publishers.
Nell, I. (2021), 'Decolonising an Introductory Course in Practical Theology and Missiology: Some Tentative Reflections on Shifting Identities', *Transformation in Higher Education* 6, available at https://doi.org/10.4102/the.v6i0.103 (accessed 7.07.2024).
Parker, E. (2022), *Trust in Theological Education: Deconstructing 'Trustworthiness' for a Pedagogy of Liberation*, London: SCM Press.
Pattison, S. (2000), *A Critique of Pastoral Care*, 3rd edn, London: SCM Press.
Reddie, A. (2008), 'People Matter Too! The Politics and Method of Doing Black Liberation Theology' (the Ferguson lecture – University of Manchester, 18 October 2007), *Practical Theology* 1(1), pp. 43–64.
Shahjahan, R. A. et al. (2022), '"Decolonizing" Curriculum and Pedagogy: A Comparative Review Across Disciplines and Global Higher Education Contexts', *Review of Educational Research* 92(1), pp. 73–113.
Swinton, J. and H. Mowat (2016), *Practical Theology and Qualitative Research*, London: SCM Press.
Tuck, E. and K. Yang (2012), 'Decolonization is Not a Metaphor', *Decolonization: Indigeneity, Education & Society* 1(1), pp. 1–40.
Tuhiwai Smith, L. (2021), *Decolonizing Methodologies*, 3rd edn, London: Bloomsbury.
van Beek, A. M. (2010), 'A Cross-cultural Case for Convergence in Pastoral Thinking and Training', *Pastoral Psychology* 59, pp. 471–81.
von Balthasar, H. U. (1988), *Theo-drama 1: Theological Dramatic Theory* (vol. 1), San Francisco, CA: Ignatius Press.
von Balthasar, H. U. (1990), *Theo-drama 2: Man in God* (vol. 2), San Francisco, CA: Ignatius Press.

Index of Names and Subjects

addiction 128
advocacy 24, 25, 64, 109, 112, 156, 176, 195, 201, 217, 218, 219
Anglican 1, 30, 32, 64, 80, 85, 105, 108, 110, 111, 112, 120, 150, 157, 180, 181, *see also* Church of England
Anglo-Catholic 124
anti-racism 189, 195
Assemblies of God (AOG) 1, 2, 121, 122, 126
Association of Clinical Pastoral Education (ACPE) 161, 170, *see also* Clinical Pastoral Education (CPE)

Baptist 1, 7, 13–17, 30, 85, 105–16, 120
bereavement 9, 10, 128
bilingual 119, 147, 149, 170
Black, black 2, 120, 121–3, 190–8, 227–8
Botswana 1, 3, 173–6
brown 190–8

care home(s) 78, 80–3, 85, 86, 173, 175–7, 211
Catholic 30, 31, 58, 59, 62, 94, 95, 120, 161, 175, 185 *see also* Roman Catholic
chaplaincy model 2–3, 7, 8, 29, 30–4 39, 40, 42, 43, 60, 62, 64, 65, 66–76, 105, 108, 110, 113, 118, 119, 120, 144–50, 160–4, 169, 170, 179, 180, 181, 183, 185, 194, 198, 223, 224, 225, 228
charismatic 180, 185
child, children 61, 71, 78, 84, 138, 154, 174, 177, 189, 190, 191, 192, 194, 185, 196, 197
Church in Wales 7
Church of England (CofE) 7, 19, 24, 78, 143, 189, 212, *see also* Anglican
Church of Scotland 138, 153
Church of South India 1, 91
Clinical Pastoral Education (CPE) 36, 41, 161, 170, *see also* Association of Clinical Pastoral Education (ACPE)
co-creation 230
code switching 94, 95, 96, 149
commissioned 31, 92, 113
community 3, 11, 19, 20–7, 31, 33, 36, 53, 54, 60, 61, 63, 66–9, 71–5, 78, 82, 92, 109, 110, 113, 114, 124, 129, 130, 143, 144, 149, 153, 157, 158, 173, 174, 176, 180, 182, 183, 185, 194, 197, 210, 213, 219, 229
consecrated 31
contemplative 160, 166
culture 24, 25, 32, 36, 37, 38, 44, 50, 59, 60, 61, 64, 111, 120, 129, 130, 131, 133, 138, 143,

233

145, 146, 147, 153, 161, 163,
  167, 177, 184, 192, 193, 195,
  225, 226, 228, 231
cure of souls 19, 21, 22, 23, 26

decolonize 223, 226, 227, 228,
  229, 231
dementia 2, 78–87, 173, 175, 177
disaster 152, 156
distanciation 92
diversity 2, 15, 17, 22, 24, 29,
  30, 31, 33, 34, 93, 96, 99,
  101, 103, 105, 110, 112, 113,
  114, 143, 145, 162, 180, 184,
  193–6, 208, 213, 223, 226
divine spark 168

economic 40, 42, 63, 129, 133,
  163, 179, 182
ecumenical 8, 66, 180, 181, 213
encounter 24, 34, 41, 43, 58, 59,
  62–5, 66–9, 71–6, 87, 99–102,
  106, 109, 110, 123, 125, 126,
  131, 145, 160, 161, 163–6,
  168, 169, 179, 181, 182, 183,
  184, 185, 186, 228, 230
end of life 9, 49, 50, 80, 86, 146,
  169, 199, 200, 201, 203, 205
equality 12, 15, 29, 30, 105, 123,
  196, 225
evangelical 39–42, 147, 180, 181,
  185
Evangelical 58, 59, 62, 149
evangelism 124, 143, 147, 150,
  180, 181, 183, 185, 186

facilitator 217–18
fire-tender 160–71
formation 3, 14, 24, 49, 55, 56,
  70, 73, 108, 166

gathering/s 69, 83, 84, 160, 163,
  164, 190, 213

gay 3, 14–17, 130, 132, 137, 139,
  140, *see also* sexuality
gender 12, 16, 26, 53, 121, 123,
  126, 130, 133, 161, 163, 199,
  200, 201, 203, 204, 205
generic 30, 93, 94, 95, 113, 149,
  150
Gospel, gospel 22, 39, 40, 61,
  62, 67, 75, 106, 129, 133, 144,
  145, 146, 157, 195
governance 7, 10, 13, 16, 36, 40,
  42, 44, 45
gym 128–34, 138, 139, 154

healthcare 1, 2, 7, 8, 10–13,
  15–17, 36–44, 59, 73, 107, 120,
  121, 123–6, 147, 160, 230
Hong Kong 1, 36–45
hospice 1, 2, 49, 50, 51, 53, 54,
  55, 56, 163, 199, 201, 203,
  204, 205
hospital 7, 9, 10, 14, 15, 36–44,
  51, 118, 119, 121, 123, 125,
  143–50, 154, 155, 160–3
hospitality 22, 26, 31, 32, 67, 75,
  76, 97, 98, 99, 102, 111, 112,
  120, 179–82

illness 15, 51, 52, 53, 54, 56,
  125, 128, 164, 165, 182
image, imagery 55, 58, 63, 145,
  161, 163, 169, 170, 193, 194,
  196, 197, 217, 218, 219, 220,
  228
inclusive 3, 16, 30, 33, 75, 91,
  133, 140, 145, 149, 150, 162,
  194, 213, 223, 229, 231
India, Indian 1, 91, 94, 225
institution, institutional 7, 19–27,
  30, 36, 37, 38, 41, 66, 92, 105,
  108, 109, 113, 124, 143, 145,
  147–50, 162, 167, 190, 191,
  214, 223, 229

integrity 21, 26, 27, 32, 33, 91–6, 99, 100, 105, 106, 109–15, 131, 149, 185
  theological 92, 93, 99, 106, 109
interfaith 92, 93, 95, 96, 98, 213
interpathy 149
interpreter 148, 217, 218
isolation 2, 72, 176, 177, 182, 223

L'Arche 210, 211, 213, 214, 216, 217, 219, 220
later life 86, 87, 175, 177
lay, non-ordained 2, 68, 78, 80, 180
learning disabilities *see* persons with learning disabilities
LGBT 12, 15, 16, 17, 132, 139
liberal arts 19, 20, 22, 26, 27

marginalized 33, 58, 161
maritime 156
mental health 41, 42, 128, 140, 148, 154, 155, 162, 182, 199, 200, 201, 204
Methodist 2, 66, 67, 79, 80, 85, 143, 179, 180
Missio Dei 33, 109, 144, 148, 150
mission, missional 2, 20, 22, 24, 25, 26, 32–4, 37, 39, 75, 100, 106, 108, 109, 124, 143, 144, 146, 147, 149, 156, 157, 181, 182, 185, 202
missionary 3, 37, 39, 40, 44, 106, 122, 143, 144, 145, 146, 147, 148, 149, 150, 185
mortality 2, 49–56, 148
multifaith 2, 29, 30–4, 40, 91–3, 95–6, 98–102, 105, 150, 161, 170

narrative 7, 49, 50, 52, 54, 55, 56, 58, 65, 75, 76, 99, 100, 101, 102, 121, 149, 164, 165, 166, 167, 169, 170, 209, 213, 214, 223, 226, 228, 230, *see also* stories
  theology 166
networking 25, 26
NHS (National Health Service) 1, 7–17, 36, 37, 40, 42, 44, 49, 92, 95, 96, 118, 119, 121, 123, 124, 125, 144, 145, 146, 147, 150, 161, 177, 184
Nigeria, Nigerian 1, 2, 58, 59, 60, 61, 62, 63, 64, 230
nursing home 1, 79

offshore 3, 152, 153, 154, 155, 156, 157, 158
oil and gas 1, 152, 154, 156, 157, 158
ordained 19, 21, 38, 80, 92, 108, 121, 121, 124, 126, 153, 179
organizational 1, 7, 9, 12, 31, 38, 41, 42, 67, 69, 73, 74, 75, 83, 180, 213, 219

partnership 115, 179, 181
pastoral care 8, 24, 25, 29, 33, 34, 43, 62, 63, 66, 67, 70, 91, 128, 144, 145, 146, 149, 157, 176, 177, 181, 184, 197, 199, 201, 203, 204, 205, 223–8, 230
patient-centred, patient-directed 162, 167, 169
peer ministry 157, 158
Pentecostal 120, 122, 125, 149
person-centred 8, 73, 94, 119, 208, 209, 217, 220
persons with learning disabilities 207–14, 216, 218, 220
pioneer 66, 122, 143, 17
police 1, 2, 29–34, 129
policy 9, 12, 15, 16, 41, 42, 50, 64, 107, 176, 184

post-secular 115
prison 1, 37, 58, 59–65, 79, 105, 106, 107, 109, 110, 113, 114, 115, 129, 163, 170, 230
professionalization 7, 8, 10, 17, 37, 39, 40, 51

racial justice 194–5
racism 3, 189, 190, 191, 192, 193, 195, 196
re-storying 167
retail 179, 180, 183, 185
Roman Catholic 80, 85, 122, 126, 134, 157, 180, 181, 208, see also Catholic

sacred 62, 143, 149, 160, 161, 163, 165–70
safe space 74, 195
school 3, 36, 130, 189–98, 212, 291
Scotland 2, 83, 94, 153, 173, 175
secular 2, 15, 27, 30, 33, 37, 38, 39, 42, 52, 63, 92, 101, 105, 106, 110, 112, 114, 124, 139, 143, 148, 150, 154, 170, 175, 219, 220
secularism, secularized 21, 30, 34, 40, 44, 49, 94, 112, 113, 149
self-harm 128
sexual, sexuality 12–16, 53, 59, 114, 130, 161, 163
Shades 189, 190, 194, 195, 196, 197, 198
social care 73, 75, 78, 83, 86, 214, 216
spiritual care 3, 8, 16, 36–9, 41, 42, 44, 45, 49, 50, 52, 54, 71, 73, 93–6, 119, 120, 128, 146, 149, 152, 161, 170, 173, 174, 176, 177, 184, 204, 207–17, 219, 220

stories 24, 52, 58, 59, 61, 62, 64, 65, 71, 72, 75, 122, 126, 163–9, 191, 223, 230, see also narrative
suicide 29, 36, 40, 41, 43, 200, 201
supervision 42, 66, 170, 215

tension 39, 43, 52, 92, 93, 94, 97, 98, 107, 122, 124, 125, 126, 150, 161, 165, 179, 180, 181, 210, 213, 230
terrorism 31
theodrama 223–31
theological education 102
theological reflection 51, 81, 107, 161, 165, 166, 167, 227, 228, 230, 231
tragedy 32, 152
transitional space 160
truth-in-hand 98–9
truth-in-process 98–9

UKBHC 11, 12, 17, 45, 96, 124, 125
Unitarian 1, 128, 129, 140
United Reformed Church 85, 180
United States of America (USA) 1, 2, 3, 19, 20, 27, 96, 113, 160, 170, 213
university 1, 19, 20, 21, 22, 24, 26, 28, 131, 133, 226

values 19, 20, 21, 25, 73, 112, 119, 129, 134, 139, 145, 147, 149, 150, 182, 195, 198, 210
verbatims 161
vision 20, 22, 25, 27, 39, 58, 62, 78, 100, 109, 119, 124, 189, 225
vocation 9, 29, 43, 121, 123, 125, 160, 170, 197

Wales 2, 7, 37, 113,
welfare 29, 40, 64, 152, 184
well-being 8, 29, 33, 34, 50, 74, 80, 118, 129, 131, 148, 155, 162, 165, 167, 184, 195, 199, 201, 205, 212, 226
wellness 118, 129, 130, 133
workplace 15, 32, 33, 137, 162

youth/young people 71, 78, 84, 177, 189, 191, 192, 194, 195, 196, 208
YWAM 143

Zambia 122

www.ingramcontent.com/pod-product-compliance
Lightning Source LLC
Chambersburg PA
CBHW022048290426
44109CB00014B/1023